Drawings

SARAH RAPHAEL was born in East Bergholt, Suffolk in 1960. She graduated (with first class honours) from Camberwell School of Art in 1981. Her work was widely exhibited with great success; first in group, and then in solo shows at the Christopher Hull Gallery, Agnew's, and finally at Marlborough Fine Art. Her paintings have been sold to a number of public collections, including the Metropolitan Museum of Art, New York; the Fitzwilliam Museum, Cambridge and the National Portrait Gallery. Her *Childhood Cube*, made originally for the Millennium Dome, was bought by the Museum of Childhood in London, and is now a prominent part of the permanent exhibition there.

In 1993 she won the inaugural Villiers David Prize, which enabled her to spend time working in the Australian desert. In 1996 she was the winner of the NatWest Painting Prize. She lived in London with her three daughters, Natasha, Anna and Rebecca. Sarah Raphael died in January 2001.

SARAH RAPHAEL

Drawings

With appreciations by

Frederic Raphael, Clive James and William Boyd

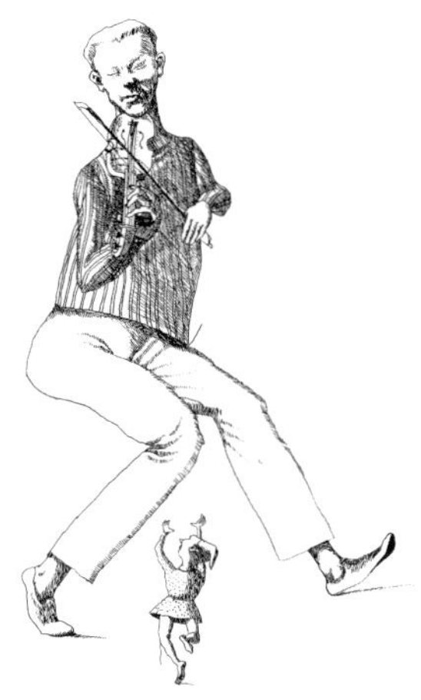

CARCANET

First published in Great Britain in 2004 by
Carcanet Press Limited
Alliance House
Cross Street
Manchester M2 7AQ

A CIP catalogue record for this book is available from the
British Library
ISBN 1 85754 662 8

The publisher acknowledges financial assistance from
Arts Council England

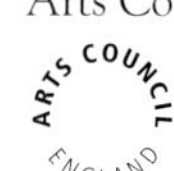

Printed and bound in England by SRP Ltd, Exeter

Contents

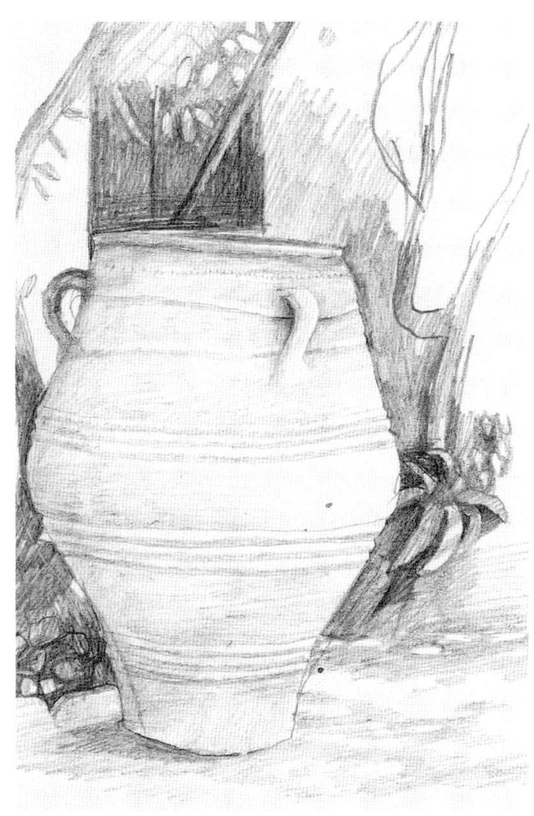

Introduction

by Frederic Raphael

You sit down to start – starting is the hard part – there is your model, like a maze of formless confusion. You look and look, the brush in your hopeful hand, your palette an ordained muddy marsh only you can negotiate; you slave at the terrain – you forgot your map; you can't find your way, but you start anyway, pretending to know your way around. Making marks, squinting in a professional sort of way, wanting something to happen, wanting to feel better, sure there is nothing here but dirty colours and a confusing, elusive reality ready to surrender to your eager gaze.

When Sarah wrote about art, which was rarely, it was in entirely unpretentious terms, but with a clarity and candour, an unfailing perception of the real nature of making, which is translated, in the work itself, into a pitiless sympathy with whatever is being depicted. When she writes of 'pretending to know your way', it chimes entirely with other forms of art, especially fiction but also, I suspect, acting. The way in which the artist addresses him/herself to the task is also like an athlete (or a golfer or a batsman), not with the certainty that all will go well, or even where anything will go at all, but in a state of willed readiness which, in art, involves a kind of accessibility: the artist prepares by assuming a kind of knowledgeable innocence. *'Je ne cherche pas,'* Picasso famously said, *'je trouve.'* Sarah was constantly discovering new things where, to the unprimed eye, there was nothing new to be seen (one of her paintings is largely of a roll of Sellotape). These drawings range from the ordinary to the fantastic; the commonplace and the imaginary become consequences of each other.

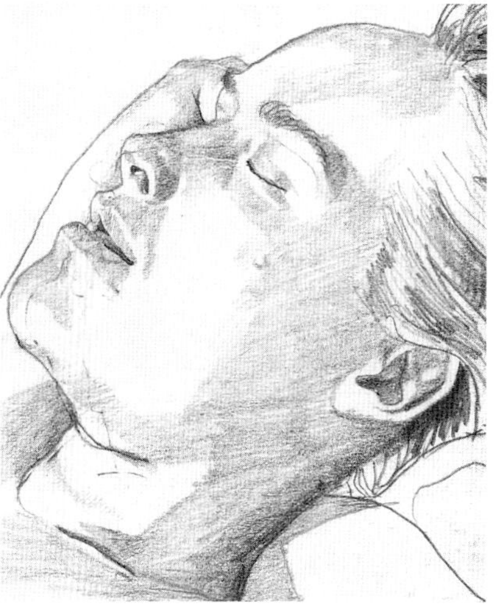

p. 31, Véronique (detail)

The only platitude in what I have quoted from her notes is, I suppose 'eager gaze'. Here a textual critic might be tempted to emend 'eager' to 'eagle': there is something keen and predatory and lofty about the artist's consideration of a subject. Sarah's drawings, of which the present volume is hardly more than a vigilantly random cull, a selection of her work from the age of sixteen, manage to catch both subject and *idea* in the same gently implacable claws:

Then you catch sight of it, the light behind the shadow of a swatch of hair, a sort of view across the hill of the forehead, a perfect little enclave right out of sight of the normal eye. But your eye gets to it, your eyes see it, your eyes search out those secret places no one else bothers to find, no one else knows that they are the start of the story that face has to tell. From then on it will just reveal itself to you, it will emerge like a landscape as the sun comes up – yes! just like that – all you have to do is look – your brushes are sharp as chisels, they tap away the crude rock.

What Sarah describes here is again what unifies many artists, in different arts: apprehension shading into comprehension. As the grasp tightens on the subject, so the problem resolves itself. In the play between style and content, the content takes form (and makes sense) in the light of style, but does not determine it. Nor must style become a barrier between artist and perception, by style becoming itself the subject: such is the limiting, and limited, characteristic of 'genre' art. Predictability, however pleasing, is typical of art, in any medium, in which our knowledge of the artist enables us to guess how he or she will shape the material. Vladimir Nabokov's stories can trump expectation because, against all the odds, and unlike most 'serious' writers, he could treasure and depict sudden epiphanies of happiness. Sarah's tragic sense of life was at one with her joy in it. Her drawings call on us to smile, as a certain accuracy always does (the mimic trades on this).

With Sarah, especially in her drawings, there is never the feeling that this view of the subject is just the kind of view Sarah Raphael *would* take of it. Every artist is sustained by some idea of his or her qualities, and strengths, but only those of the second rank always do things the way they *always* do things. When the artist begins to have a trademark, he risks becoming a tradesman: his public know what to expect of him. He ceases to make it new. The purity of Sarah's work lies in the direct play between the subject and the artist's play specifically with *it*. Sarah honoured, sought out, found what was unusual in the usual thing.

There is tenderness and callousness here, as you can see in the drawings of Sarah's children, whom she loved so much and to whom she gave so much time. But if, at the moment when she was drawing them, one looked like some pouting primitive creature, that was how she portrayed her. Comedy is an integral part of Sarah's tragic sense of life: she was immensely serious, and full of laughter. Proud, dedicated and, too often, in pain from persistent migraine, she suffered cruelly (to the point of being ashamed of it), but I associate her with happiness. The work carries no tragic tag and sells no sorry vision (how different from Edvard Munch, for instance, whose genre was the horror, the horror!, and never transcended it): Sarah knew the pain, but also the comedy, and their fragile proximity. She never turns the attention back from the work to herself, or to what she 'must be feeling': nothing is more exaggerated in assessing an artist's work than the notion that 'passion' certifies genius and should be manifest in its work. These drawings are often like a dance in which levity is the proof of mastery.

The mark of genius is to refuse – no, *ignore* – the cataloguer's categories. All the great Greek tragedies had been written by the time Aristotle listed

p. 26, Natasha (detail)

(more or less correctly) what their ingredients should be. No one ever wrote a masterpiece after he had supplied the recipe. Sarah found time, in her too-short life, to be a brilliant teacher, because she never showed anyone what they should do. She herself became exasperated, when she was six years old, by a well-intentioned teacher at St Paul's Girls' Preparatory School, who actually *drew over* something she had done.

At Bedales, she owed a great debt to Christopher Cash, himself a painter (in the Camden Town tradition), who had the instinctive wit to recognise her quality and to do nothing but put himself, and the studio's materials, at her disposal. 'Ah, talent!' he said, and left it at that.

Sarah's greatest teacher was the tradition of art itself and her vigilant admiration of those – Matisse, Balthus, Cézanne, Pollock – in whom she saw something first to amaze and then to instruct her, and finally to leave behind. She did not imitate; she assimilated and digested what went before, and around her, in art and in life. She always drew; those slim fingers were made for that.

Greece was the primal influence. She was never so happy, all her life, as on the island of Ios, in the Cyclades, where we first went in 1962. Ios was then a depopulated paradise. Her drawings and paintings, huge and tiny, made constant use of Greek motifs. I have always beside me the painting on a block of wood of a Greek warrior (with something of the amazon about him/her) which she gave me for a birthday. Ios she always called 'that place'.

As the tourist avalanche hit Greece, the island changed, but never lost its lure for Sarah, who painted and drew it through all the stages of its evolution into a touristic babel of voices, and noises. She kept patience with all the changes. An artist such as Sarah finds subjects everywhere; she saw the form in anarchy, and the turmoil in the apparently static (how mutable the human face is!). The catchpenny cafes and the loud hedonists that thronged to Ios were all enjoyable to her: she filched their essence in her work and they never felt a thing.

Her earliest, easiest, drawing book when we were poor on Ios was the unmarked sand itself. We have a few feet of film in which she is dancing naked on the beach, three years old, and drawing horses (or are they donkeys, of which there were then many on Ios in the days before anyone ever saw a wheel there?) between skippy steps. The horses had short bodies and fat bellies, with saddles and dangling stirrups, *her* horses.

Later that year, we drove through the Peloponnese. At Mycenae, we walked up under the gate, with the stretched lions reaching up on either side of the sacred stone on which their front paws rest, and Sarah stood and looked at them, while I rambled on about Agamemnon. That night, in her drawing book, she drew more horses, but now they had longer bodies and smaller heads. The lion gate had taught her to revise her visual vocabulary. The interplay between the given – the great continuum of art history – and the still-to-be-found –

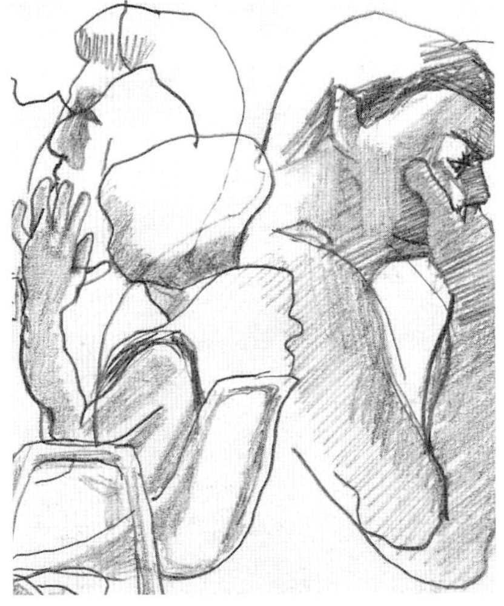

p. 32, Study of people at Far Out café, Ios (detail)

her own contribution to it – procured the balance in Sarah's work between what was there to the eye and what her hand and mind contributed to seeing it better, differently, more truly.

Preciousness creeps in when discussing art. The truth of it, however, is born of vigilant callousness. Sarah understood that the loneliness of the artist resembles that of the spy, and even of the thief: the more attentive she was, the clearer, and more useful, the report; the defter the hand, the more one gets away with, the easier to pick the essential lock, or thread the maze.

Michael Ayrton watched Sarah working one day, in her teens, and said, with glum generosity, 'I expect she'll be better than me.' The three of us went out drawing one afternoon, when he was staying with us in the Dordogne, and sat on a hillside below the hilltown of Belves. Michael was not well (he died that same year) and after a while could no longer sit on the grass without pain. As we packed up, he said, 'We've looked at it long enough, we can make up the rest.' He saw that Sarah was not convinced. 'If you look carefully, you'll see you've already got it in your head.' Michael's style took care of the details; but Sarah never had a style in that sense, and wanted to look and look. I loved Michael, and his drawings, but I have a notion Sarah was right: after you had seen it all, she always found more to see.

Solitude is an artist's best company (not that Sarah was good at guarding hers, or her ideas, which is why they were sometimes stolen) and the best inspiration: she liked praise as much as the next man or woman, but never repeated a motif or a manner because the public or her gallery liked it. Success was a thrill, but not a purpose. When her Australian desert pictures won prizes and were quickly sold, she was pressed to paint more, and (since the big paintings were done from studies, but in the studio) she could well have done so, but she would not pander to a market, though she was glad to have one. There was nothing priggish or attitudinising in her integrity: she just had it.

Her apparent variety of styles *was* her style: unlike, say, John Minton, with her, versatility was never a symptom of facility without inner conviction. In her painting, one thing led to another, and sometimes to another style, not least when the agony of her migraine headaches drove her to see a maelstrom of pigmented pain, and to find art (but not relief) in the radiant order in which chaos was made visible to her.

The meaning of her work was always the work itself (she refused all 'explanation' and resented its attribution). Her 'Strip' series mimicked and transcended the strip cartoons she always loved in children's comics, and typical of that sublime parody was her use in them of 'speech balloons' in which nothing intelligible is contained. The work was the work was the work.

Sarah's drawings were, I suppose, her notebooks. But only rarely does an image get repeated, let alone re-heated, in any recognisable way, in finished paintings. There is only the occasional specific study, for instance for the

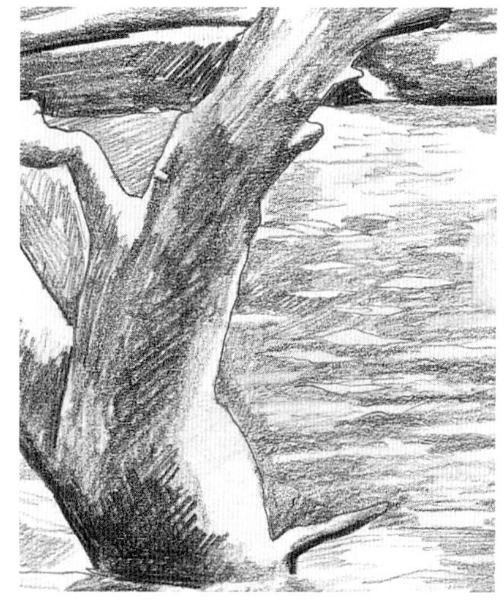

p. 72, 'Glory Creek' (Australia) (detail)

peasant boy leading his bullocks through a wood. This issued in a wonderful large painting which was interpreted, in an essay by a nun, Sister Wendy Becket, who is also an art critic, as illustrating the Christian theme of 'and a little child shall lead them'.

Sister Wendy's analysis was as well-argued as it was well-intentioned, and Sarah was enraged by it. In the first place, she protested, her images were not illustrative: like Bishop Butler, she believed that a thing is what it is, and not another thing. Responses are one thing (they can be intelligent or fatuous) but *interpretation* is always reductive. In the second place, Sarah insisted that she was not a Christian, and resented having her work appropriated to garnish a Christian message.

Jewishness was not a religious matter for Sarah (maybe that is her parents' fault, since nor is it for us), but a practical posture from which, sometimes at least, to read the world and, more particularly, its inhabitants. She was particularly impressed, in her teens, by Jerzy Kosinski's novel *The Painted Bird*, about a little Jewish boy in Poland during the Nazi occupation, and responded to it, but in no illustrative spirit, with a series of paintings in which terror finds an objective correlative in images that verge on the lighthearted, and which have, it seems, nothing to do with Jews or Poland or the war.

Sarah's pity for the persecuted made her angry, but her anger never made her violent, still less clumsy: she was outspoken, on many matters, but only through indignation, never to advance a theory, a dogma or a partiality: never. Fierce in defence (not least of her daughters), she had no use for malice. Every line of her work speaks for her humanity, but she never congratulates herself for the fineness, or finesse, of her responses. There is, as Byron said of his own *Don Juan*, no *scheme* in what she did: its silence says all she has to say.

I have always thought that Montaigne's famous quotation from Terence, '*Nihil humanum a me alienum puto*' was as much Sarah's motto as his. We pass by his *château* when we drive from Bordeaux to our house in the Dordogne, where Sarah found beauty not only in the landscape, but also in jettisoned bathing towels and lolling rows of tobacco plants. All the unremarkable furniture of life *là-bas* – an open barndoor, a twist of wooden staircase, an empty chair, a fallen towel – spoke of the presence of what was *not* in the frame. She caught the spirit of the place – *any* place – but also the spirits in it. It occurs to me, from this, that Montaigne's embrace of all human life was declared in a reclusive tower where he could rely on his sympathies not being tested by the intrusion of other human beings.

If Sarah had a religion, it was art. ('I sometimes think I should never have to do anything but paint.') But her art was not for its own sake, nor was it immune to extraneous inspiration. Indifferent to doctrine, she could maintain her Jewishness fiercely; never more so, in visual terms, than in the Pamyat drawings, which were a response to the rise of anti-Semitism in post-USSR

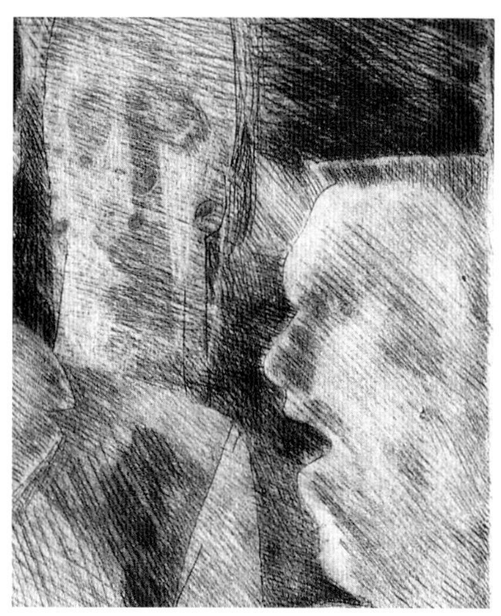

p. 36, 'Pamyat' (detail)

Russia. The drawing on p. 36 is a small, marvellously elliptical, study for the several huge pencil and charcoal drawings which avoided all propaganda, and resentment, but spoke in their terrible silence of the glib malice of what sentimentalists always call 'ordinary people', as if that certified their common decency; it may, as it may their common savagery.

These very large works were a response almost as immediate as that of Picasso to the bombing of Guernica. There was in Sarah a kind of pity for what frightened her; that is how she could encrypt it with such elusive, mordant accuracy. *Guernica* was an overtly purposeful work: it was delivered by the most famous living Spanish artist in order to rally support for the embattled Republic. It is no criticism to say that it had something of the poster about it; its sombre paint seems to announce that the artist had no time for chromatic games. Sarah's Pamyat drawings do not depict anyone being abused, nor is there any loud sign of which of the crowded figures are victims, which their persecutors. John Schlesinger the film director bought one of these big drawings and hung it, since there was sufficient space, in the office used by his secretary. After a few days, she came and asked if he would mind moving it somewhere else. 'Don't you like it?' 'It's not that,' she said, 'but I feel accused; it's stronger than I am, and I can't resist it.'

Sarah was never strident, always more frail than she or we knew, conscious in a way we never quite accepted that she might not live to see her children grow up. Her prolific generosity deceived us, but not herself:

Time passes by as swiftly as sleep – minutes are charged with what they allow you to create, they are the greatest currency you possess – all you crave, the time to do that work, the precious stuff there is never enough of. The rushes of divine hope because you really believe this time, this time you've got it – and although you know it will turn out to be just another painting, perhaps a little improvement on the last, perhaps not – you still feel sure you have never done it quite so well before.

I know I should be caring about other things but I can't help thinking that this is what really counts. Rubinstein said, 'I don't love music, I *am* a piece of music'. He said he was the happiest person he knew because every day he awoke with a sense of wonder and gratitude for his genius! I'd like to say that I am a painting but I think it sounds stupid. Perhaps I am a paintbrush... Perhaps I am crazy. I can't help feeling that it is important, these paintings I keep making, I can't help believing that they matter in the world, despite all the terrible things which make it so small and irrelevant. Can we ever change anyone's mind about anything? Does any man's vision really count for anything in the end? The evening is turning decidedly poignant on me – time to stop.

On another occasion she wrote:

At times I like (almost) the idea of a state in which artists are kings and everything is geared to allowing them all the time, space and materials they need just to produce, to ponder, to look...

As my show approaches I feel a desire to retreat into the shadows and be alone, a desire never to show anyone what I do – for everything to be kept, a great mound of secrets, to be discovered one day after I am dead. I fear not getting the reaction I want and I also fear getting it. I am sure I will not be taken seriously, and I am also sure I deserve to be. I want and I fear adulation for my work, especially the smaller work which I *know* is good; I just know it.

Even as she craved a world shaped to promote the artist, she knew that it might destroy what it set out to advance. A little further on, she continued:

...The whole approval that a system geared to the arts would give me seems to jar against the image of artist as a secret observer and independent commentator on the world – not because there must be suffering to comment on but because the whole world must function along with itself – but the artist is not a citizen – the artist is not a servant, not a member of the club, not a friend, not a loyal subject, even to himself. The artist is a creature at odds with himself, at odds with his world – with no loyalties. For his loyalties mean he cannot betray -and I betray with every stroke of my brush – with every face I draw from life and use as a character in a play, every person I place out of context I have mercilessly used for my own ends – thus I will spit at you even as I caress you or I will not be true. I will not hesitate to use your face, your hands, your worlds, your secrets, your needs and losses, if they make up part of a picture. I cannot be loyal to what art means if I am afraid of that, even if I fear death, or loss, or pain, or hurt pride. The seeking of approval can be the death of art, the acquiring of it can mean the end of progress – the beginning of repetition. Acclaim, not money, can ruin the flow of growth, lack of it can embitter the heart. There is no salvation for us – Thank God – we must be what we are, we must laugh at the labels which we pick up on our travels, we must not believe them, nor fail to have a good look at them and who has stuck them to us.

I regret my need to be approved of and loved – even my need to be comforted – just as I treasure my growing capacity to actively love, not just for what I can get but for what it gives to my soul to do so. And I treasure the warrior within me which, so tired from motherhood, from trying to be free of my past, still plays, light and mischievous, with elements and symbols, long after everyone else is asleep, long after I have finished being the me you think you know.

Sarah was, and is, a true artist.

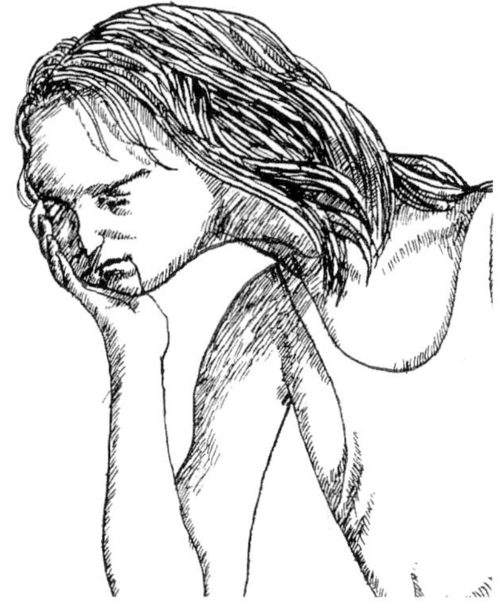

p. 84, 1995 (detail)

Sarah Raphael

by Clive James

One day it will be part of British art history that Sarah Raphael died young.

Today, on the day of her funeral, everyone who knew her must cope with the first loss – the loss of her physical presence. Perhaps the cruel law of chance that took her so soon was trying to make up for its early prodigality in giving her everything. She was brilliant, she was beautiful, and she had the generous, unstudied charm that does not always go with those gifts: being down-to-earth when you are so favoured can't be easy, but she could always manage it.

Once, when I first knew her, I was looking though a stack of dauntingly authoritative paintings leaning against the wall of her studio and I ventured to suggest that 'Sarah Raphael' wouldn't quite do as a name: 'Sarah Michelangelo' might be more appropriate, or even 'Sarah L. da Vinci'. The gag got a laugh – she looked more than usually lovely when she was laughing, which she usually was, even while she worked – but there was a thoughtful addendum. 'You really think I'm quite good, don't you?' I really did, and nobody who had seen any of her work thought anything else.

Which brings us to the second loss, the one that will affect many people who never met her, and eventually whole generations to come, because rarely since Rex Whistler was killed in Normandy in 1944 has there been a deprivation so calculated by fate to impoverish the future.

Right from her first phase, she looked destined to put into reverse the dire expectations for the next round of young British art: she could draw, her canvases had more in them the longer you looked, and there wasn't a dead shark in sight. At Camberwell School of Art (where she went after Bedales) she was a star student, but there was no surprise in that. She had been born into a cultivated household – her father is the writer Frederic Raphael, two of whose books she illustrated – which is always a help towards an apparent precocity, although later on things tend to even out. The real surprise was in her thematic range. Precocious wasn't the word for it. An historical synthesis is usually something that artists attempt only later on, as the final prelude to their achieved individuality. In the initial stages they work through one influence at a time. Young Sarah seemed to have been influenced by the whole European tradition all at once, and to have absorbed the lot.

The first thing of hers I ever saw was a postcard reproduction of one of her big oil-paintings. The postcard was a magic window on the past. On the other side of the window were Cossa's frescoes in the Schifanoia palace in Ferrara, and Paolo Uccello's Green Cloister in Santa Maria Novella in Florence. All the colours and characters of the Quattrocento were there.

But when I went to her first big solo exhibition – at Agnew's, in 1989 – I found that she was already out of that phase and into something less crowded, rather in the way that the young Picasso, having proved that he could paint a whole night-club full of people, switched his attention to individuals. The first picture of hers I bought was a huge oil with almost nothing in it except a centrally placed oval mirror framing her self-portrait in the act of painting: the one and only time, as far as I know, that she used her own good looks as a subject. It was the opposite of conceit, because the other thing in the picture, down in the foreground, was a grotesque homunculus that she had borrowed from Velasquez, just as she had borrowed the idea of the painter painting himself from Rembrandt.

The picture was a set of quotations, but the arrangement and the execution were all hers, and typically luscious even in their austerity. It was a picture about chance, about beauty being a fluke. But there was no fluke in the technique, and the picture was also about that: about an abundant young talent discovering how spareness, too, could be a means of expression. It was a bravura piece: look what I can do. It was also a renunciation: look what I can leave out, see how I can discipline myself to serve the purpose.

Barely managing to fit my wrapped trophy into a taxi, I already knew that it would be the last of her big pictures that I would ever be able to afford. The millionaires were already moving in. New York's Metropolitan Museum had made a purchase. Every possible prize, except of course the Turner, was getting set to drop into her lap. If you do the rounds, you run into a lot of young artists who are going to be something. But she was already something.

Like all her admirers I wanted her first flush of enchantment to go on for ever, but she was too serious to stay with a winning streak. On the face of it, her next phase looked like a total abnegation. Suddenly her pictures were drained of colour. Nothing remained except greys, dark greens and chilly blues, and the paint itself was acrylic, almost military in its determination to be non-seductive. But you didn't have to look long to see why. The subject matter was terror.

There was no overt violence: many of the pictures just showed people walking in the park. But something was going to happen to them, or they were going to do something to someone else. Like those interrogations in Harold Pinter's early plays that lead you to nothing except a realisation of what it feels like to be helpless, these pictures summed up the anxieties of modern history without having to mention it.

They were so mature that there seemed no way forward, and no need to seek it. She had discovered something uniquely hers. Regrettable for its bleakness, admirable for its truth, it was a personal manner so powerful that it would have served most artists for a lifetime.

Then she transformed herself yet again. A working visit to the Australian desert brought all the colours back with a rush. But this time the colour was without form, except for the way that a new and ravishing pointilliste technique (it was as if a re-born Seurat had met Clifford Possum Tjapaltjari over cocktails) arranged individual grains of red dust and molecules of stone into a resplendent Mandelbrot set, a polychromatic map for chaos. Some of the paintings were enormous and all of them were tremendous. In 1995 the buyers went at them like a lynch mob. At Agnew's I walked slowly so that someone with a lot more loose change would beat me to the one I wanted most. It was fabulous, with a price-tag to match.

While painting my portrait she had given me a frightening lecture on how little of the money a painter gets to keep after the gallery takes its cut, but by now she was such a hit that freedom beckoned. She could have – she always could have – just painted away in a style the well-heeled public had learned to like, while exploiting her glamour in the glossies to boost the market. But she wasn't like that.

There was another metamorphosis, into a kind of neo-pop summa that looked as if the sixties were getting a re-run on a bigger screen, in a better theatre. Miniature motifs were repeated and counterpointed endlessly: Philip Glass had taken up embroidery. (In 1998, she moved to Marlborough Fine Art for 'Strip!'; her last exhibition, 'Small Objects in Transit', etchings and monotypes, closed there last month.) She was having fun, but it was easy to predict that she was getting ready for whatever would happen next.

Until now, there was always something that was going to happen next. My own bet is that it would have been the real synthesis – the majestic one, not that merely sensational one she started off with. We will have to guess what it would have looked like, and at the moment guessing hurts too much. One thing we can be sure of: it would have included human figures painted to a standard seldom seen in British art since the eighteenth century.

Throughout her short but lavishly fruitful career, whatever phase she was currently caught up in, she never ceased to paint portraits, and her lasting reputation would be assured by them alone. They are monumental even when small, and universal even in their solitude. The National Portrait Gallery already has two of them. In the future, when Tate Modern comes to its senses and begins to concern itself with artists instead of trends, there will be a room full of Sarah Raphael portraits so that the new young artists may flock, marvel, and resolve to do likewise. They will learn, from an artist born for greatness, that it takes more than a concept to reflect life.

No matter how far she strayed into the abstract, humanity was always her subject, and all the grief that went with it. Human grief gave the coherence to her exuberance, the chest-voice to her joy. For all her conspicuous blessings, it was part of her genius that tragedy was not strange to her: but to lose her so abruptly is a hard way to have it proved.

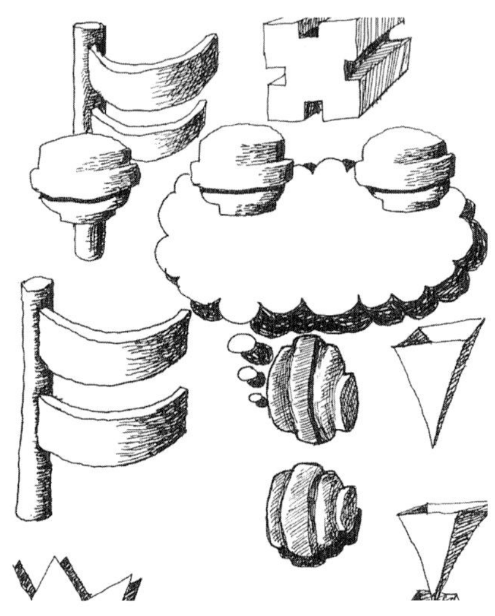

p. 101, Post-Strip study (detail)

Reprinted by permission from *The Independent*, Obituaries, 17 January 2001

Sarah Raphael

by William Boyd

'Draw your own hands. If you can draw your own hands you can do anything.' Such was the advice given to the fourteen-year-old Sarah Raphael by the sculptor, painter and all-round polymath Michael Ayrton. According to Ayrton's biographer, Ayrton recognised Sarah's seriousness of purpose even at this early age. She wanted to be an artist – she was going to be an artist – and Ayrton gave her this significant tip. It was perceptive of Ayrton to spot this aspect of Sarah – and it has to be said she eclipsed him, artistically – but the counsel was wise, however unfashionable it may now seem. At the very root of all significant art is the notion of virtuosity: good artists are better than mediocre artists – they can draw better, they can paint better, their sense of composition is better, they can do everything better. Inept artists have become very successful, in a worldly sense, but there is no disguising this basic gift when you come across it: skill, ability, touch, instinct, feeling, a sense of colour, of line, of shapeliness and so on. It shines out; it is inescapable.

I met Sarah a couple of years after Ayrton when I went to interview her father, Frederic Raphael, for a magazine. I remember, even then, there was a clear straightforwardness about her personality, a slightly daunting candour that impressed – as if you yourself were also being quietly weighed up on some private scale – perhaps this is what struck Ayrton, too? But, anyway, it's strange for me to consider now that there is no other artist, in whatever medium, that I have known for the full period of their working life. I have been, I think, to every significant exhibition Sarah had. I write this far from my collection of her catalogues but I can mentally walk myself through her oeuvre with a familiarity that is only paralleled by the all-time greats. As time went by, I came to know Sarah better (and the Raphael family), bought some of her paintings, wrote about her work for *Modern Painters* magazine and also wrote an introduction to one of her shows. It's only now that I realise I was privileged to witness the development of an artist in a unique way.

I remember particular paintings. An early, tall, thin interior with a face in an oval mirror. A group of stylised figures in front of a grassy hill. I remember also the big refulgent Australian paintings – this show being the moment where Sarah's ambitions and mastery really cohered in a dramatic way – but the one I wanted to buy was an immaculate two-foot square unfinished landscape of jungle and palm trees. And I remember vividly the 'Strip' paintings – Sarah's audacious venturing into a kind of abstraction. At the time, my initial response was that this was a mistake but I wonder now if the 'Strip' paintings will become her signature work. They were, for those who loved Sarah's confi-

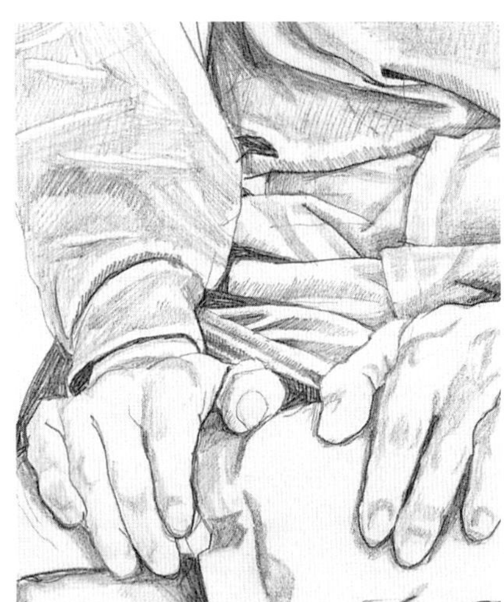

p. 27, Joe (detail)

dent, rich figuration, a swerve of huge temerity, but in their strident colours and frenetically busy surfaces they exhibited all her multifarious gifts: her patience, her craftsmanship, her minute attention to detail. Unlike most abstract painting, Sarah's 'Strips' must have been fantastically hard to paint. Stand close to one and look at the work that has gone into six square inches. Stand back and look at the finished canvas. 'Art isn't easy', Stephen Sondheim once wrote: Sarah exemplified that marriage of hard graft to nurtured ability. I don't know where she was heading but I feel that the Strip paintings heralded all manner of new directions.

And yet she always painted portraits. Like Graham Sutherland and Michael Andrews – artists who, more and more, remind me of Sarah – she could turn out a pencil sketch or a rapid oil that not only captured a likeness but were individual works in their own right. And here we come back to this idea of virtuosity. The art market, one might say, procreates the artists it deserves, but in a world where owning a video camera, or having a 'smart' idea, or instructing a team to install your installation is all that is required to merit the appella-tion 'artist', the notion that you might sit down with a pencil and sketch pad for a couple of hours to draw your child, or try to capture the essence of a beach in Greece with some watercolours, seems positively antediluvian. No matter – all this will pass, and faddy ephemera faster than most. Criteria of judgement do apply in all artistic endeavours, I'm happy to say, insofar as what is bad can be demonstrably singled out as third-rate or inferior and arguments about its third-ratedness and inferiority can be mooted and analysed – whether the work in question is a novel, a film, a play or a painting, etc. (What is not *understood* is another more complex matter, however.) It could be argued, in fact, that much of the nature of contemporary art is an attempt to evade or marginalise these criteria. If you never draw, your drawing skills will never be judged. Yet it is no surprise, I feel, that the Pantheon of great twentieth-century British artists is almost entirely dominated by (a) painters and (b) figurative painters. The reason is that you can tell how good they are, yourself: you don't need the imprimatur of a gallery or a dealer or a patron. A Lucian Freud, a Michael Andrews, a Frank Auerbach, a David Hockney a Francis Bacon or a Graham Sutherland is replete with the absolute confidence of its making. You may like some better than others but you cannot deny their individual integrity.

Looking at Sarah's work provokes the same response in me. How to define it? A kind of relaxation, a sense of calmness? Perhaps all forms of tremendous expertise, of great giftedness, signal this recognition. This person, this artist, knows what she is doing, you feel, and you want to share that discovery, to see where it takes you. The great sadness of Sarah's tragically short life is that our future voyages with her have been curtailed. She could draw her own hands. She could do anything.

Reprinted by permission from *Sarah Raphael 1960–2001*, Marlborough Fine Art (London) Ltd, 2003

Drawings

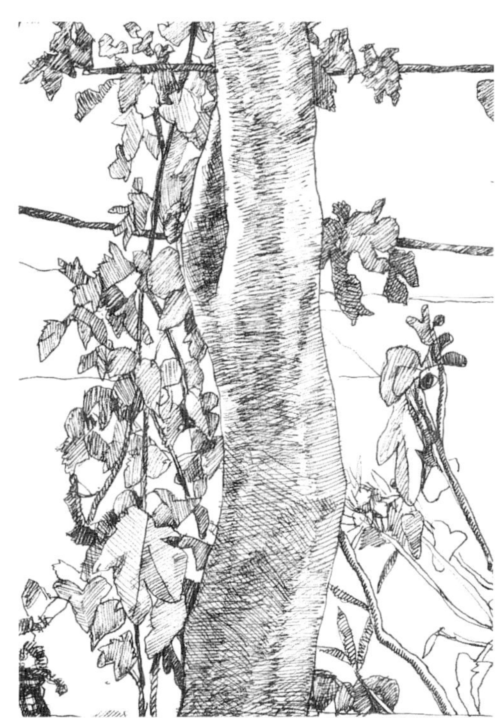

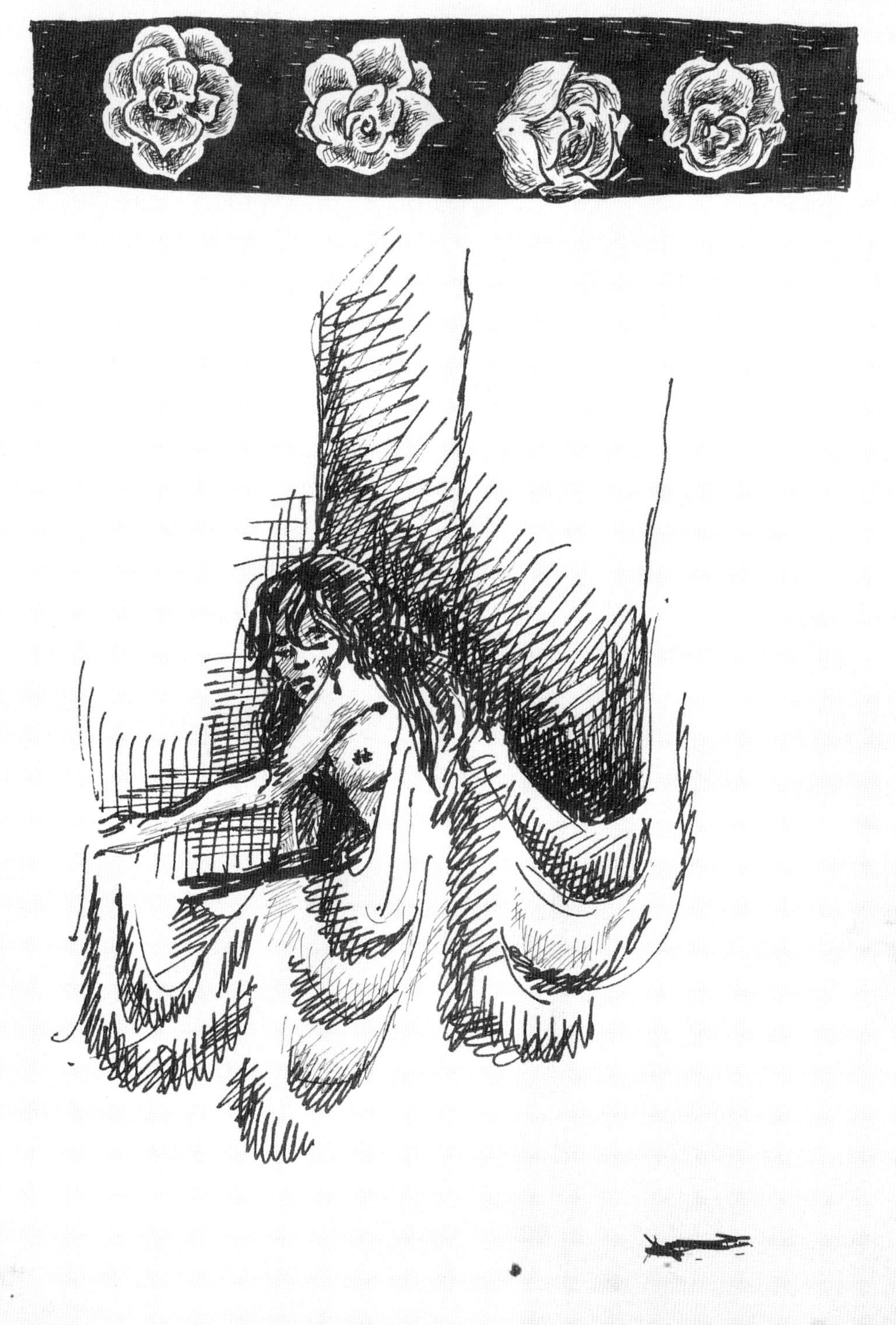

1976
pen and ink
297 × 210

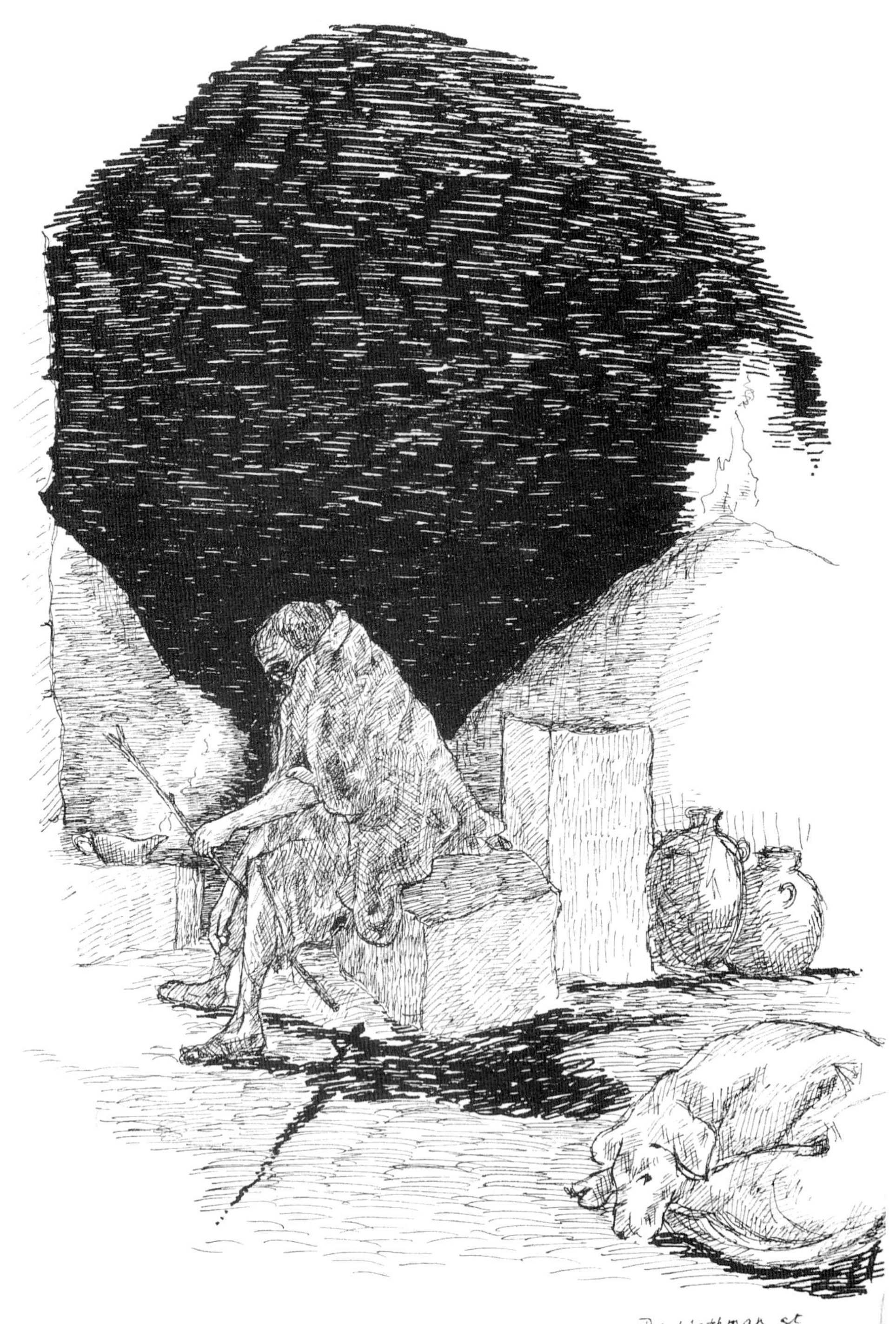

'The watchman of Mycenae'
1977
pen and ink
170 × 124

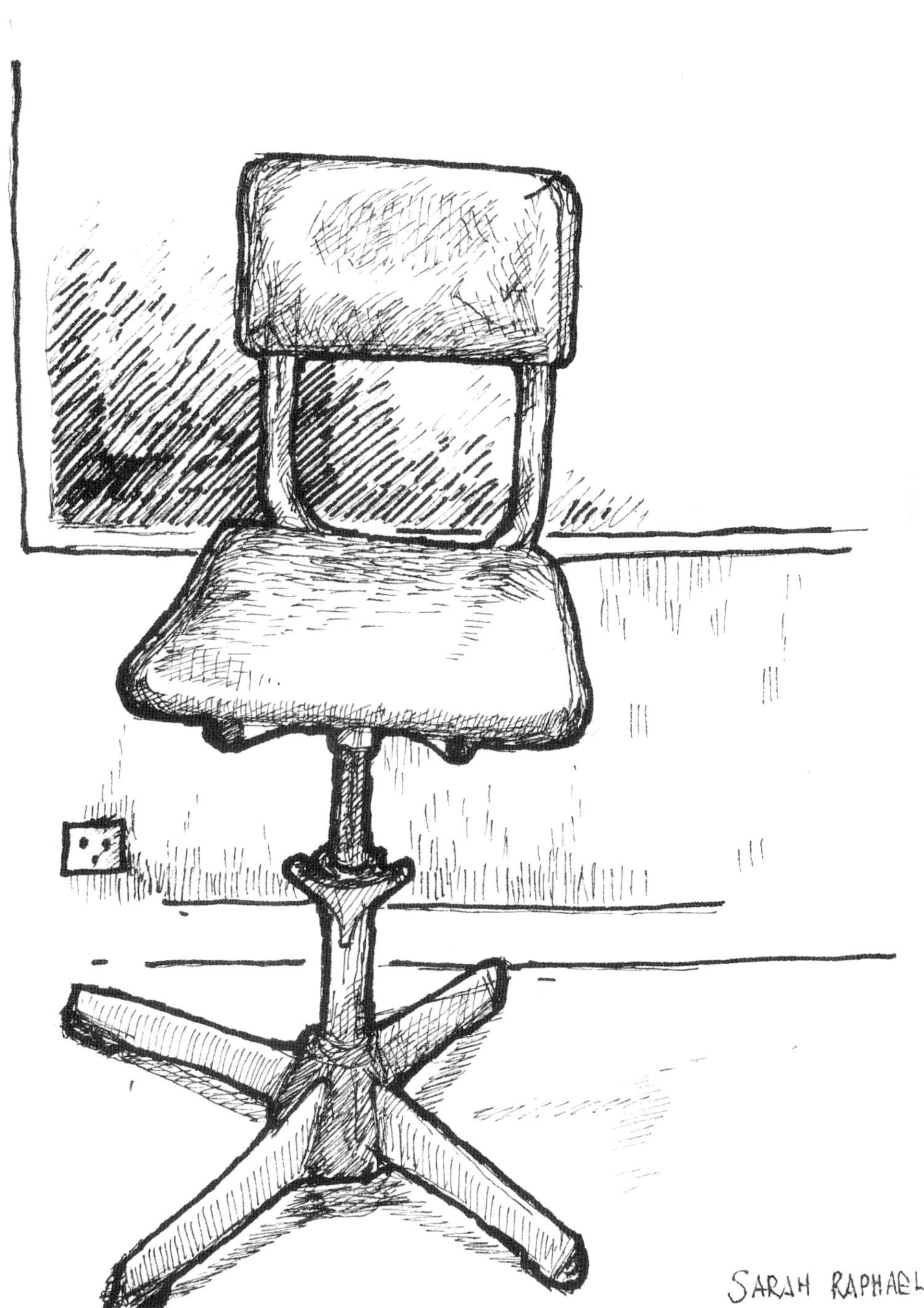

1977
pen and ink
170 × 124

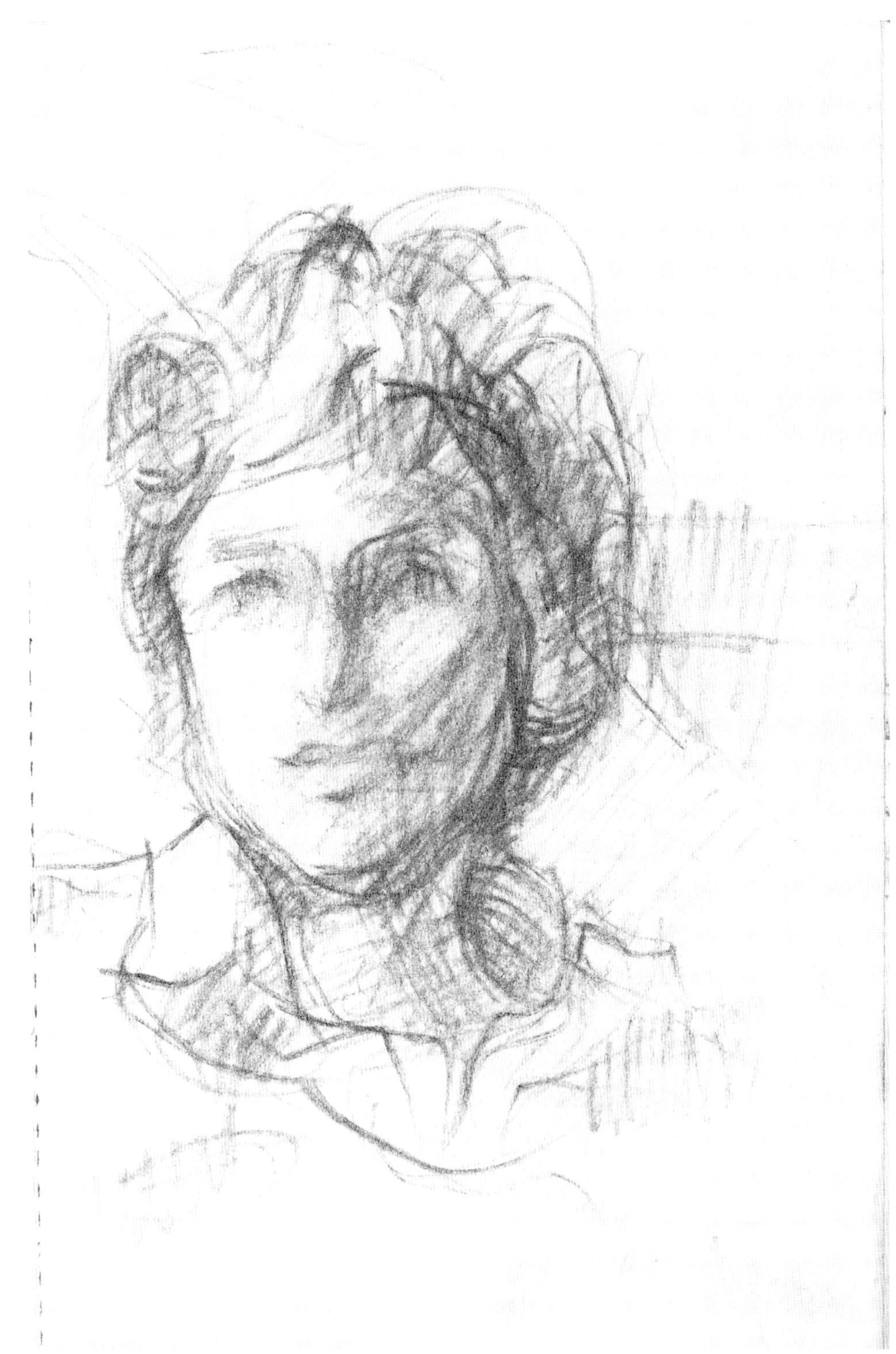

Beetle
1978
charcoal on pencil
132 × 87

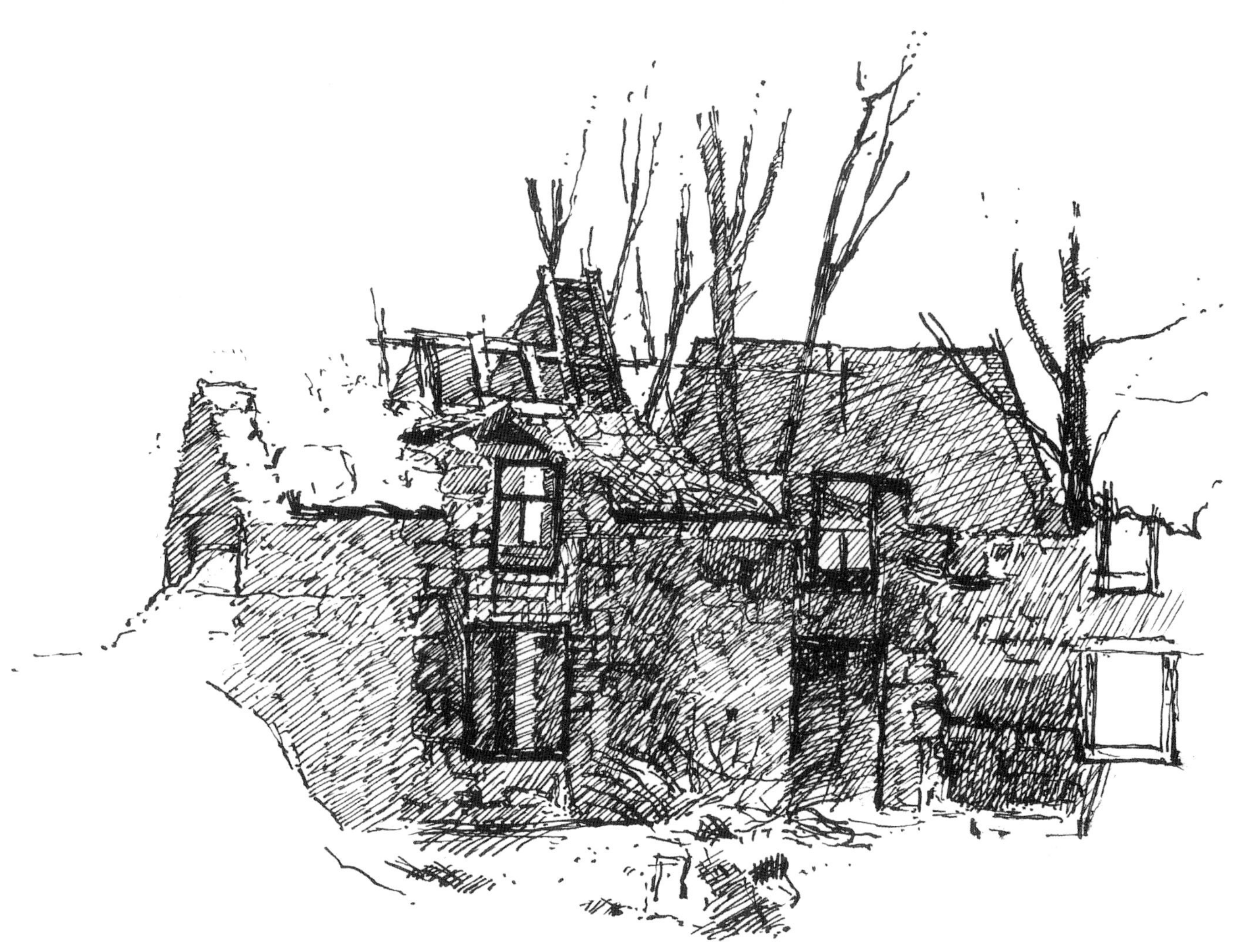

1978
pen and ink
180 × 240

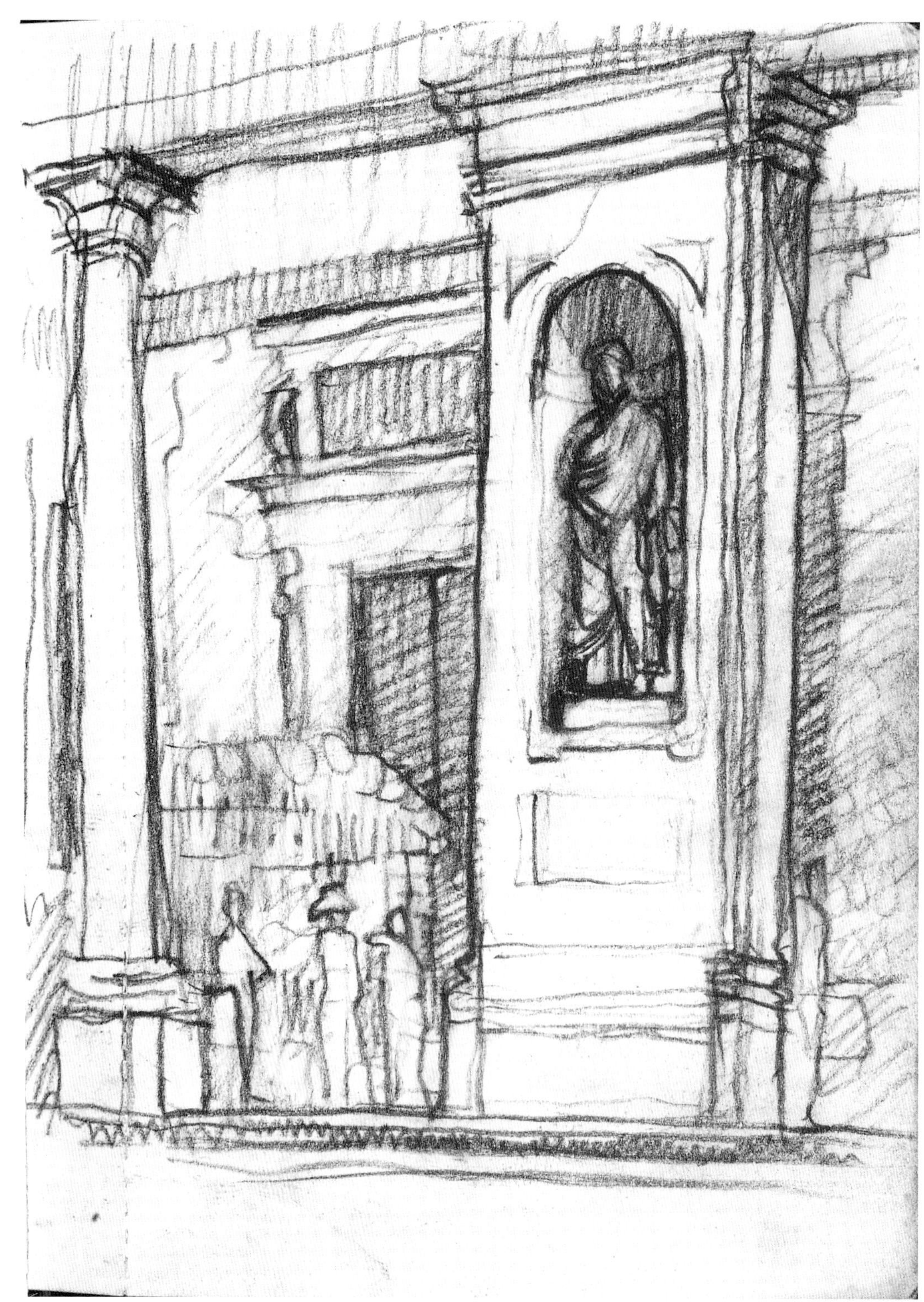

Church in Tuscany
1978
pencil
132 × 87

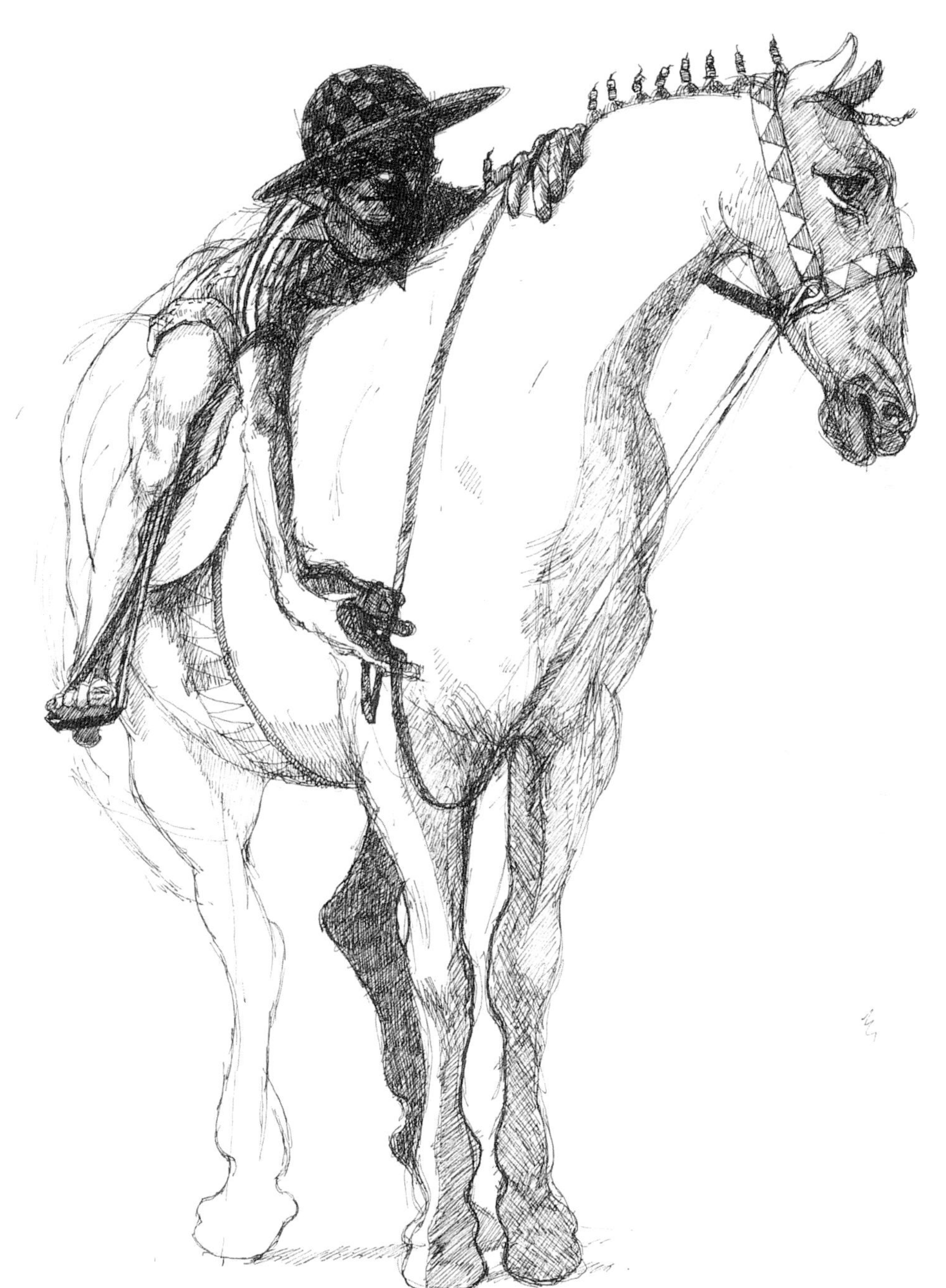

1978
pen and ink
195 × 150

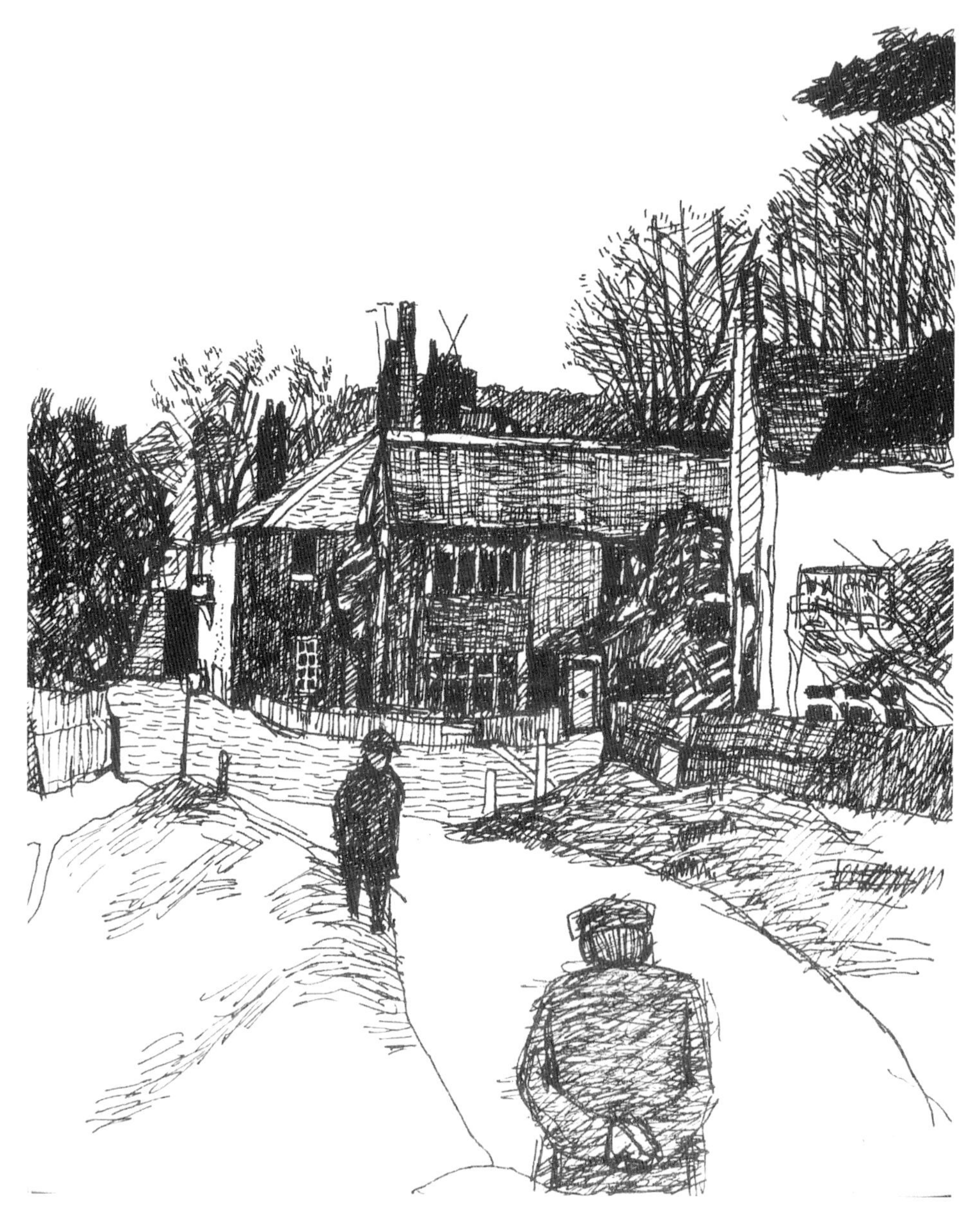

1979
pen and ink
145 × 90

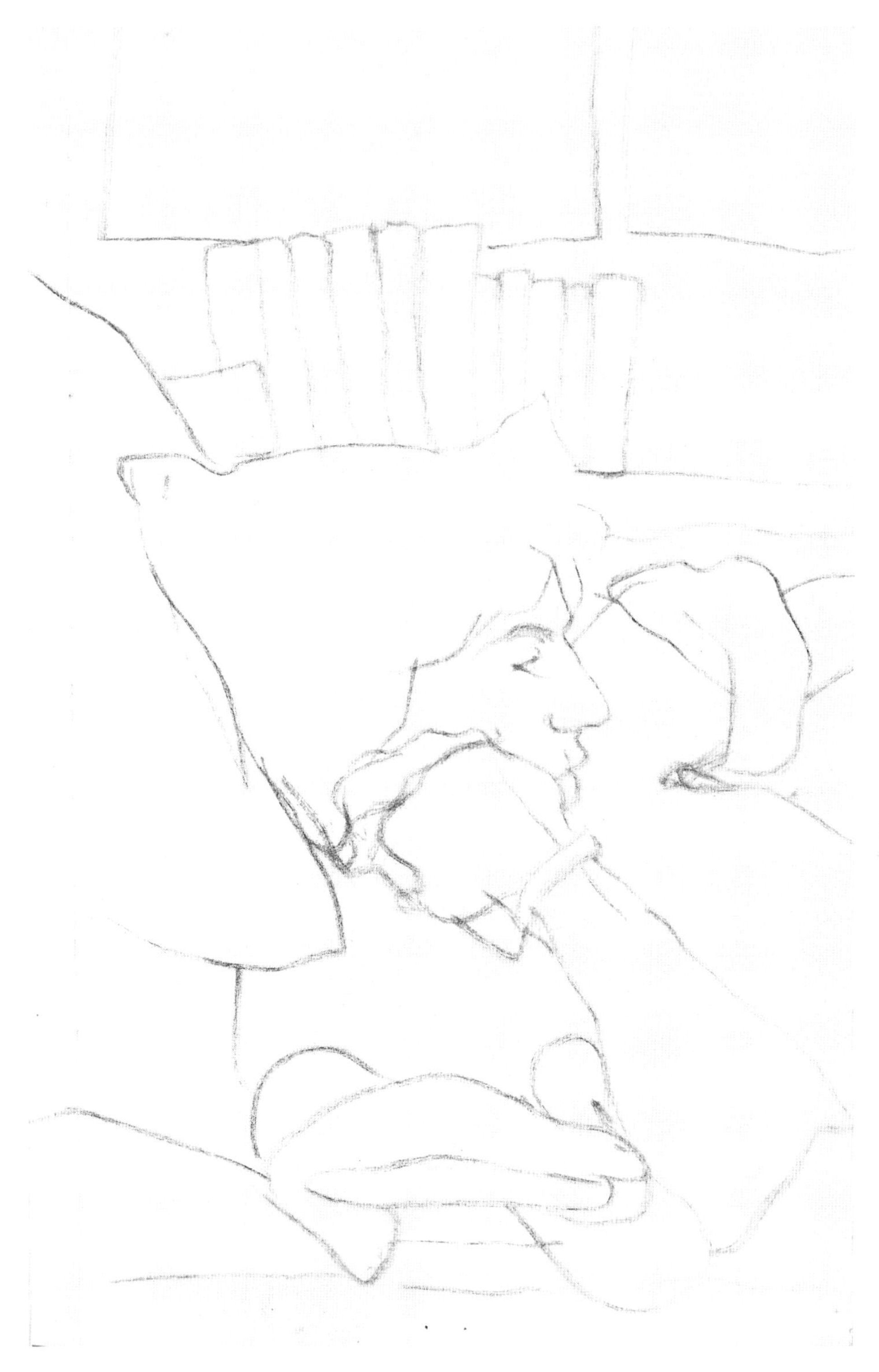

Paul
1979
pencil
145 × 90

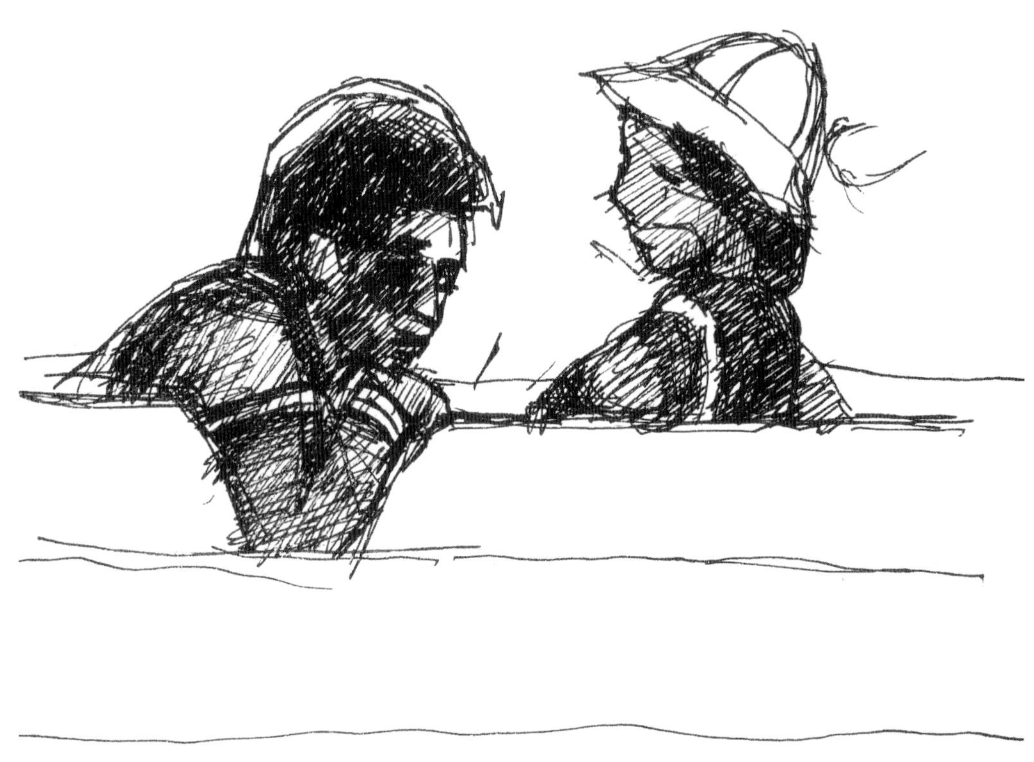

1979
pen and ink
145 × 90

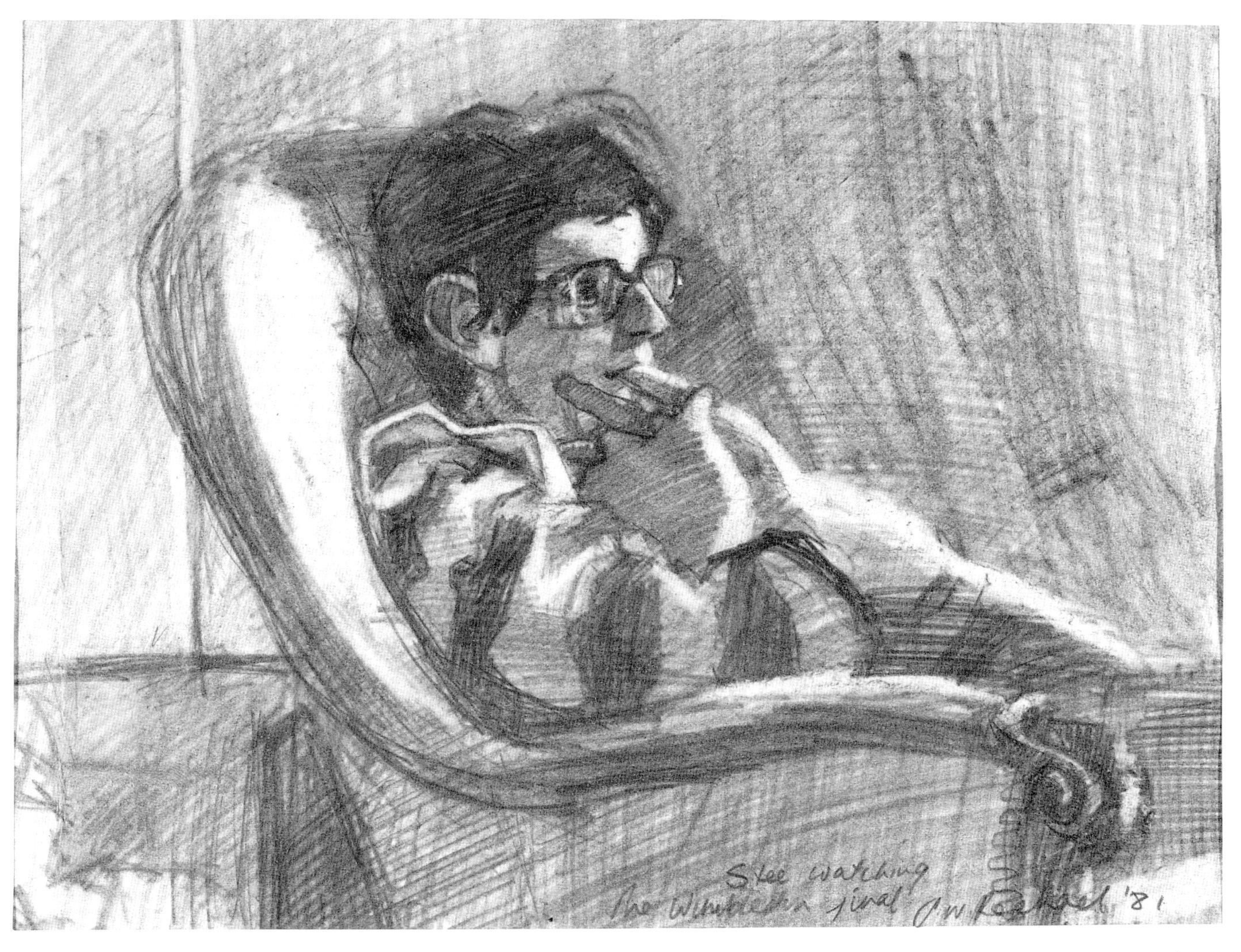

'Stee watching the Wimbledon final'
1981
pencil
160 × 225

13

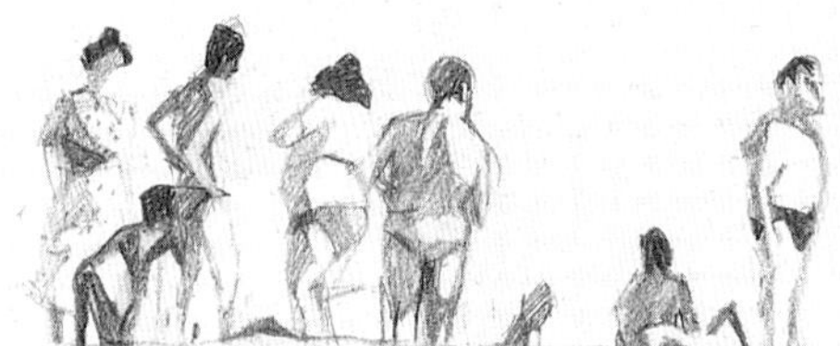

1981
pencil
295 × 200

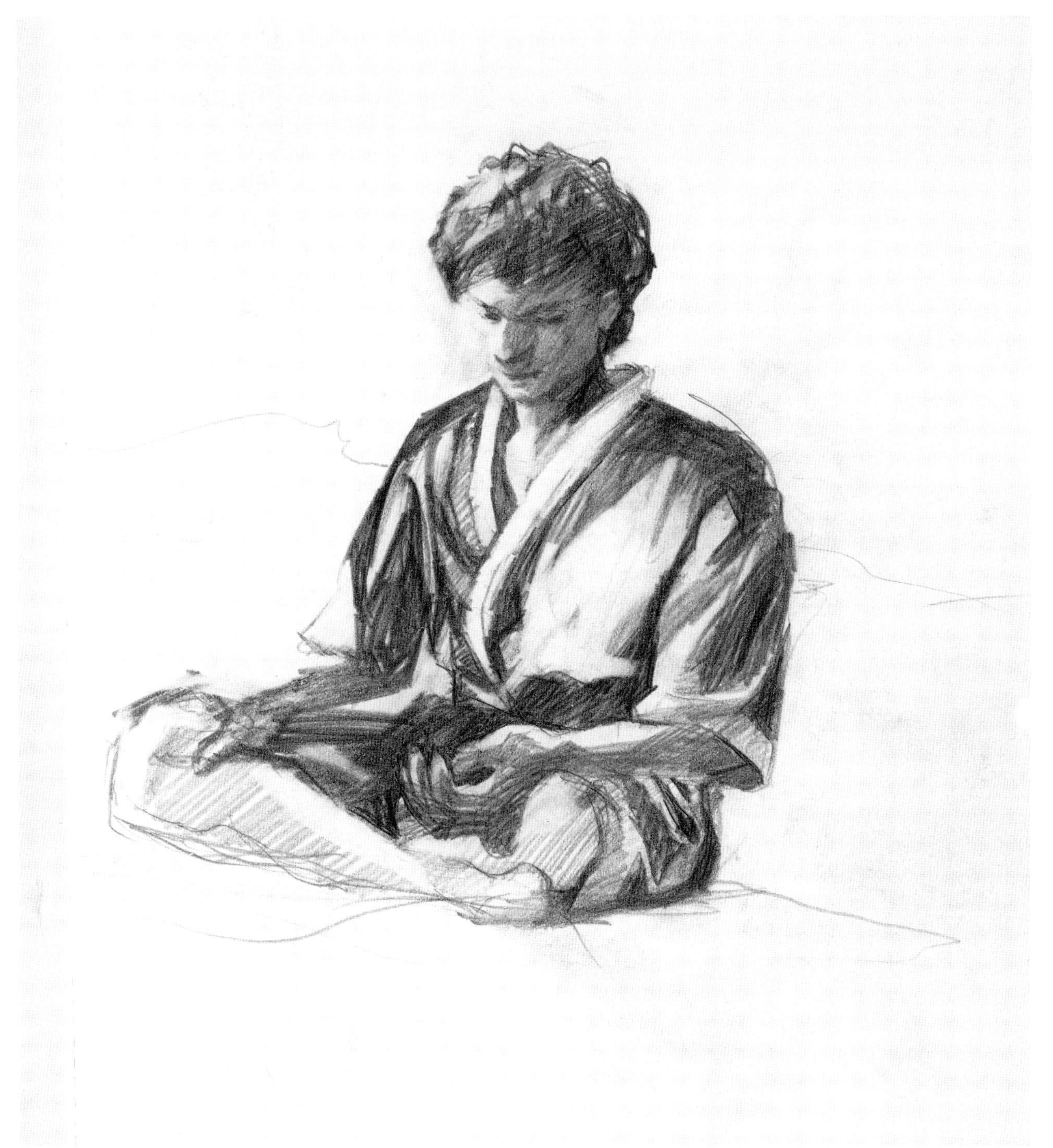

Alain
1981
pencil
295 × 200

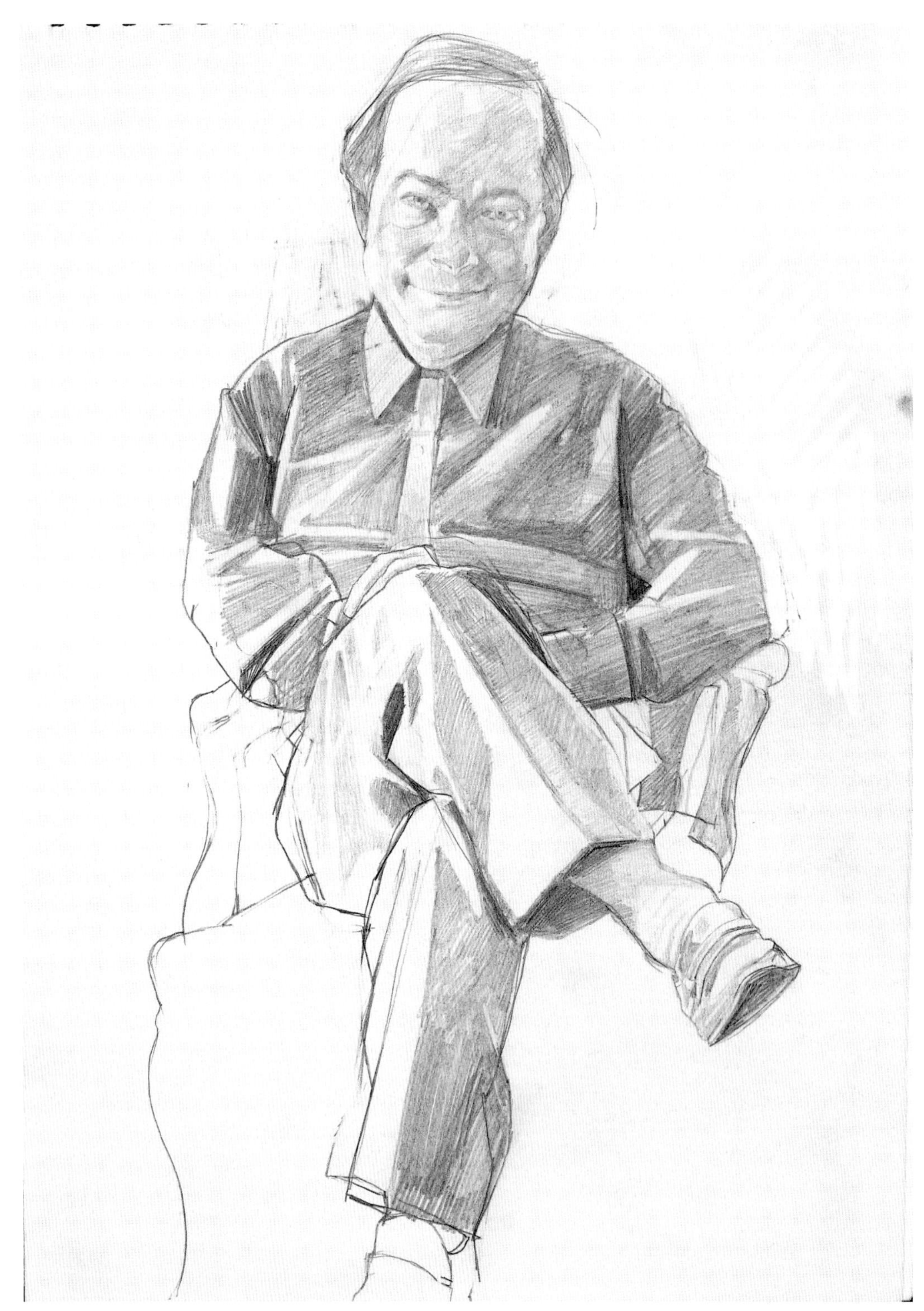

George Steiner
pencil
297 × 210

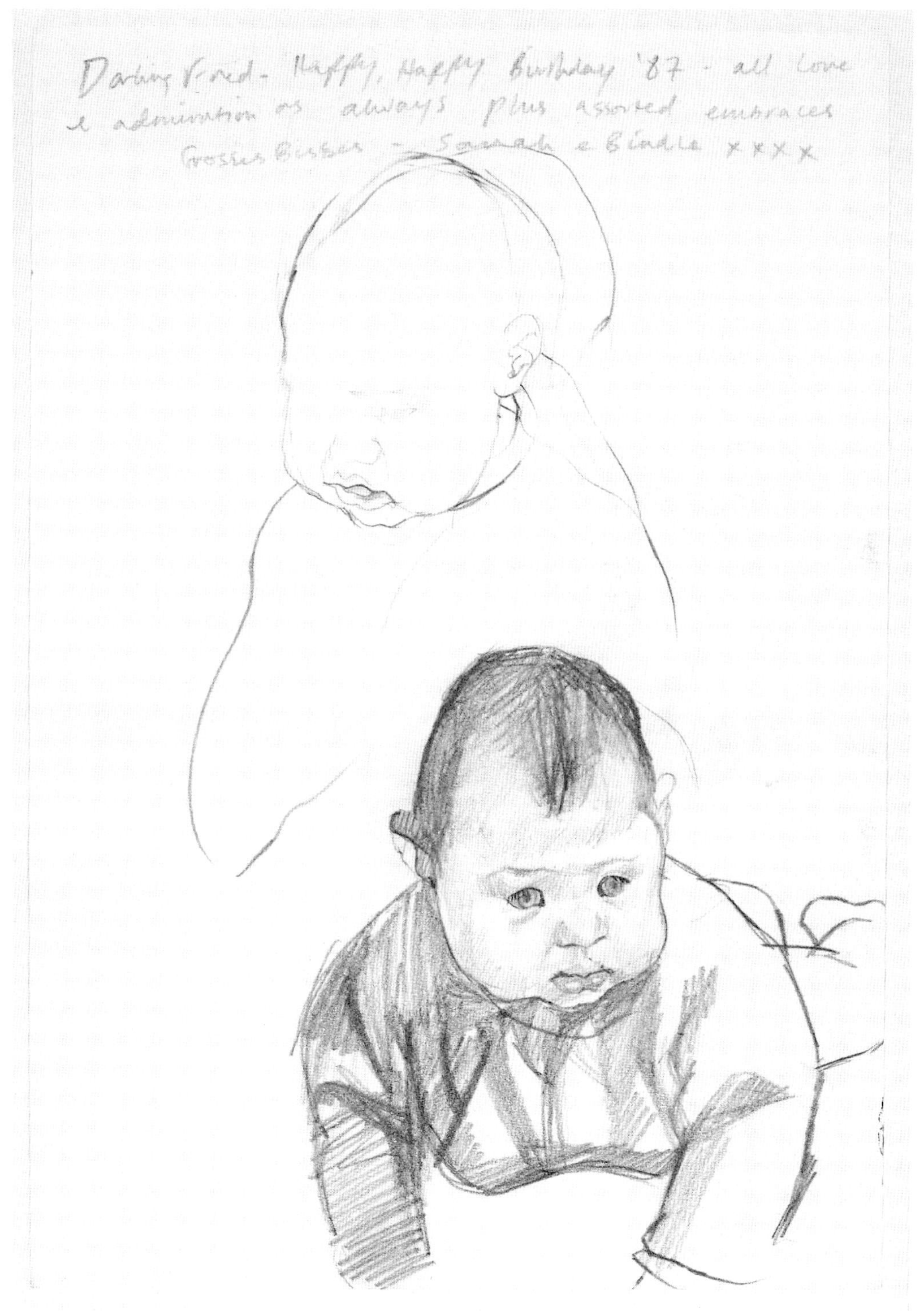

Natasha
1987
pencil
218 × 150

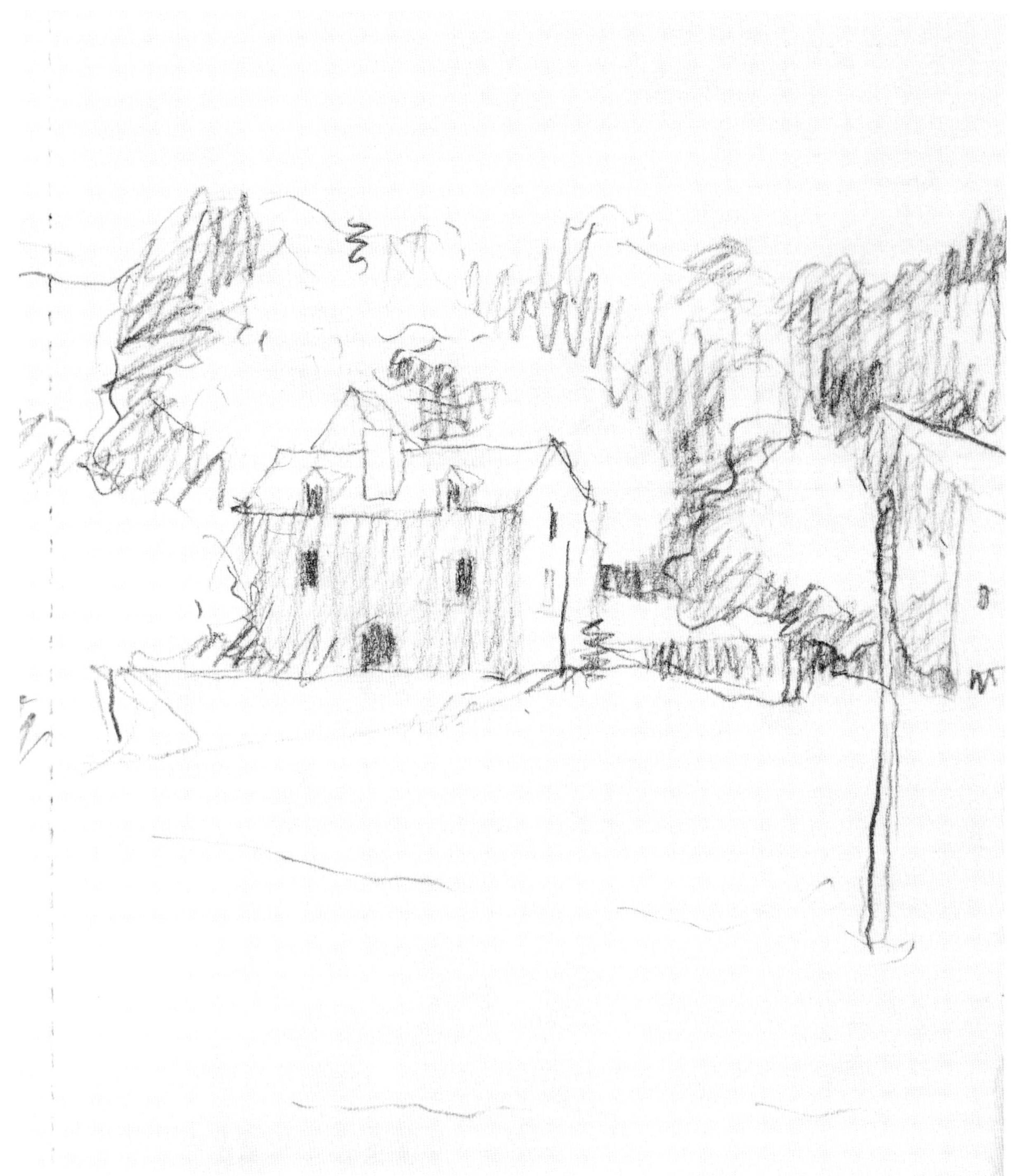

Dordogne
1986
pencil
210 × 148

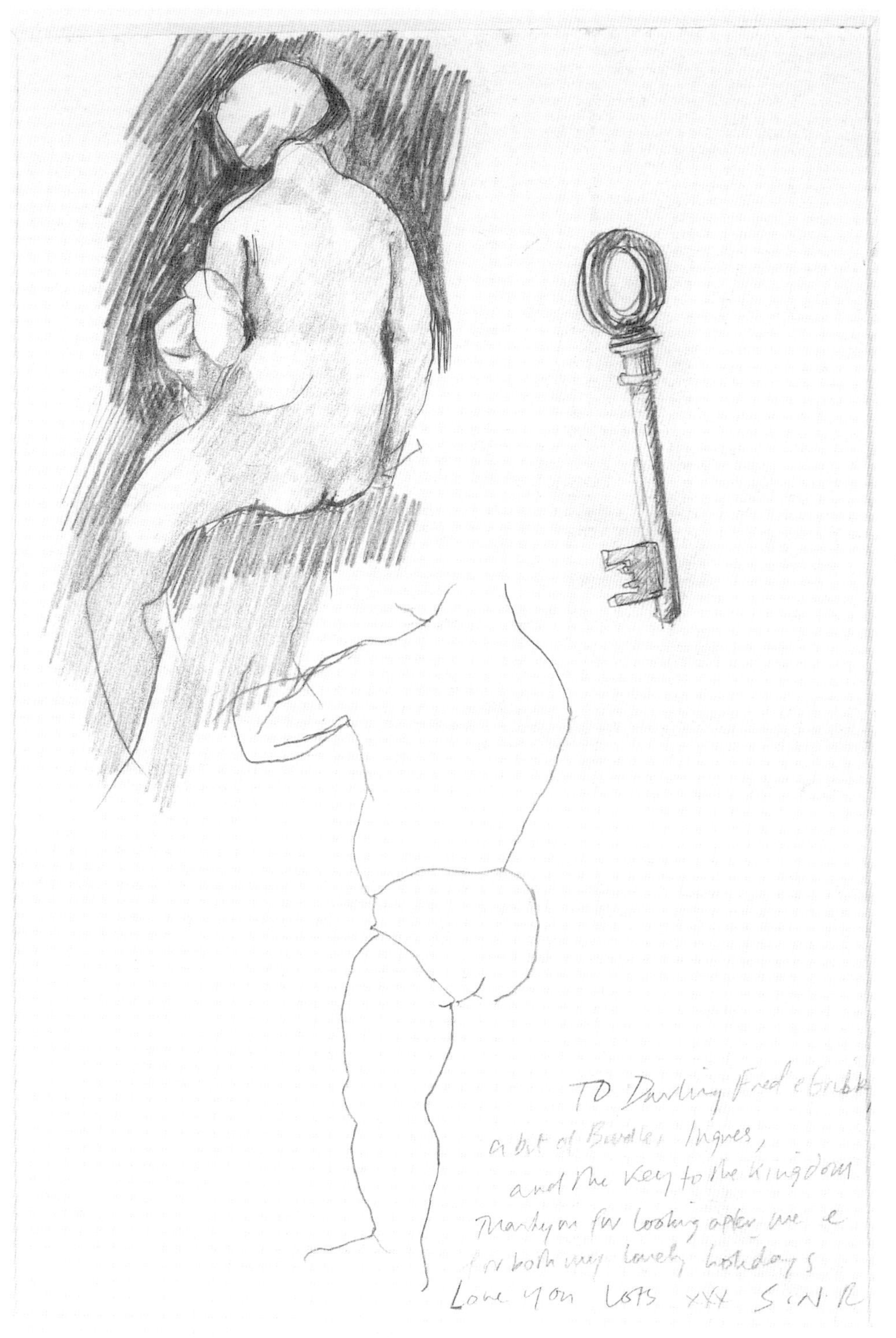

'A bit of Bindle,
Ingres, and the key
to the kingdom'
1987
pencil
200 × 140

19

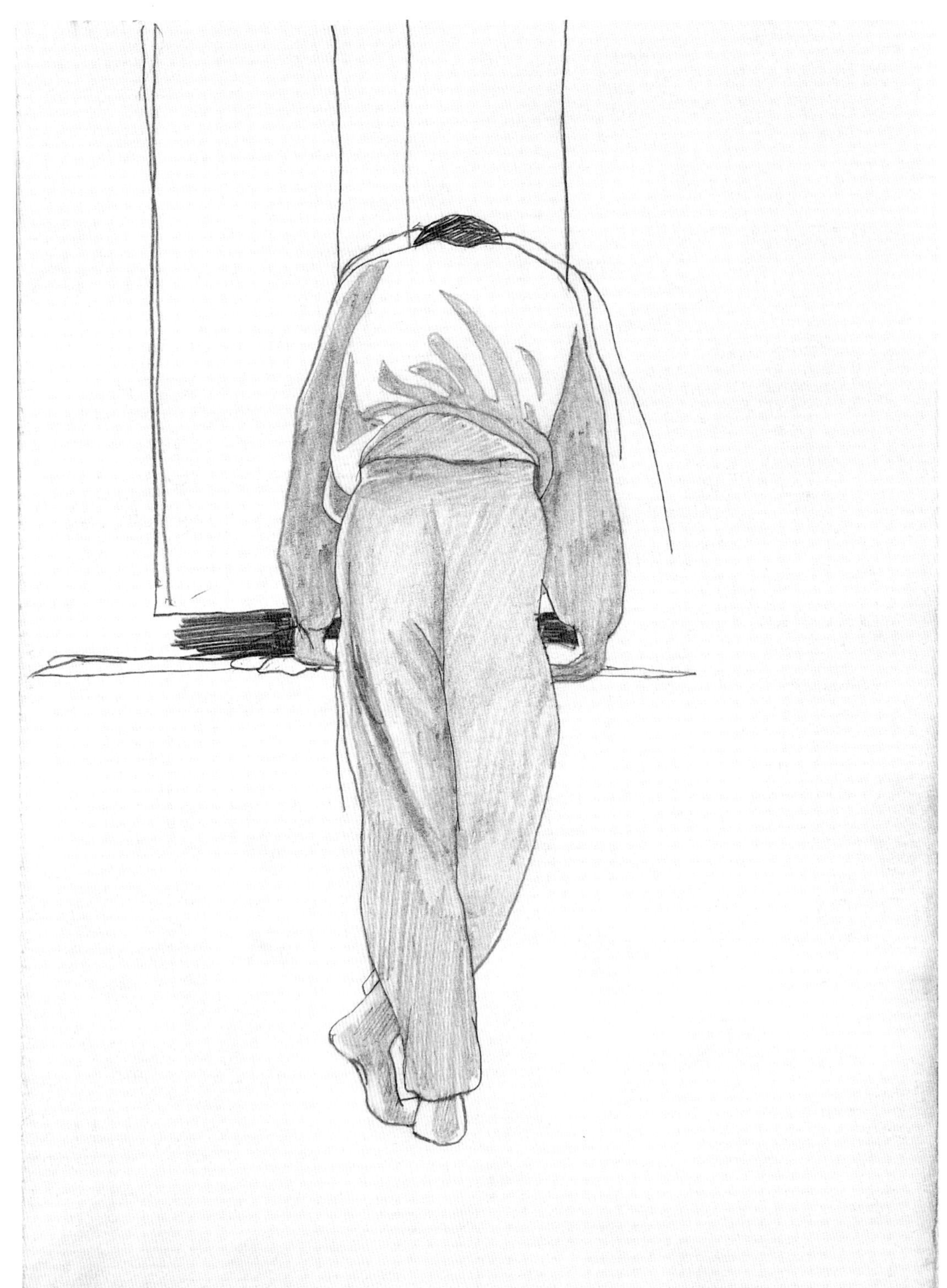

1987
pencil
210 × 148

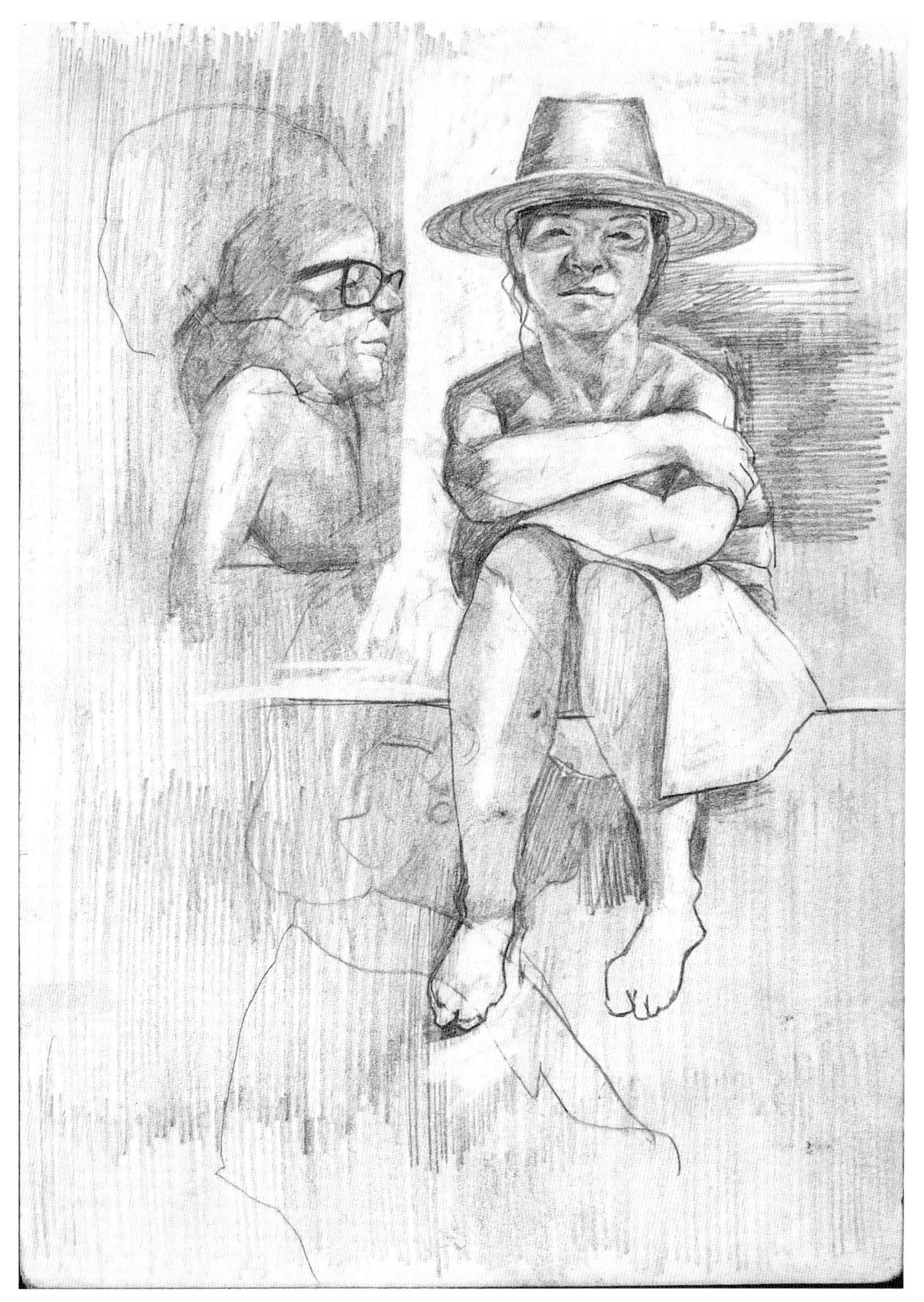

1987
pencil
210 × 148

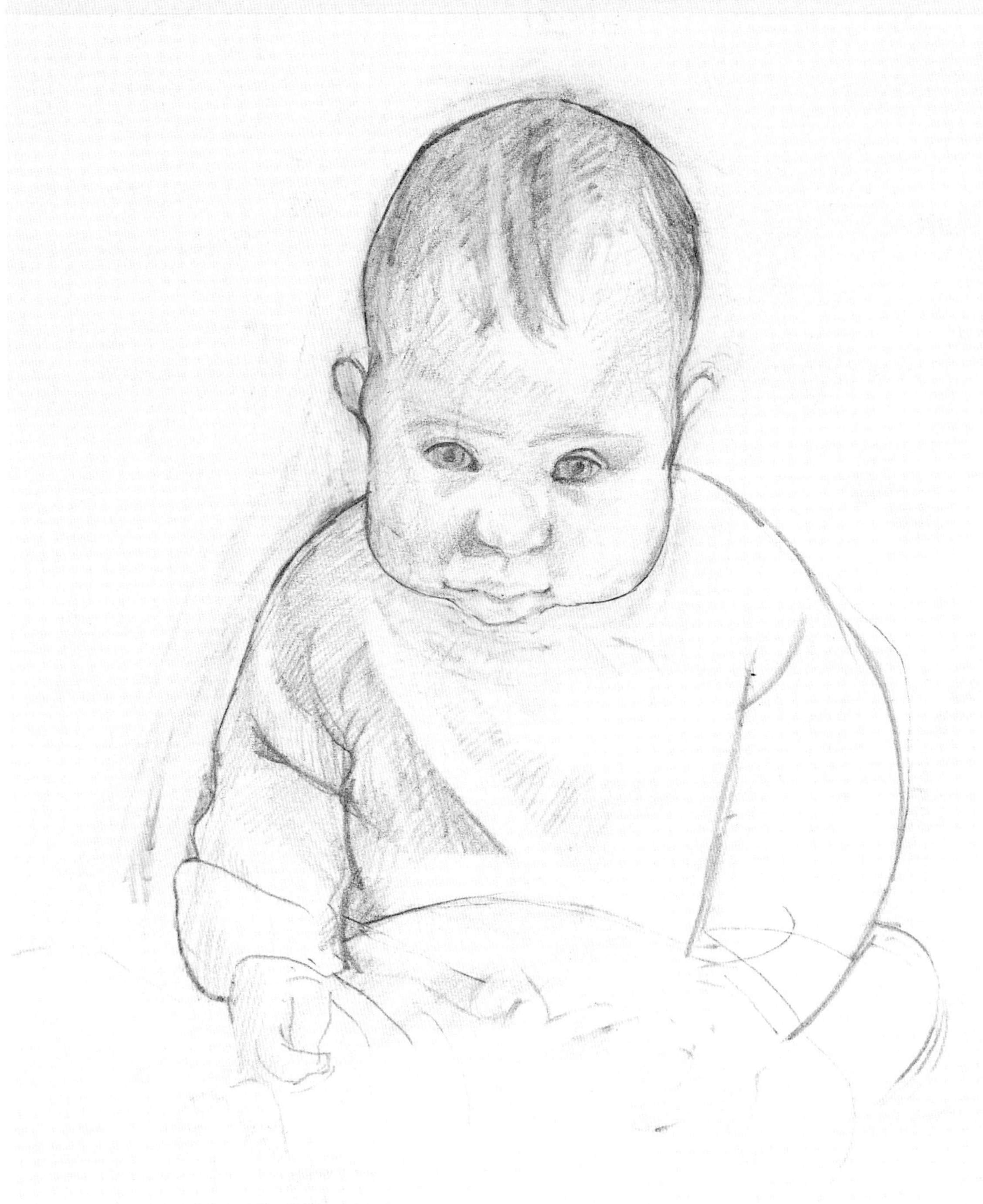

Natasha
1987
pencil
150 × 140

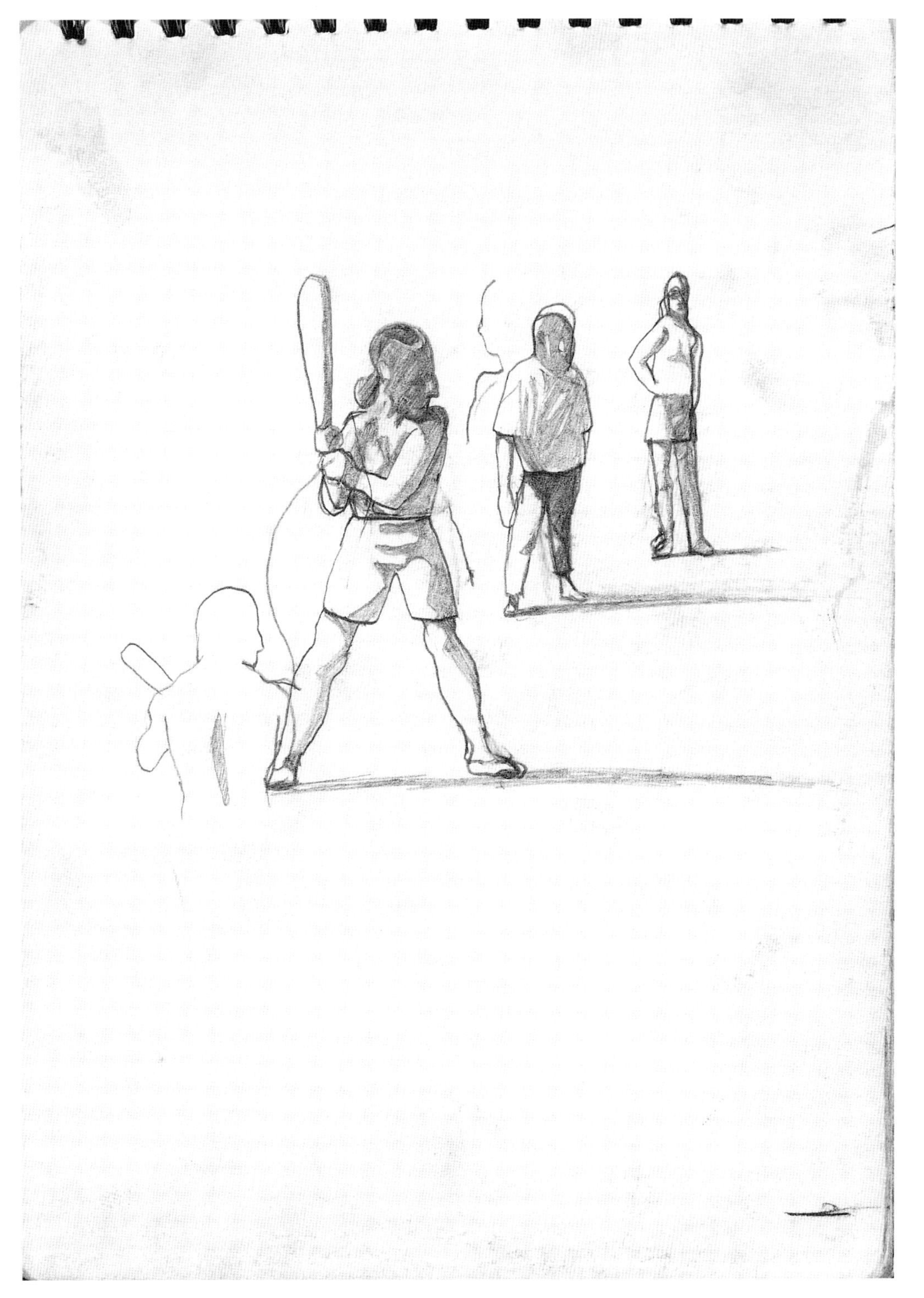

1987
pencil
210 × 148

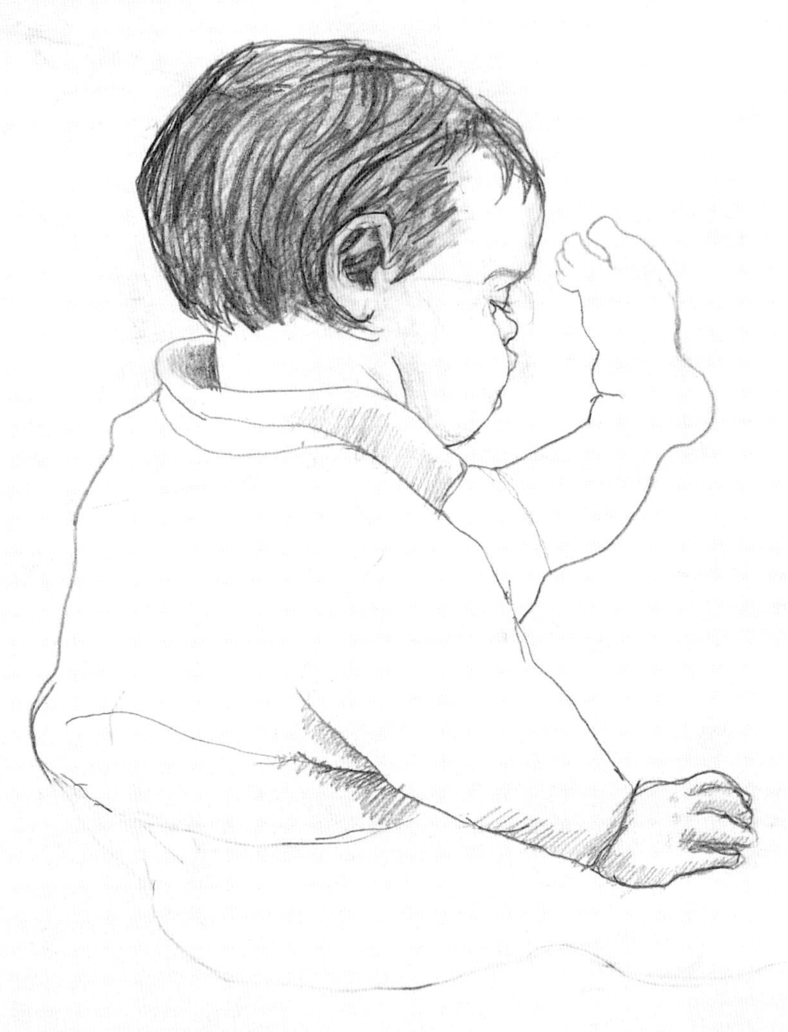

Natasha
1987
pencil
210 × 148

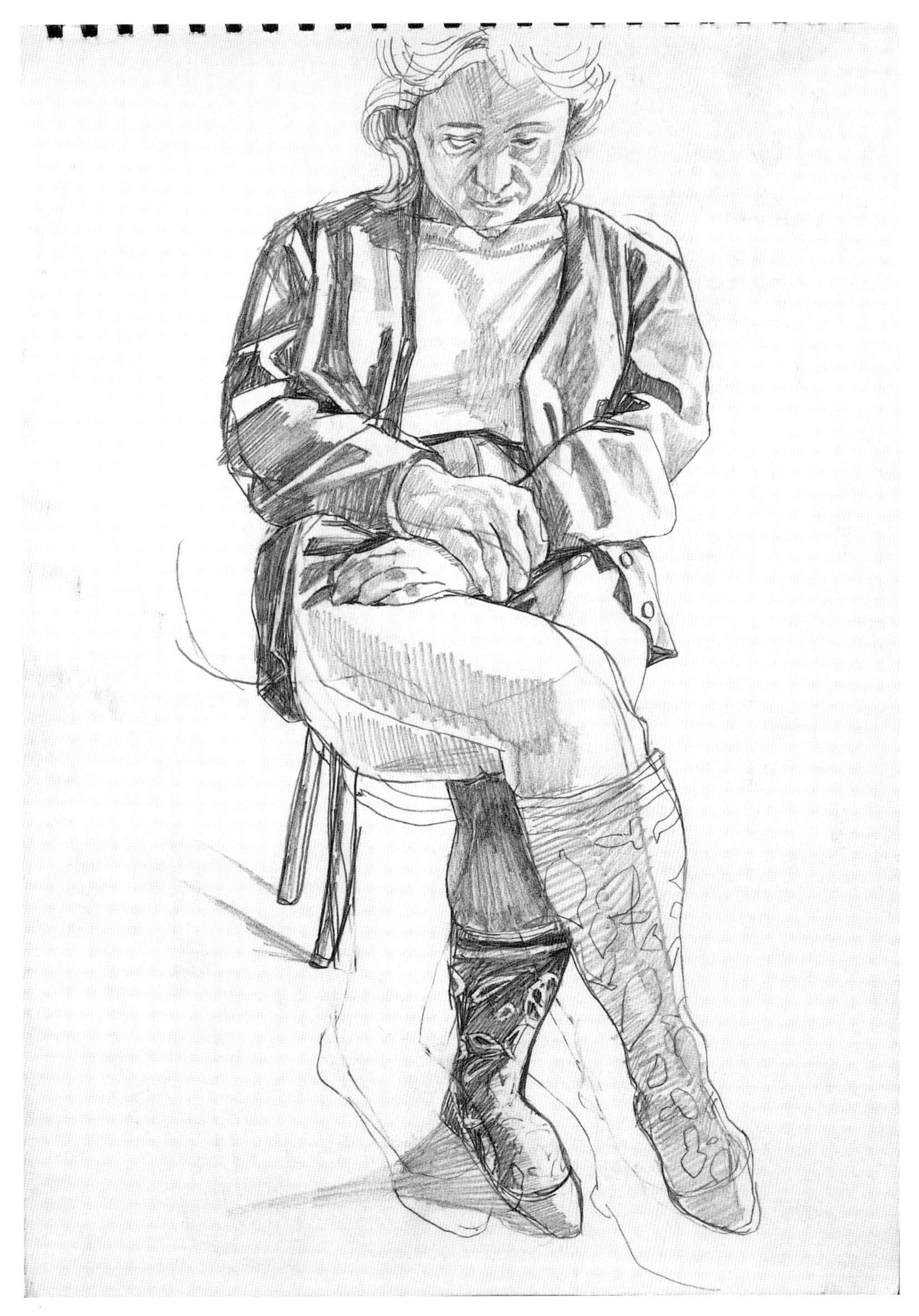

pencil
297 × 210

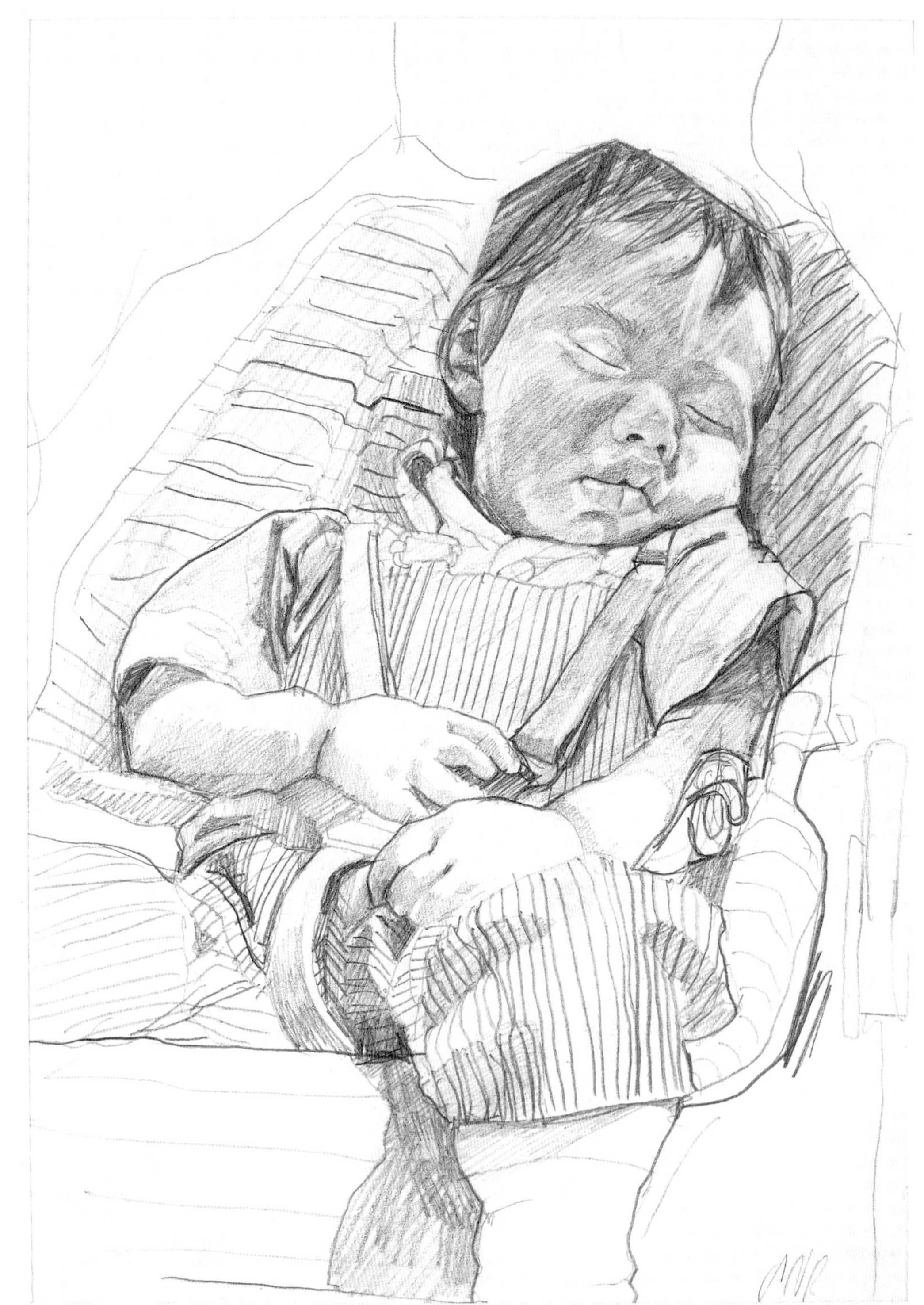

Natasha
1988
pencil
200 × 140

26

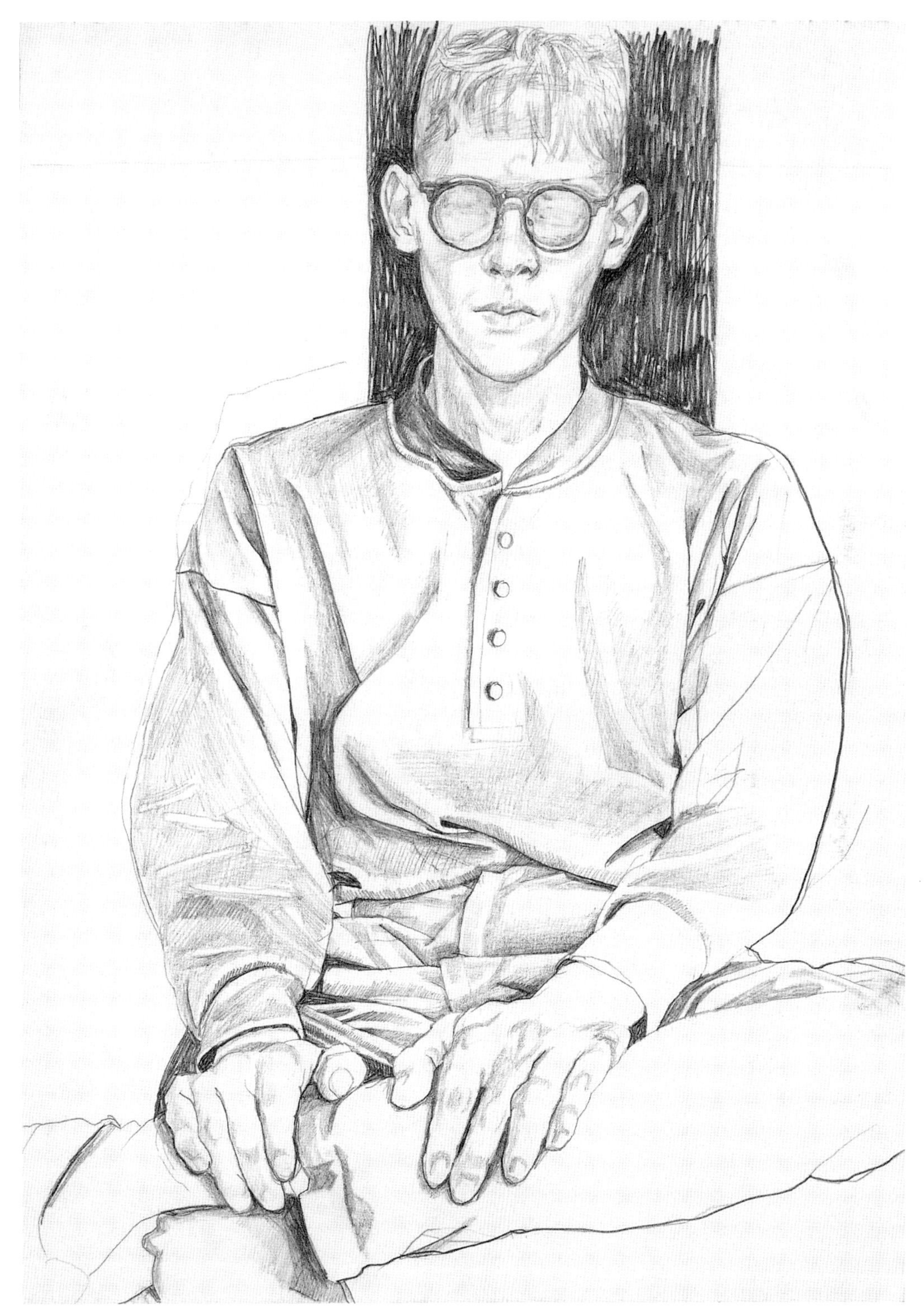

Joe
pencil
297 × 210

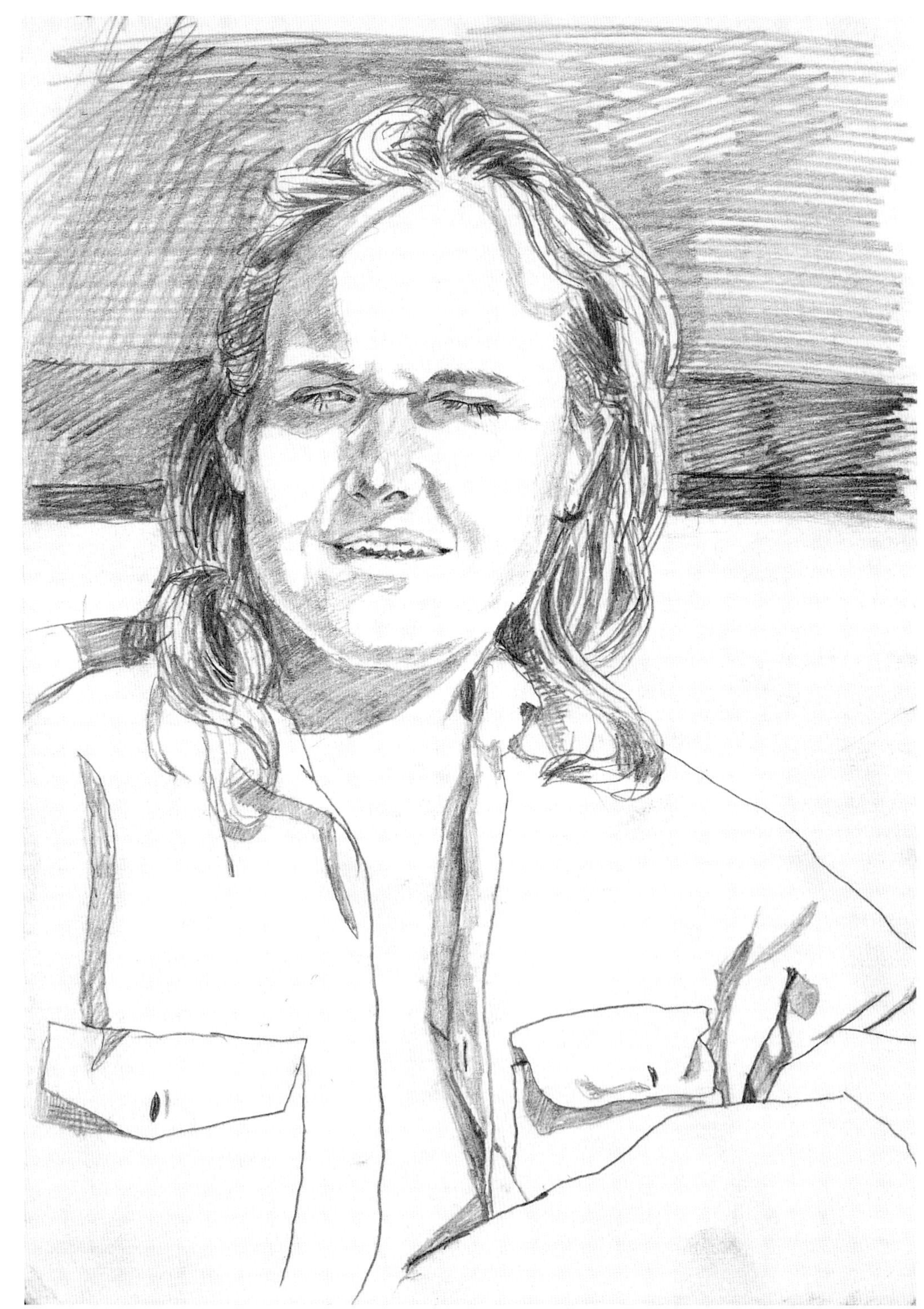

Véronique
pencil
210 × 148

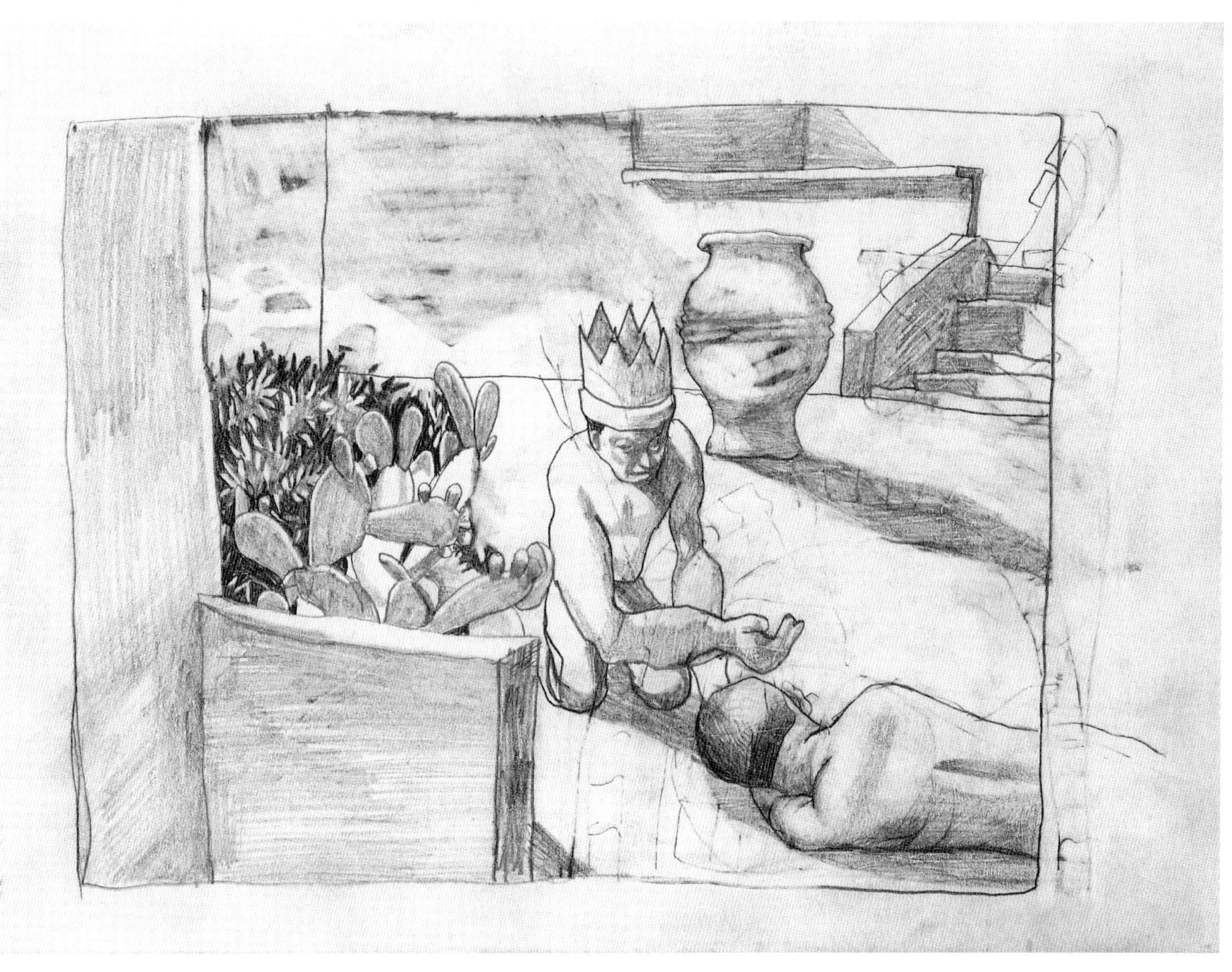

Study for *The Hidden Eye*
1988–9
pencil
148 × 210

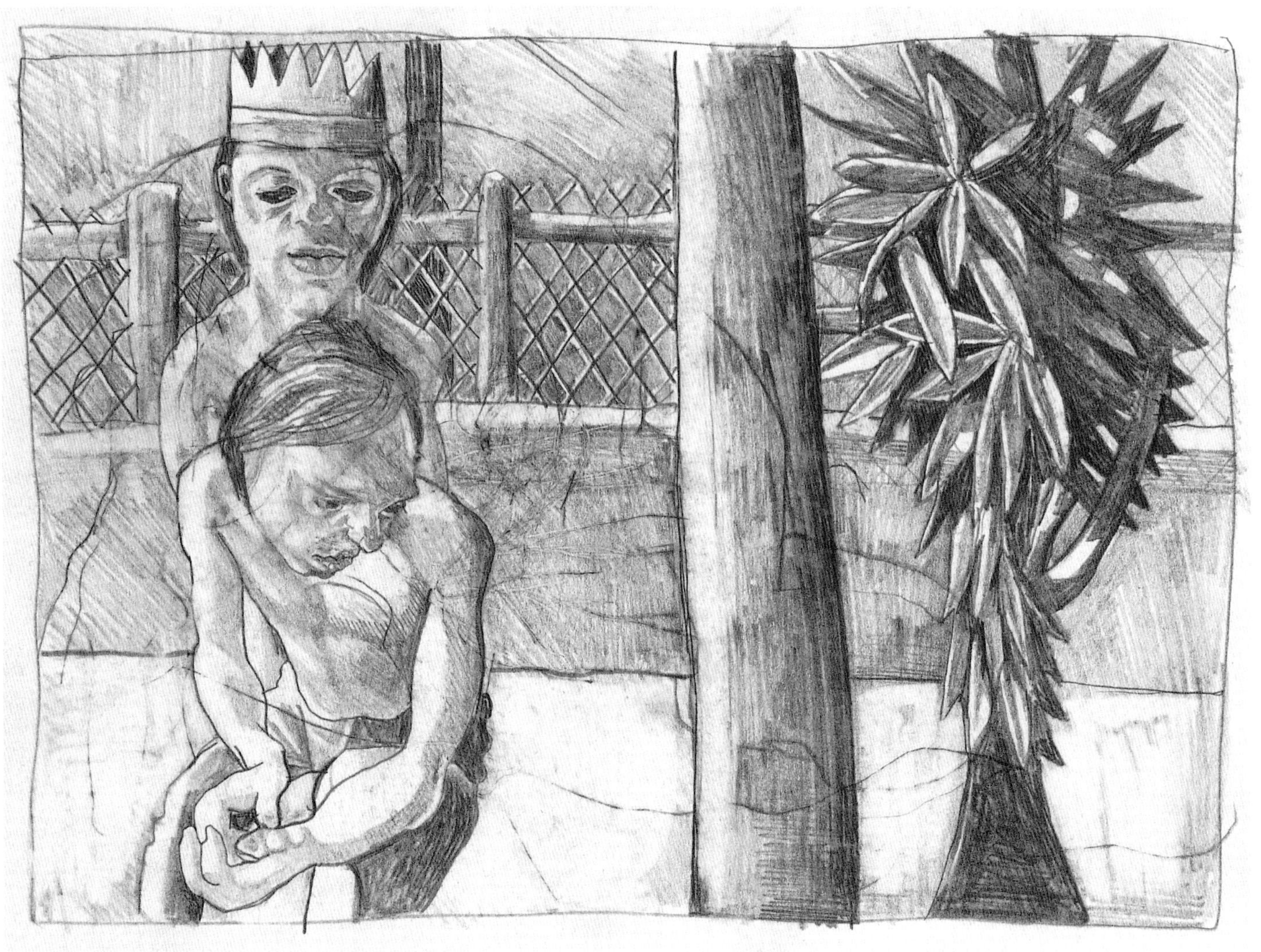

Study for *The Hidden Eye*
1988–9
pencil
148 × 210

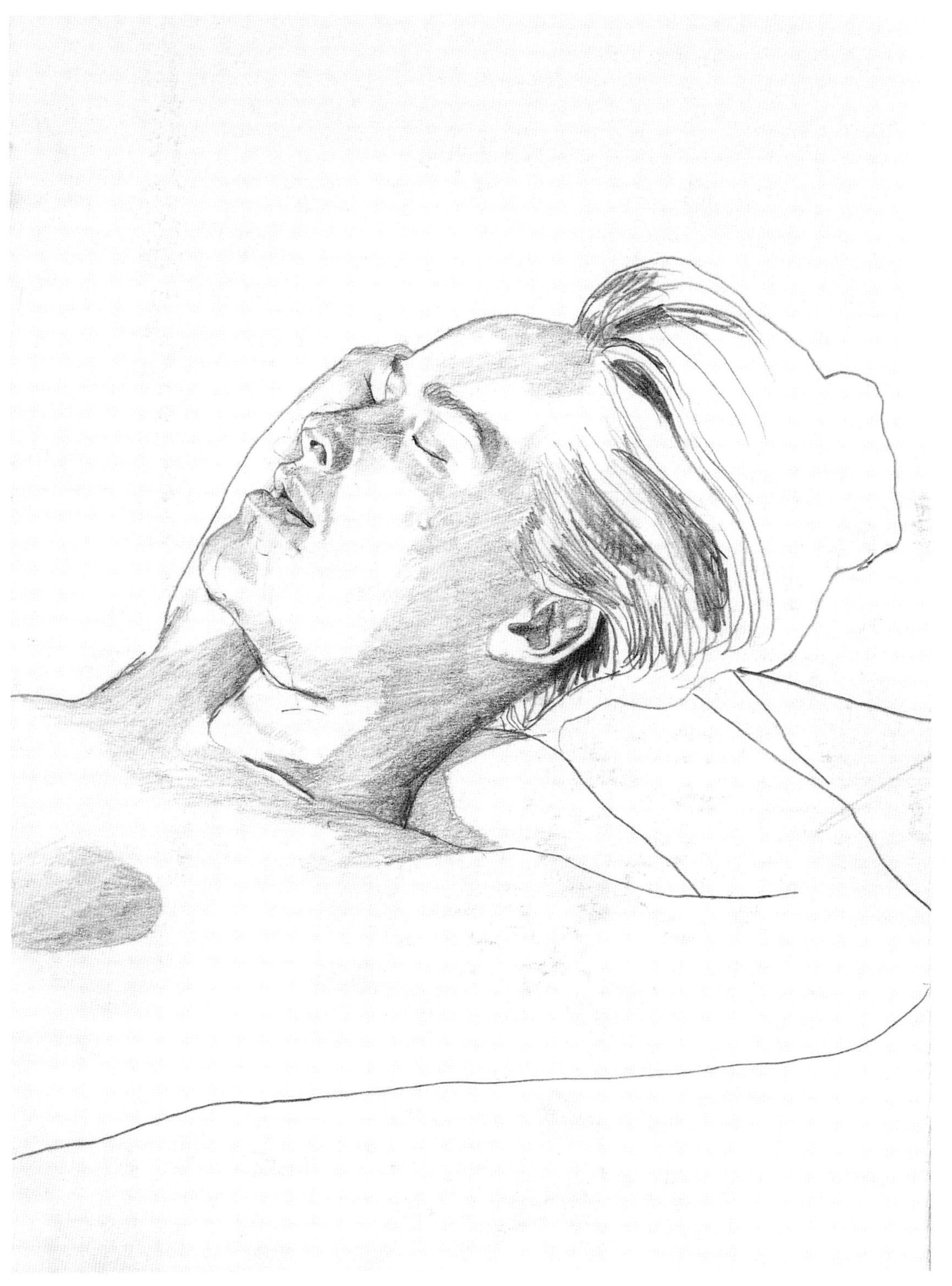

Véronique
pencil
210 × 148

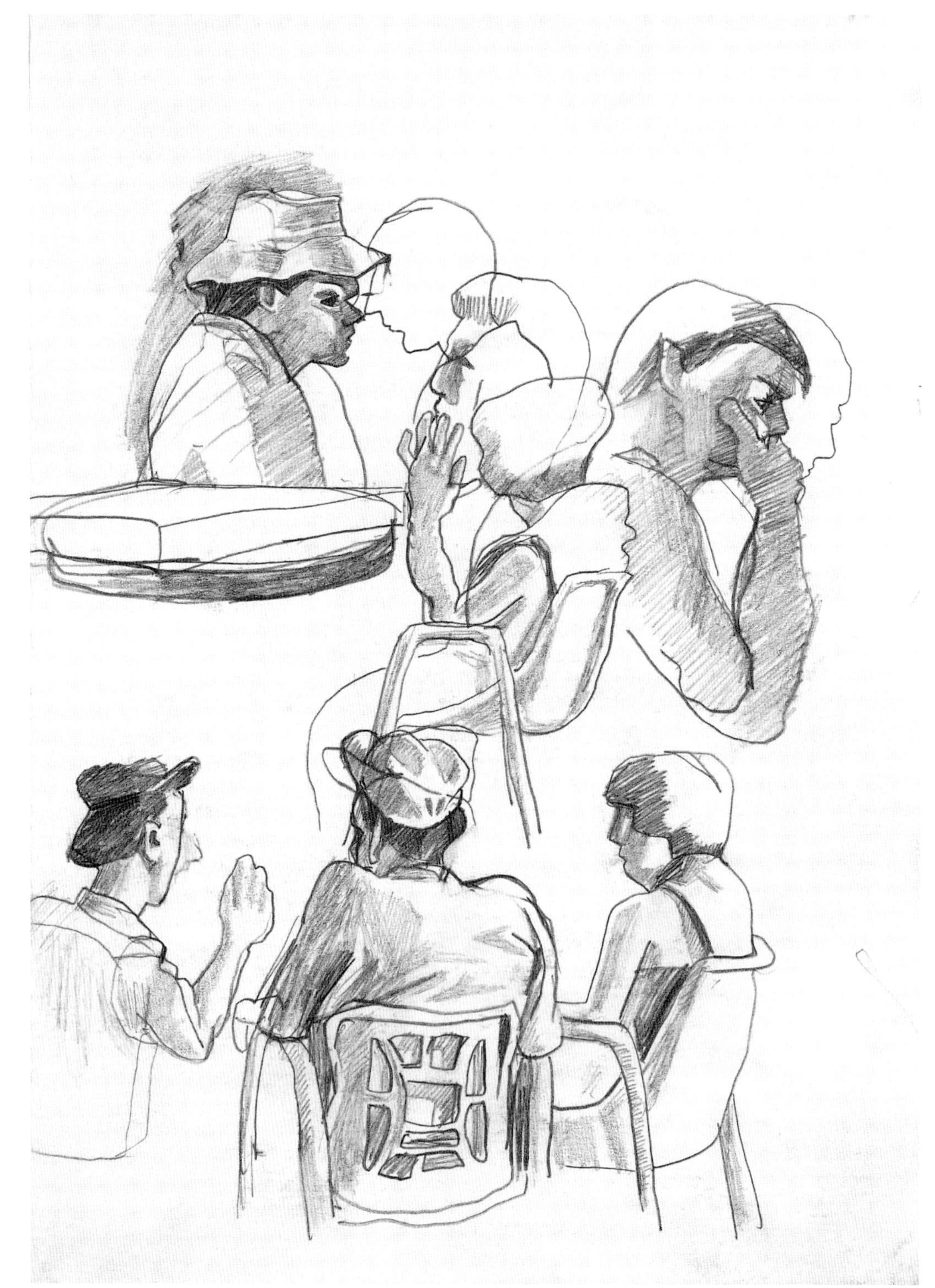

Study of people at
Far Out café, Ios
pencil
210 × 148

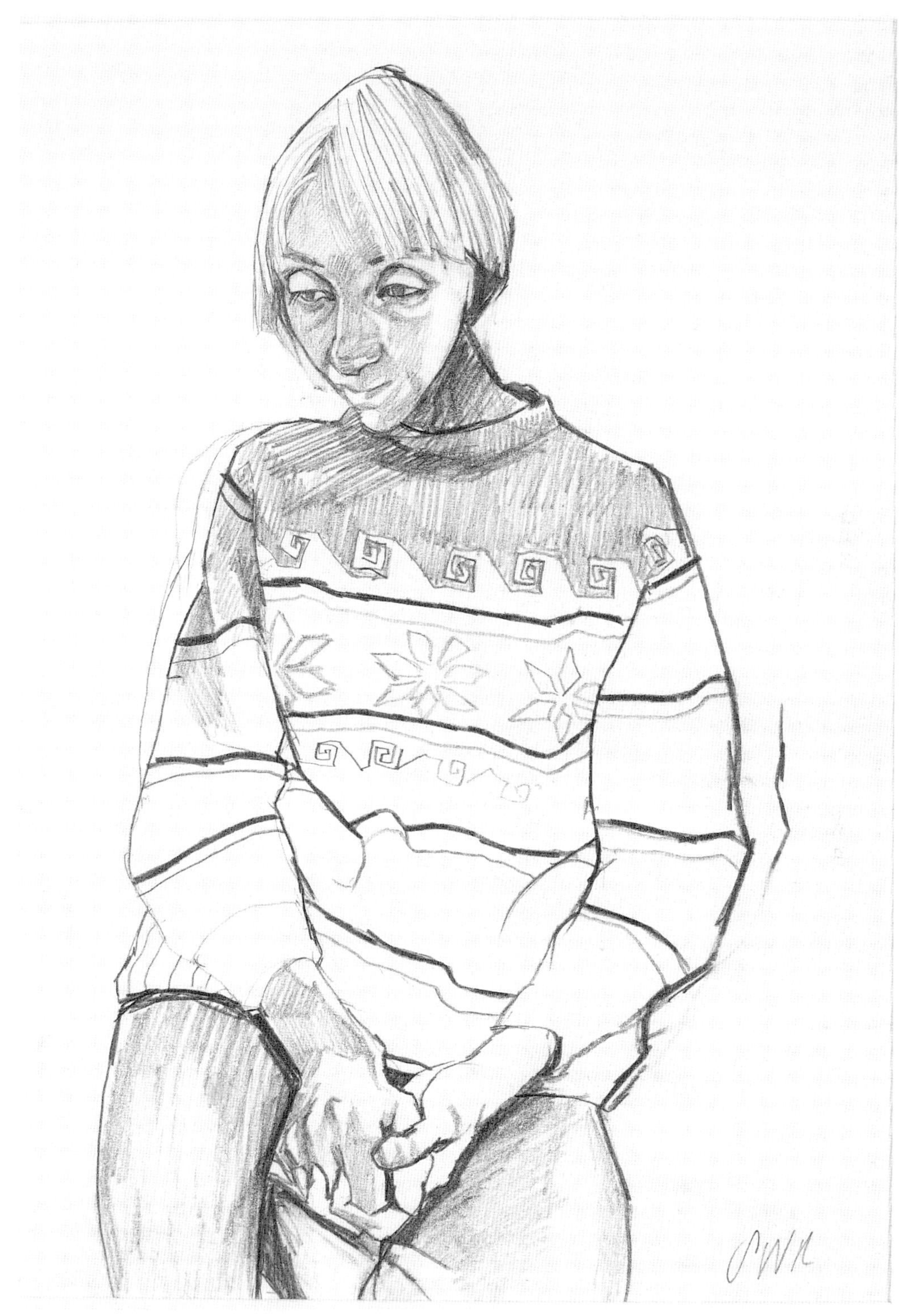

Justine
pencil
200 × 140

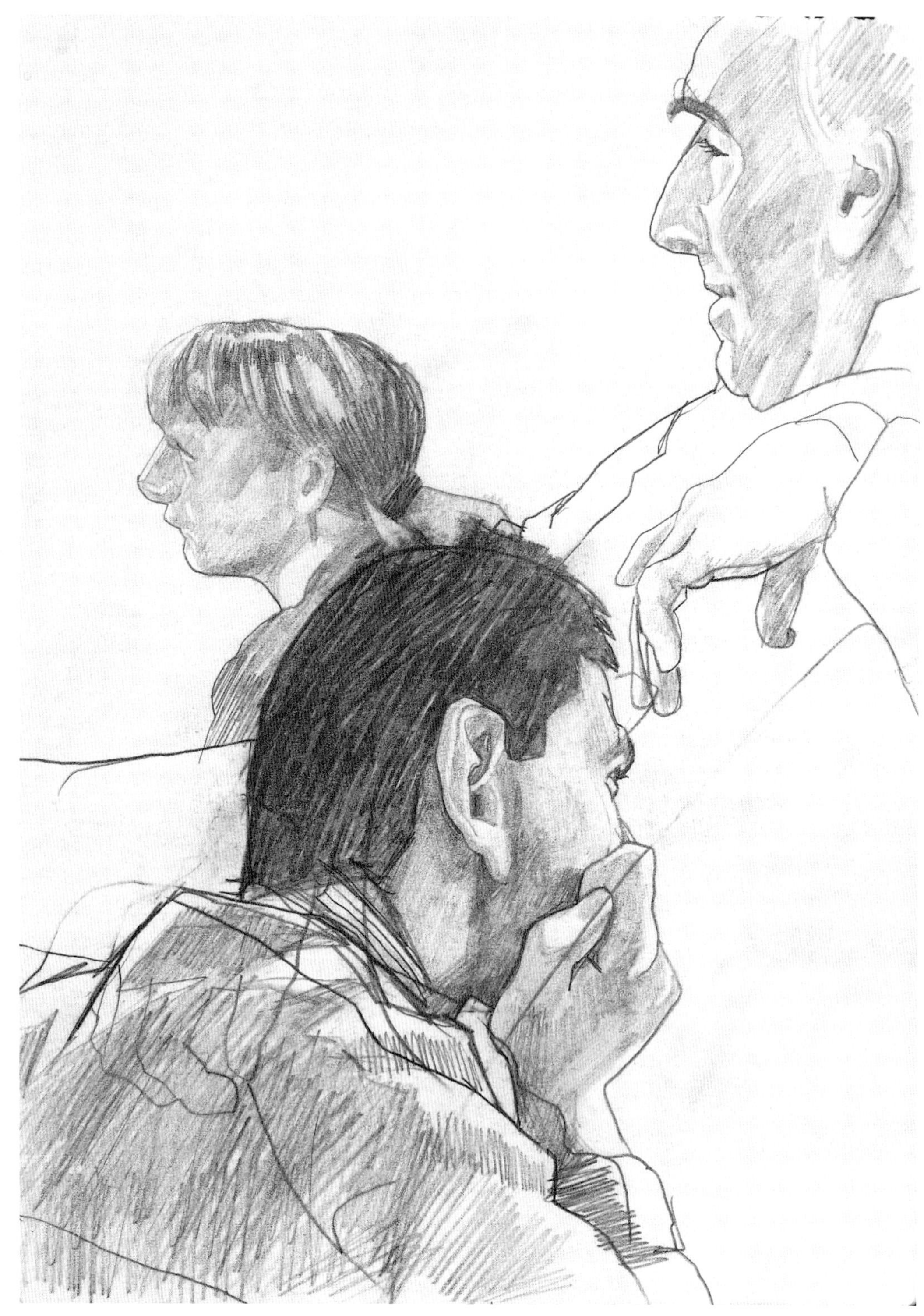

Fred, Stee and Mark
pencil
210 × 148

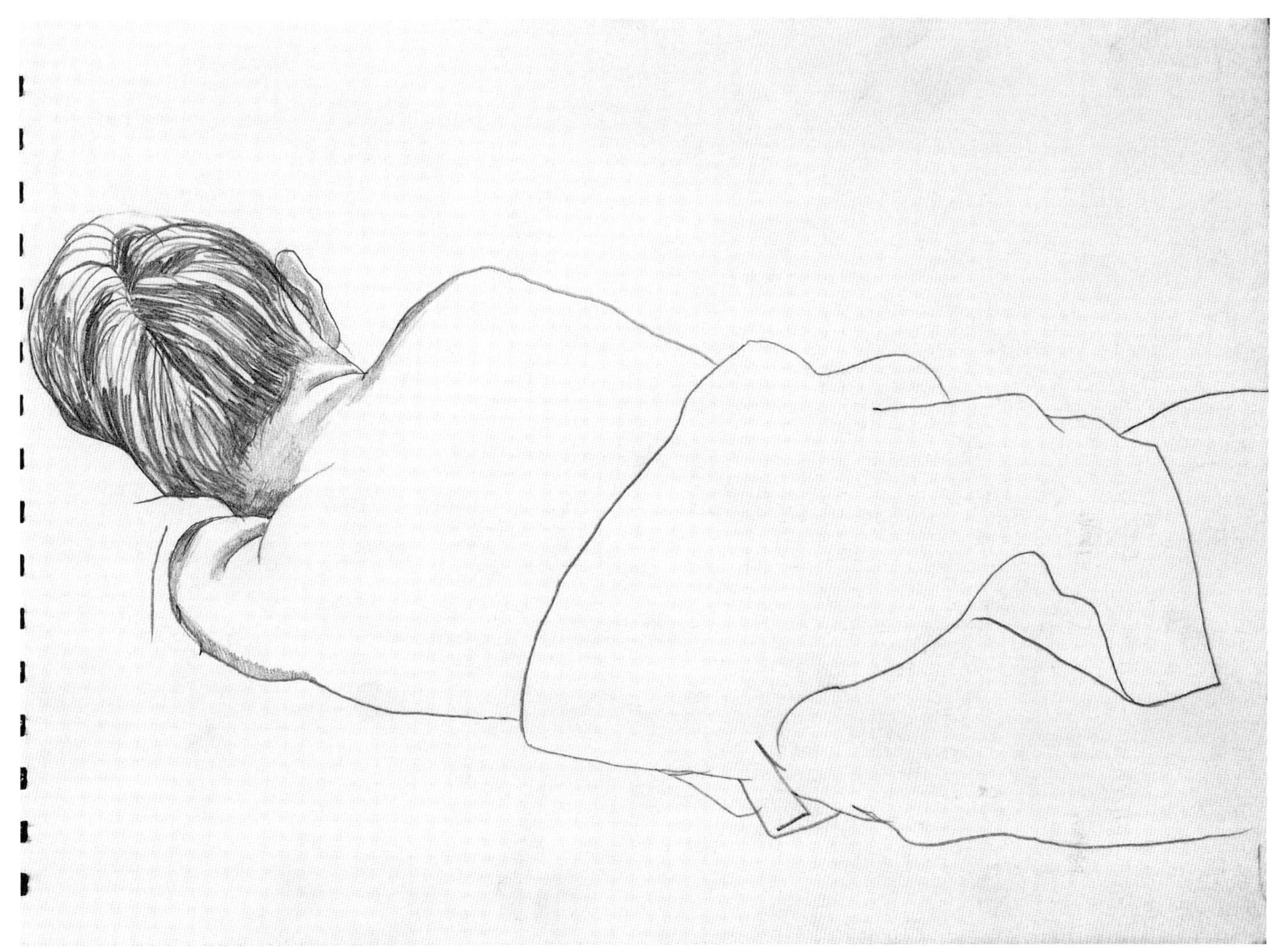

pencil
148 × 210

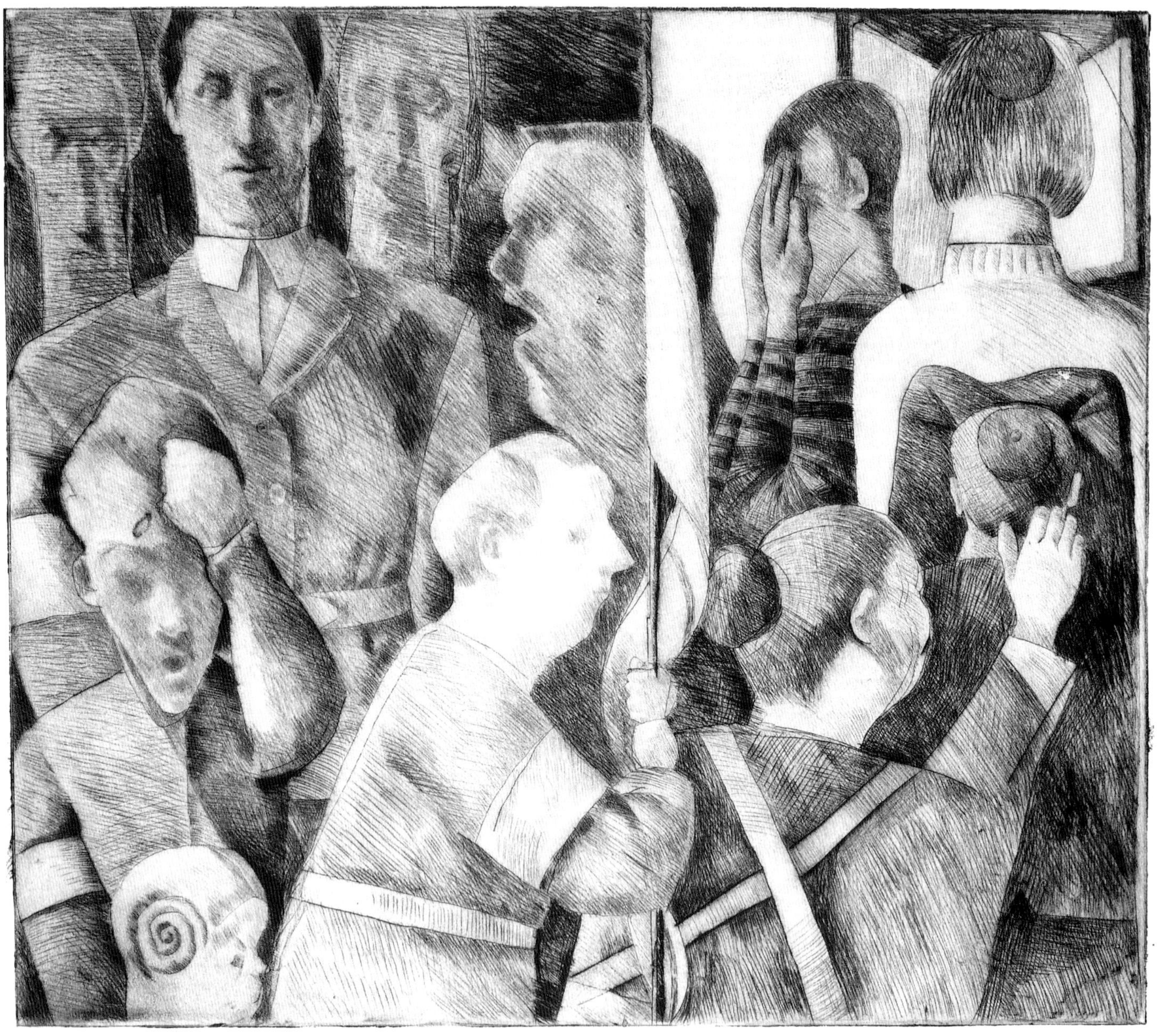

'Pamyat'
1990
pencil
170 × 200

36

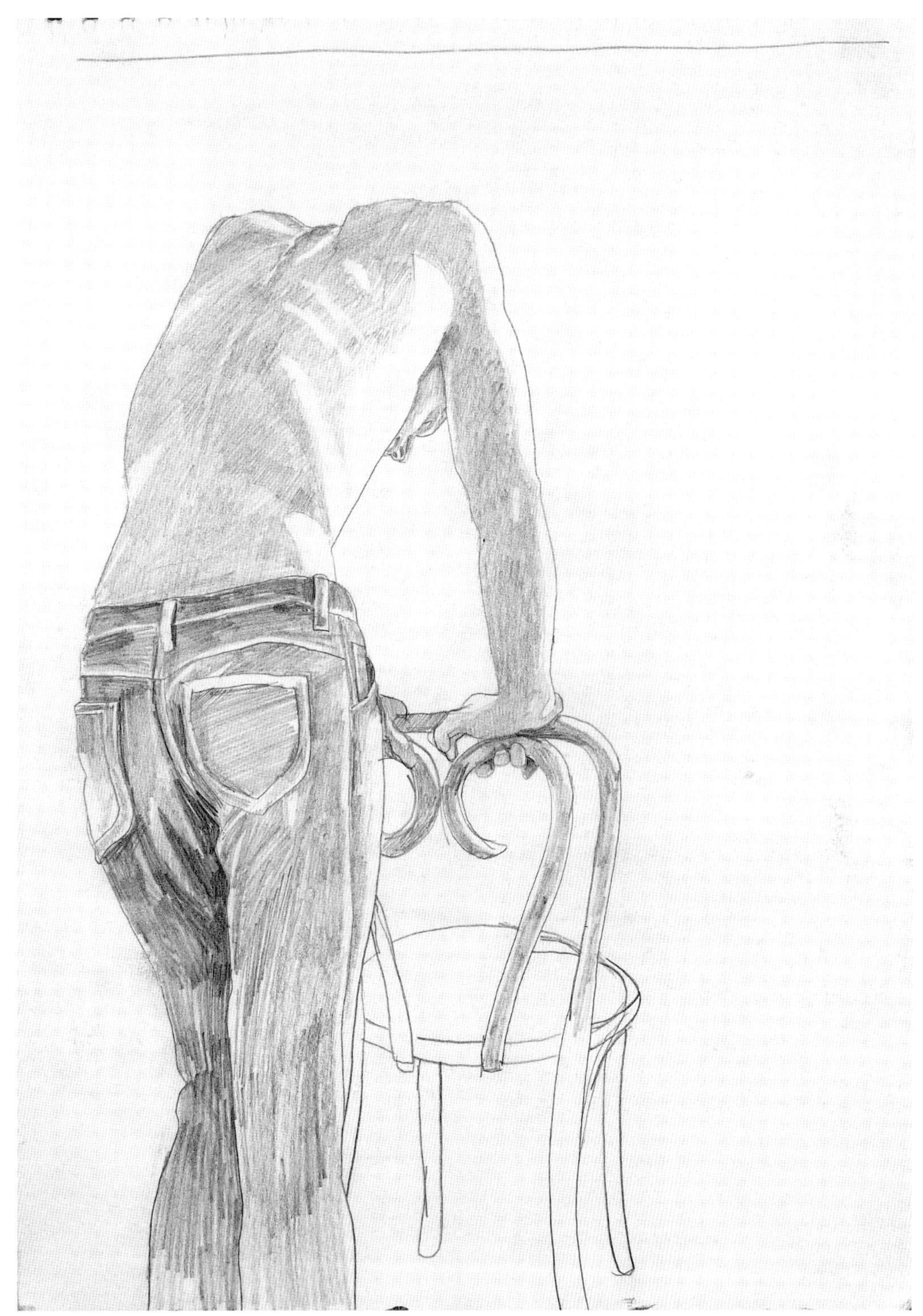

pencil
297 × 210

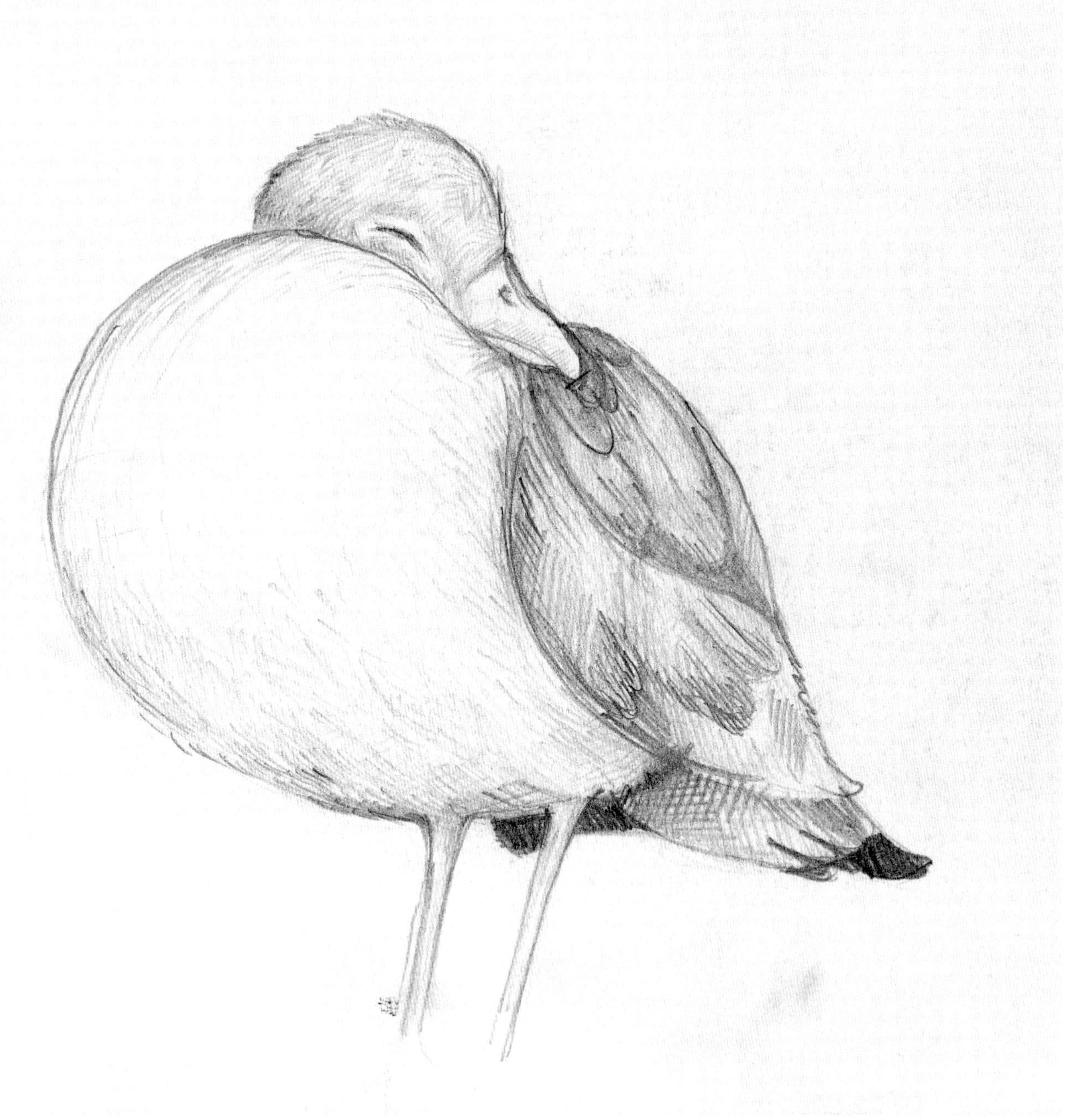

pencil
297 × 210

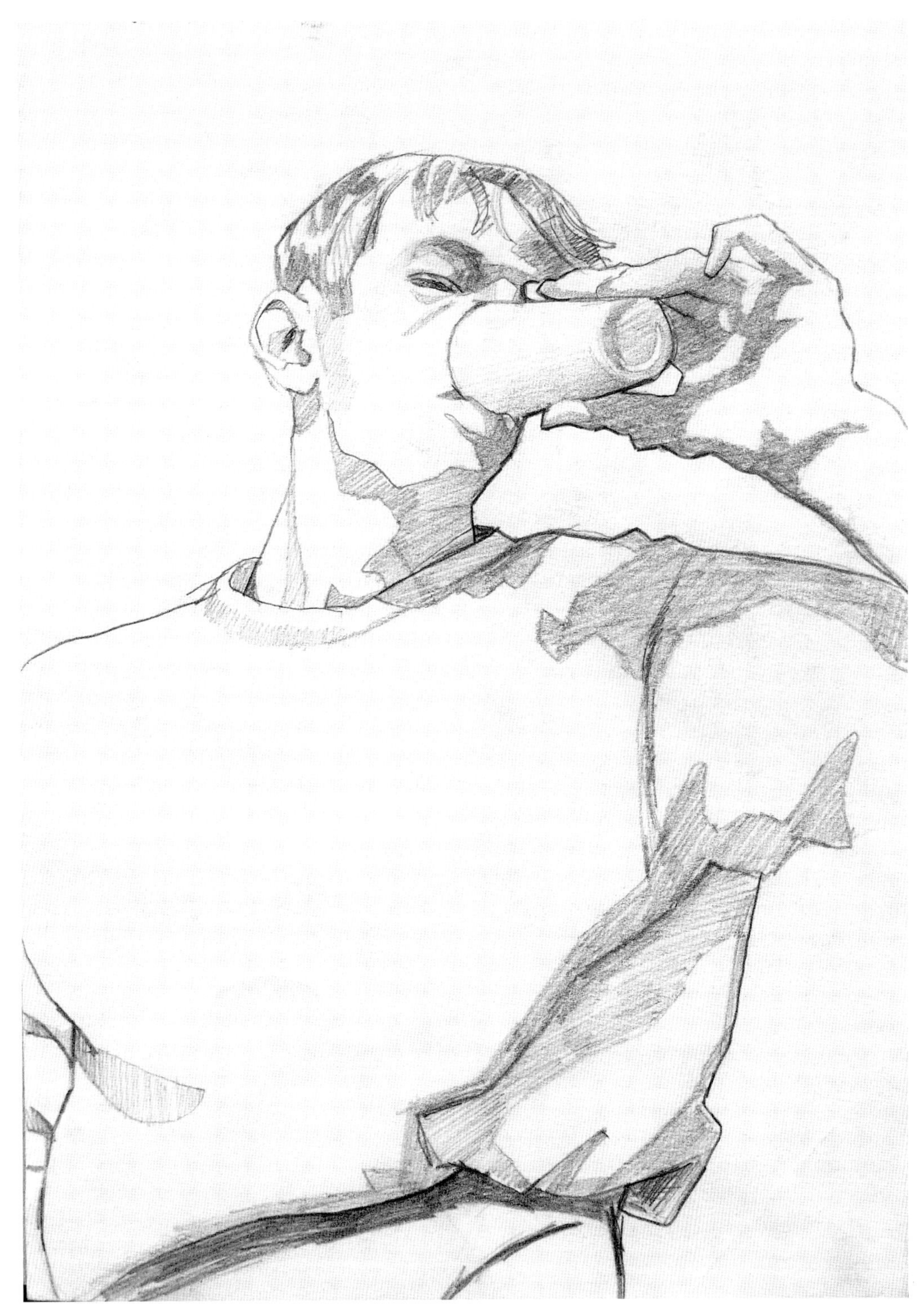

pencil
297 × 210

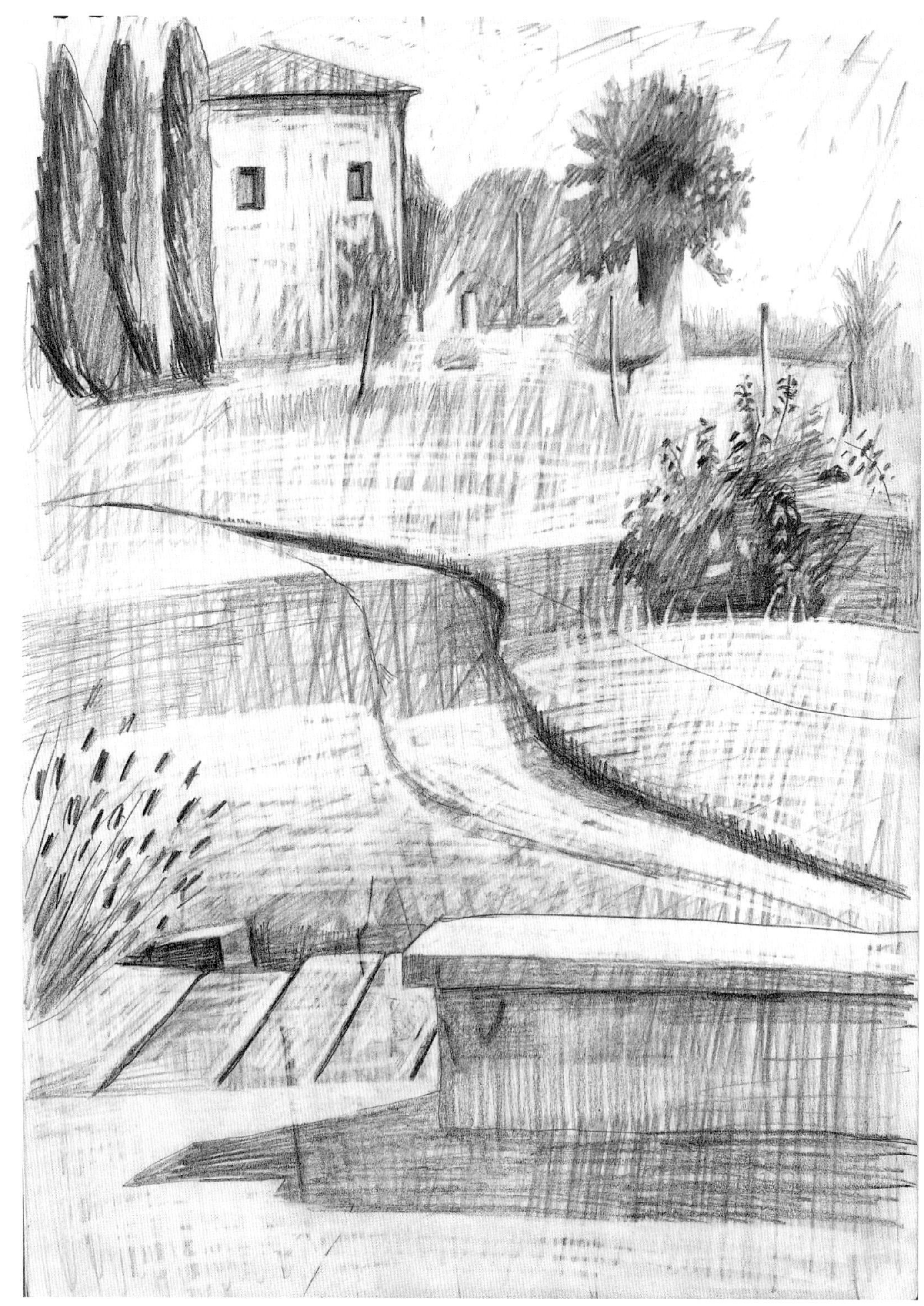

Tuscany
pencil
297 × 210

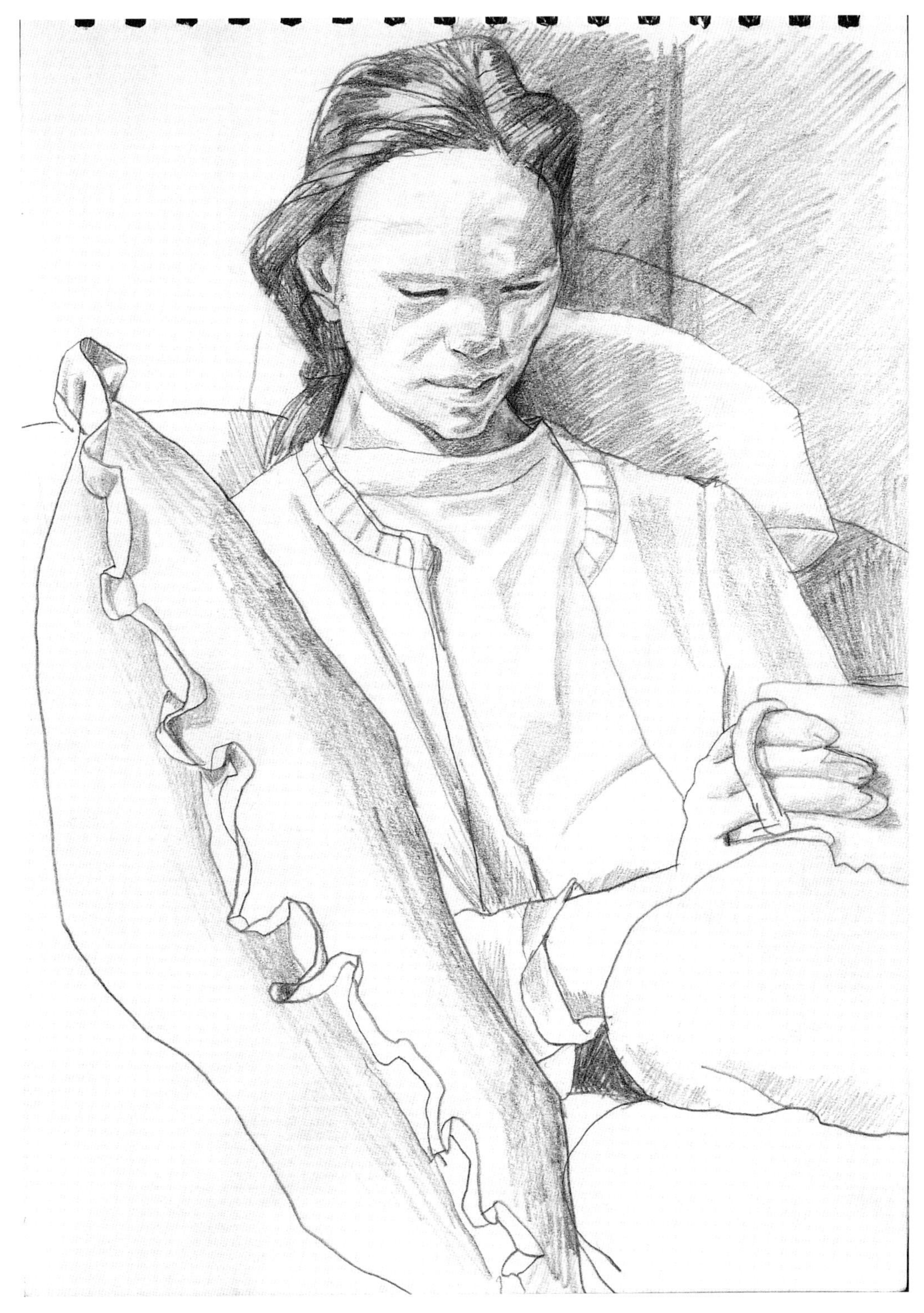

pencil
210 × 148

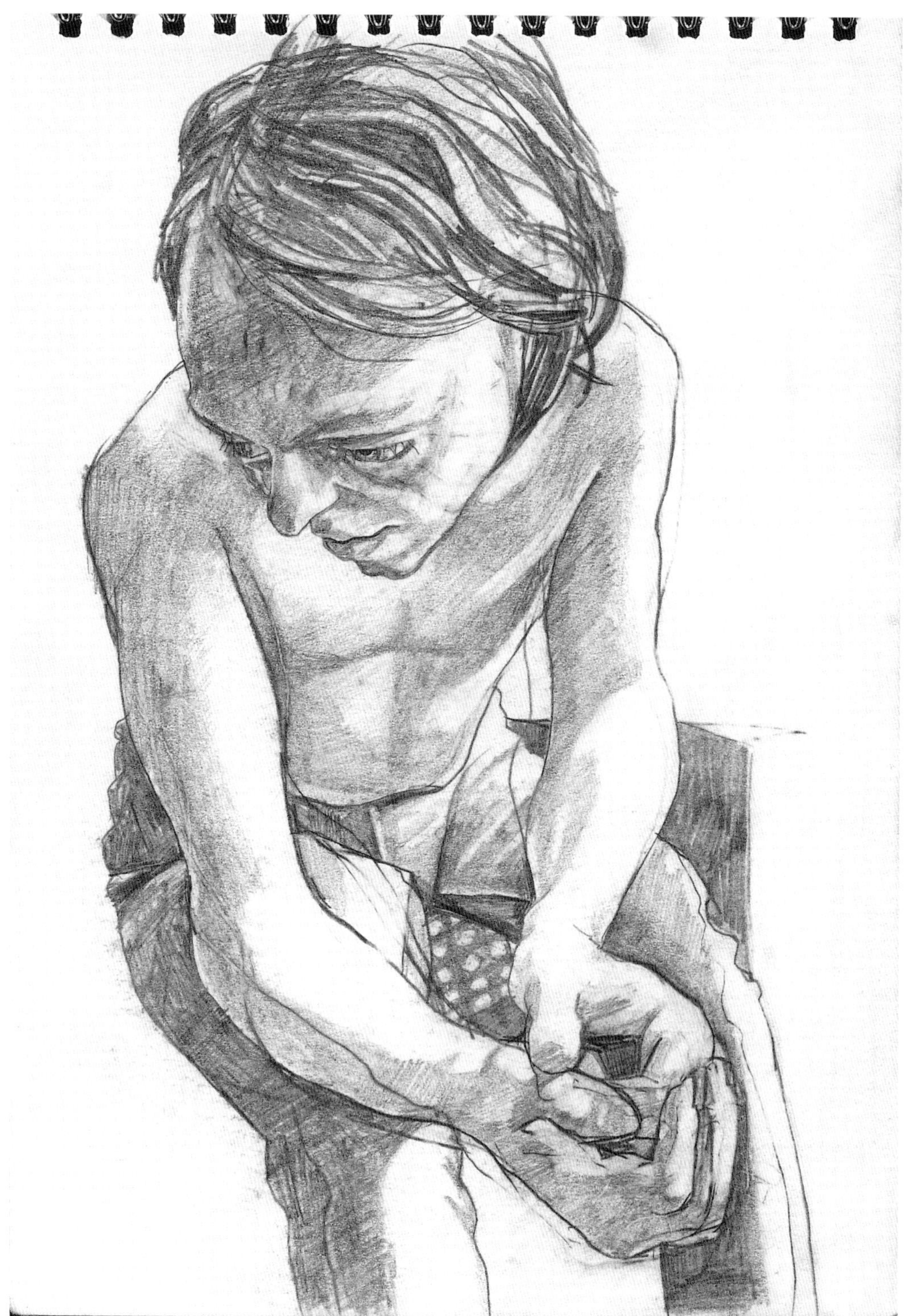

Simon
pencil
210 × 148

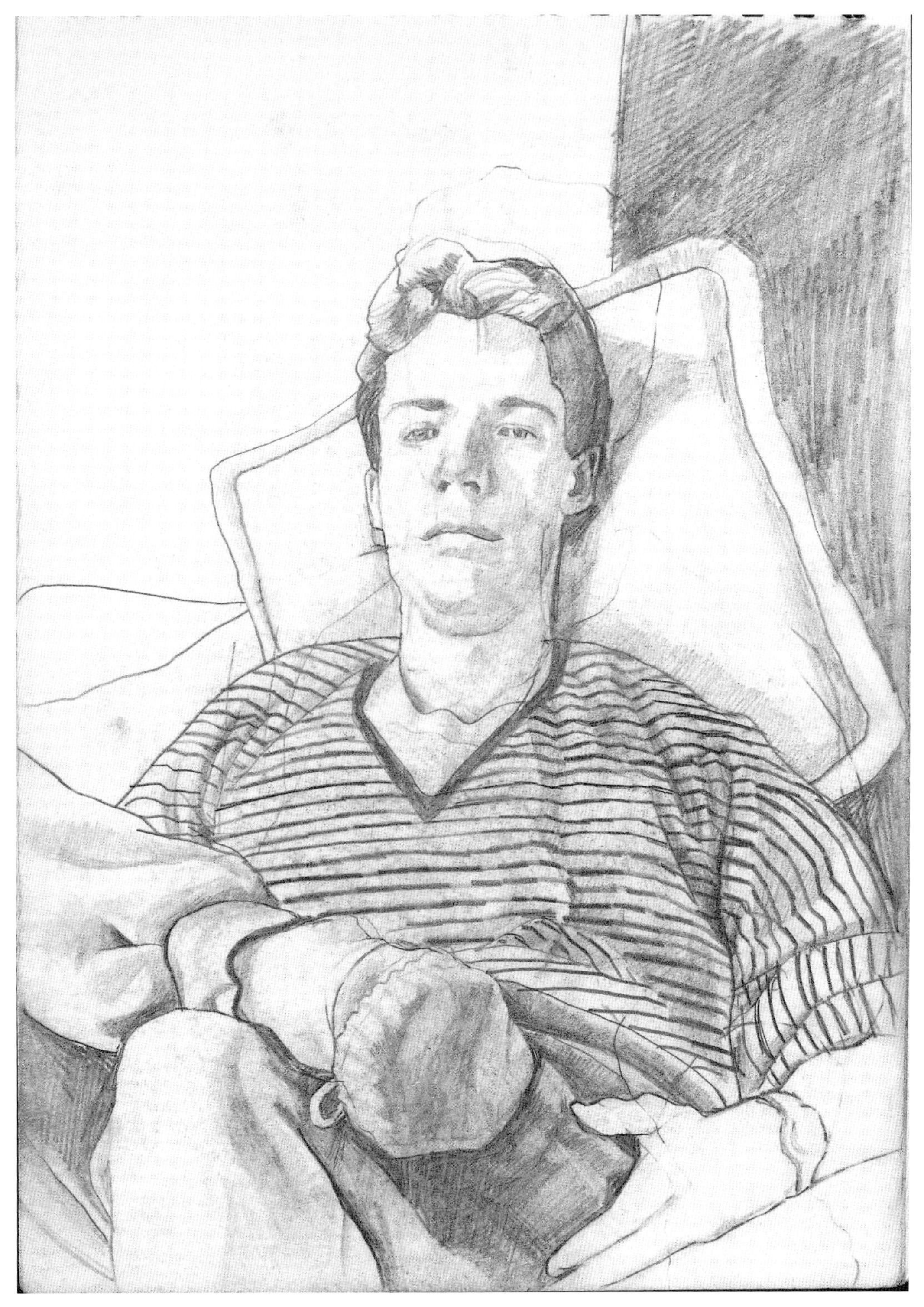

Nick
pencil
210 × 148

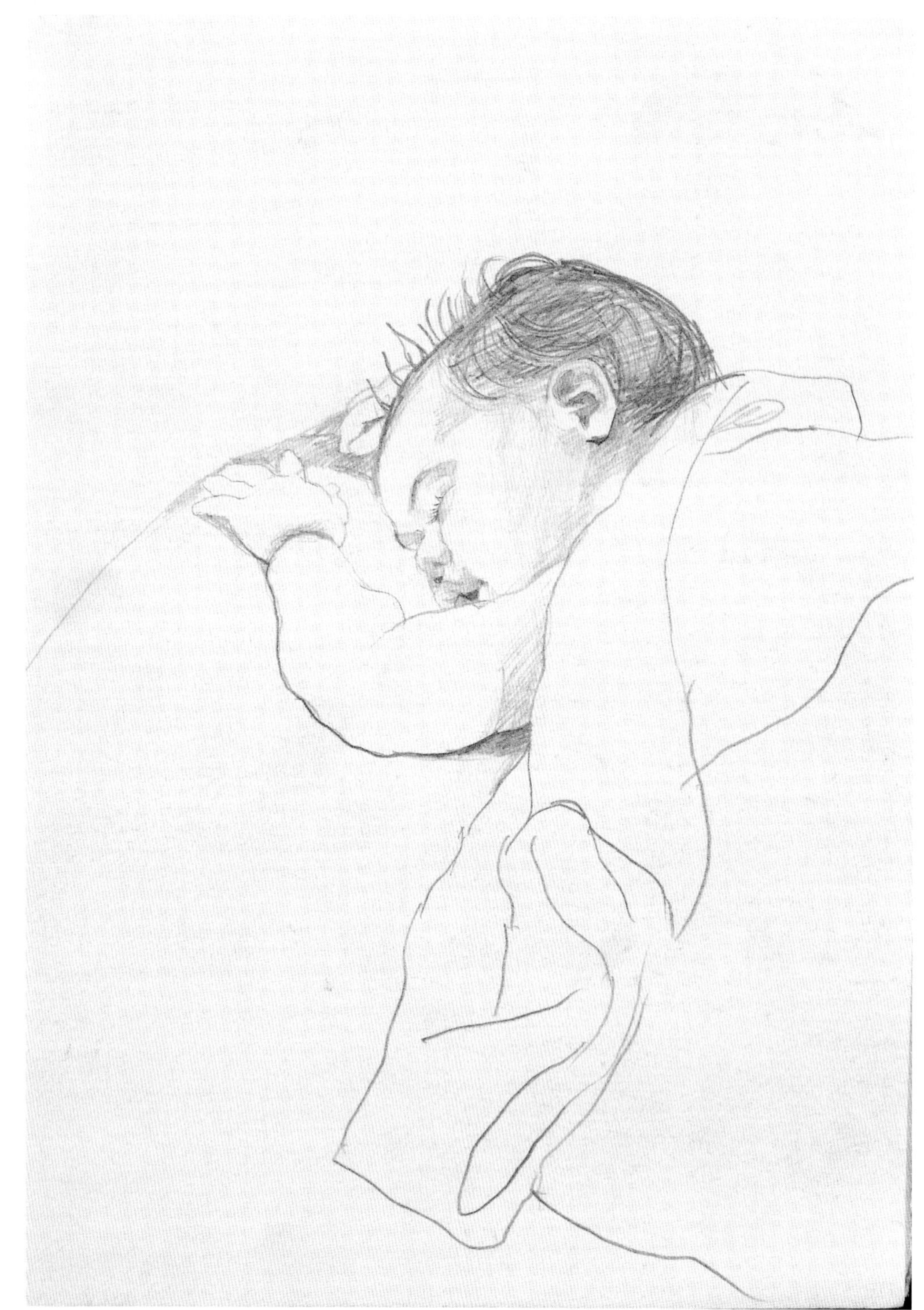

Anna
1991
pencil
210 × 148

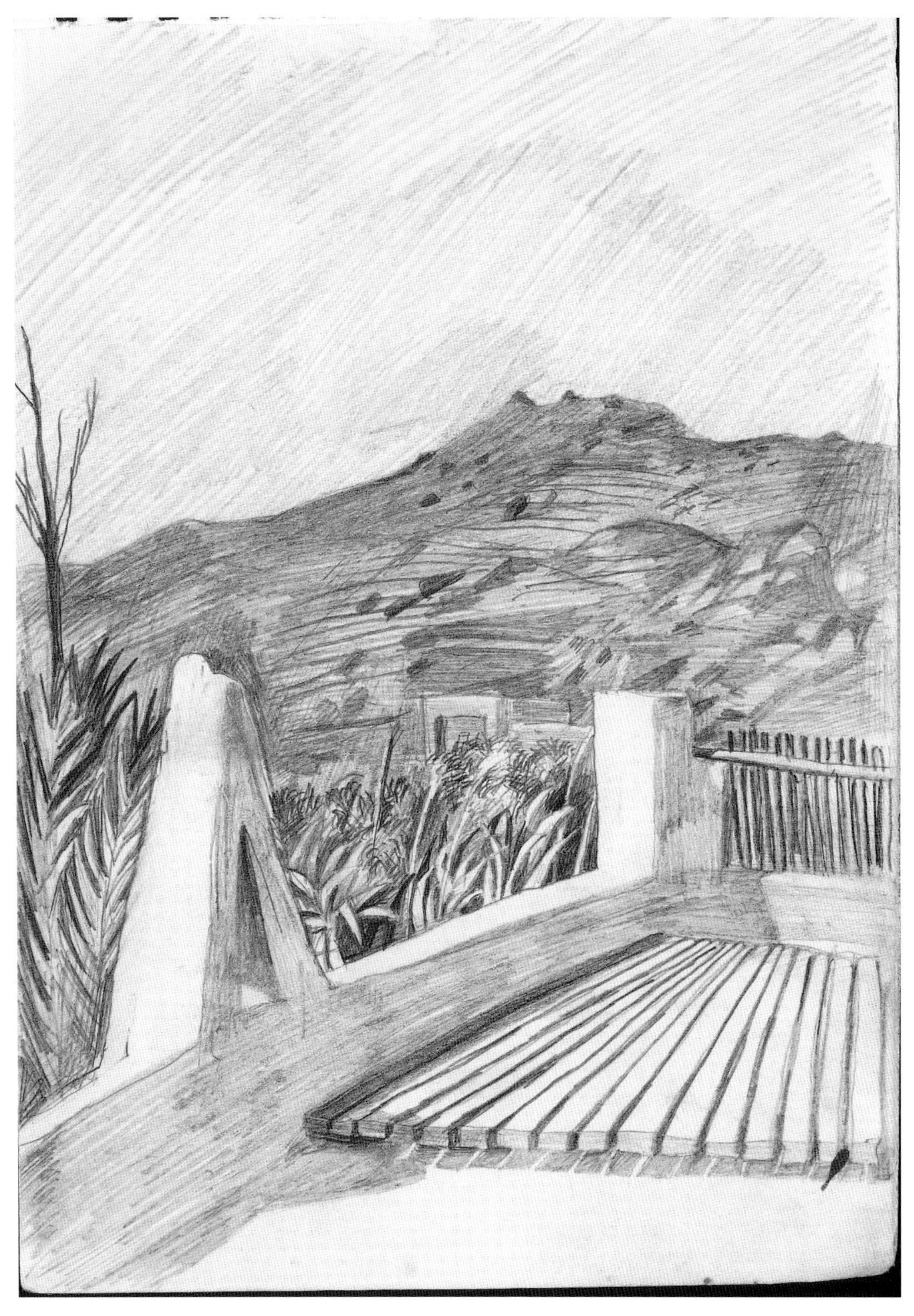

Ios
1991
pencil
210 × 148

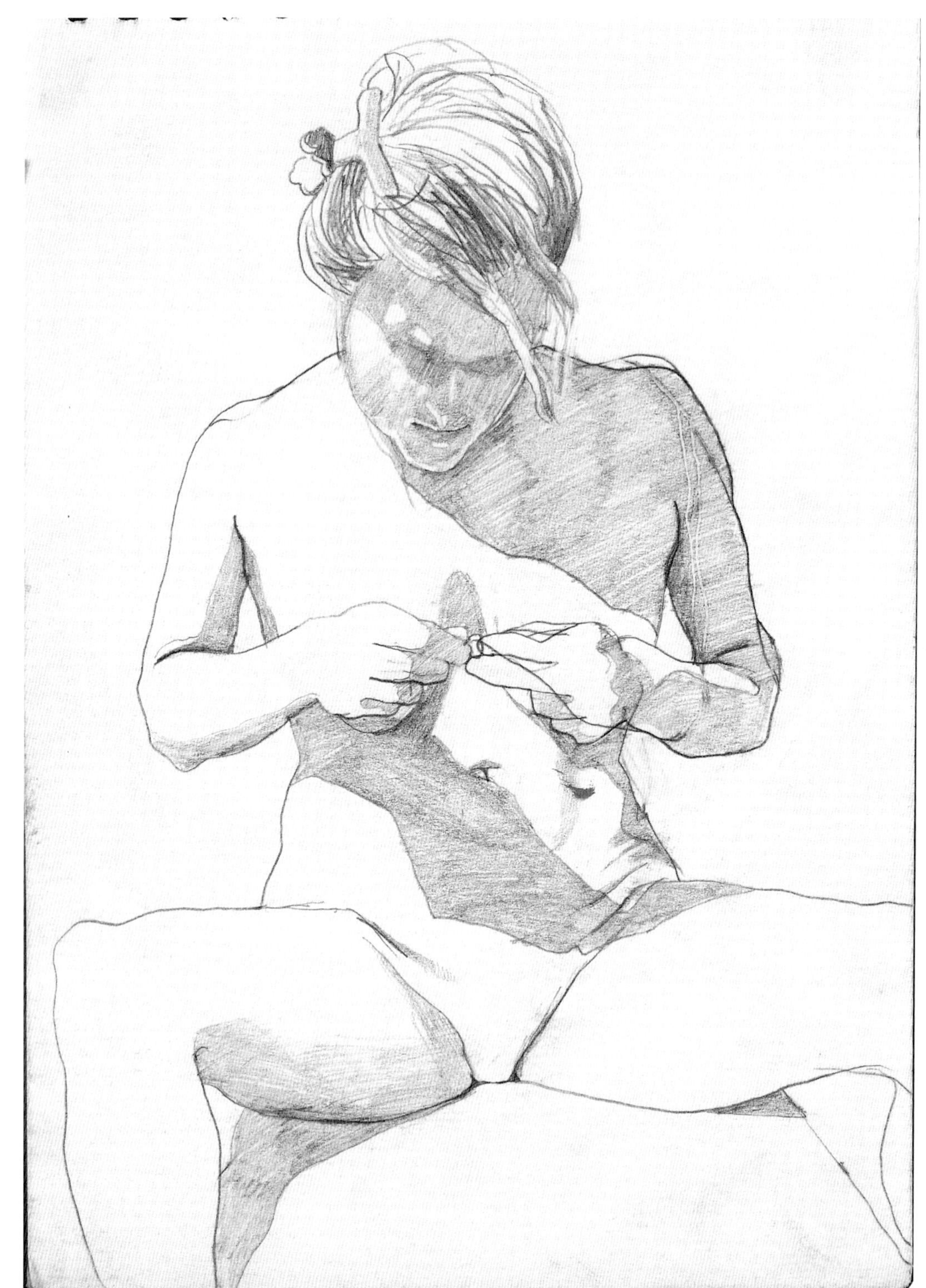

Véronique
pencil
1991 (?)
210 × 148

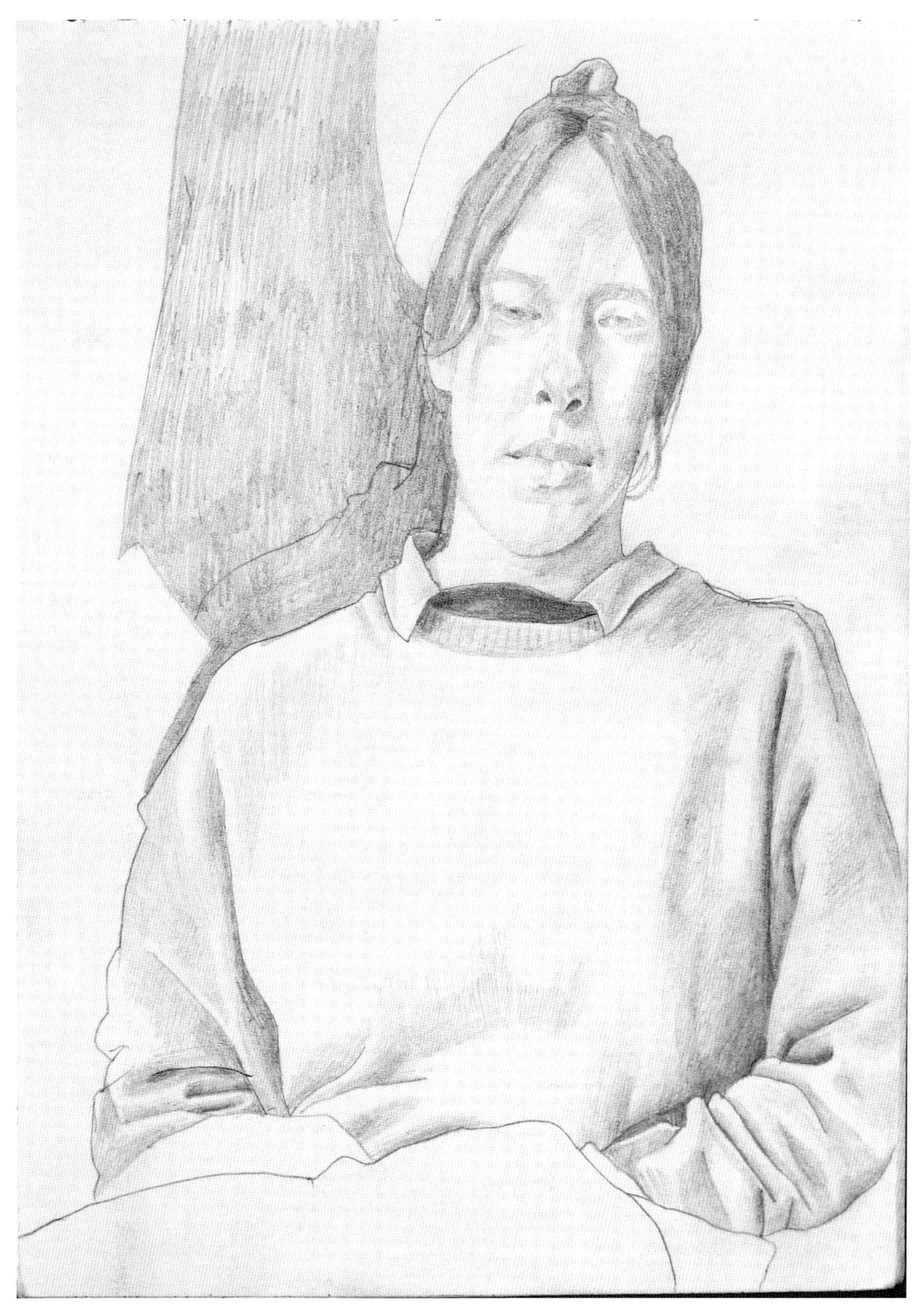

Rebecca
pencil
210 × 148

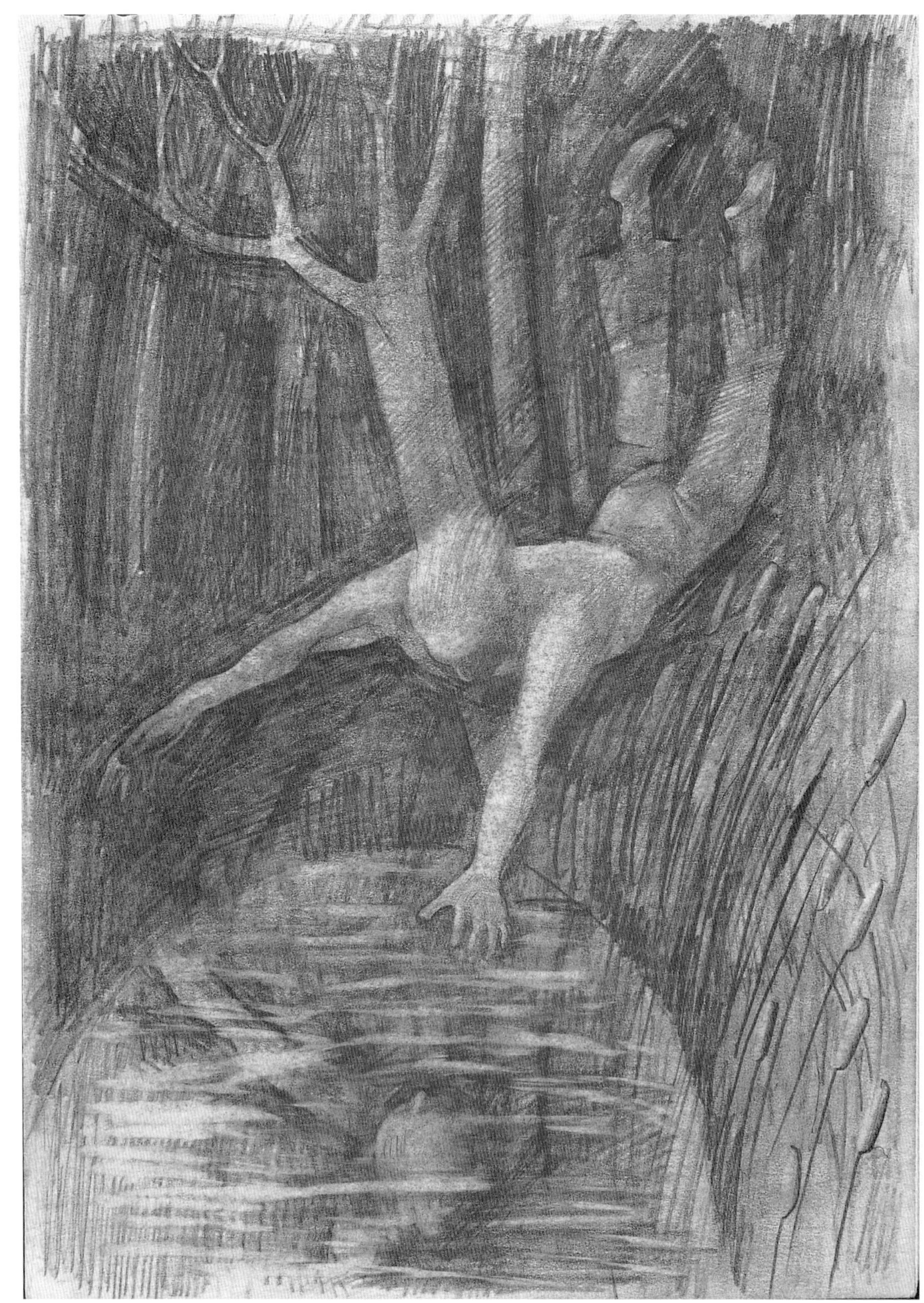

Narcissus
1991
pencil
210 × 148

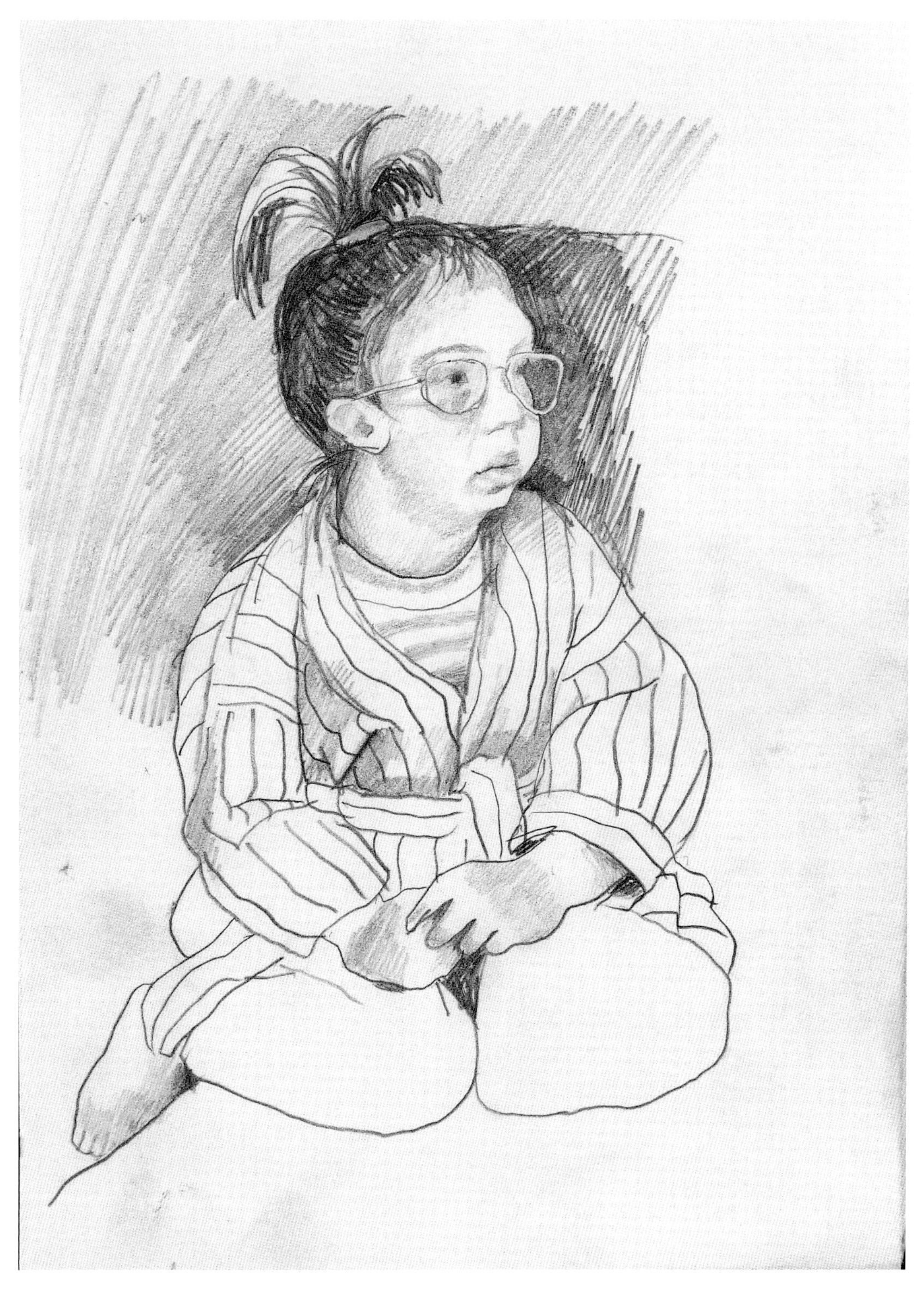

Natasha
1991
pencil
210 × 148

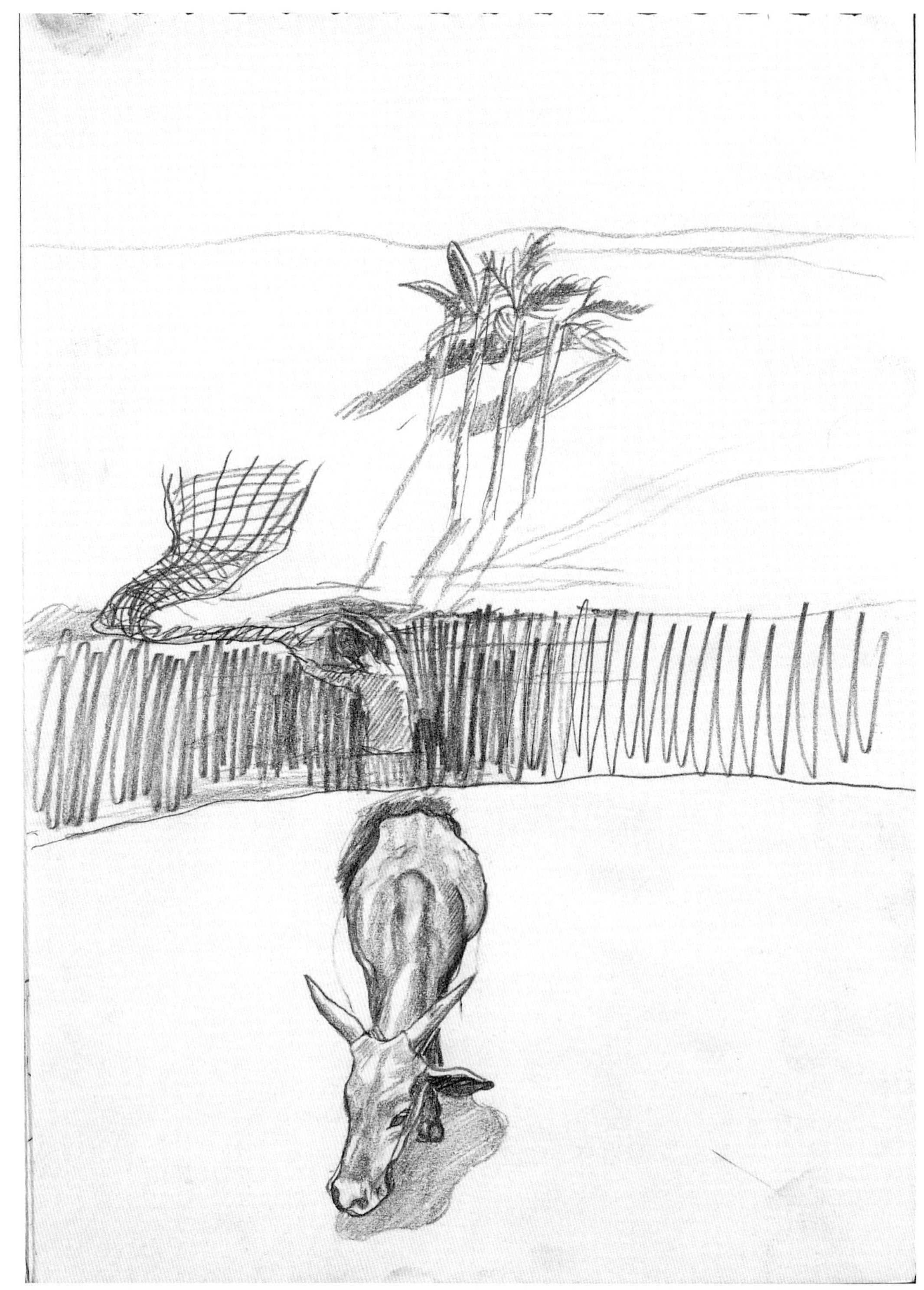

Goa (?)
pencil
210 × 148

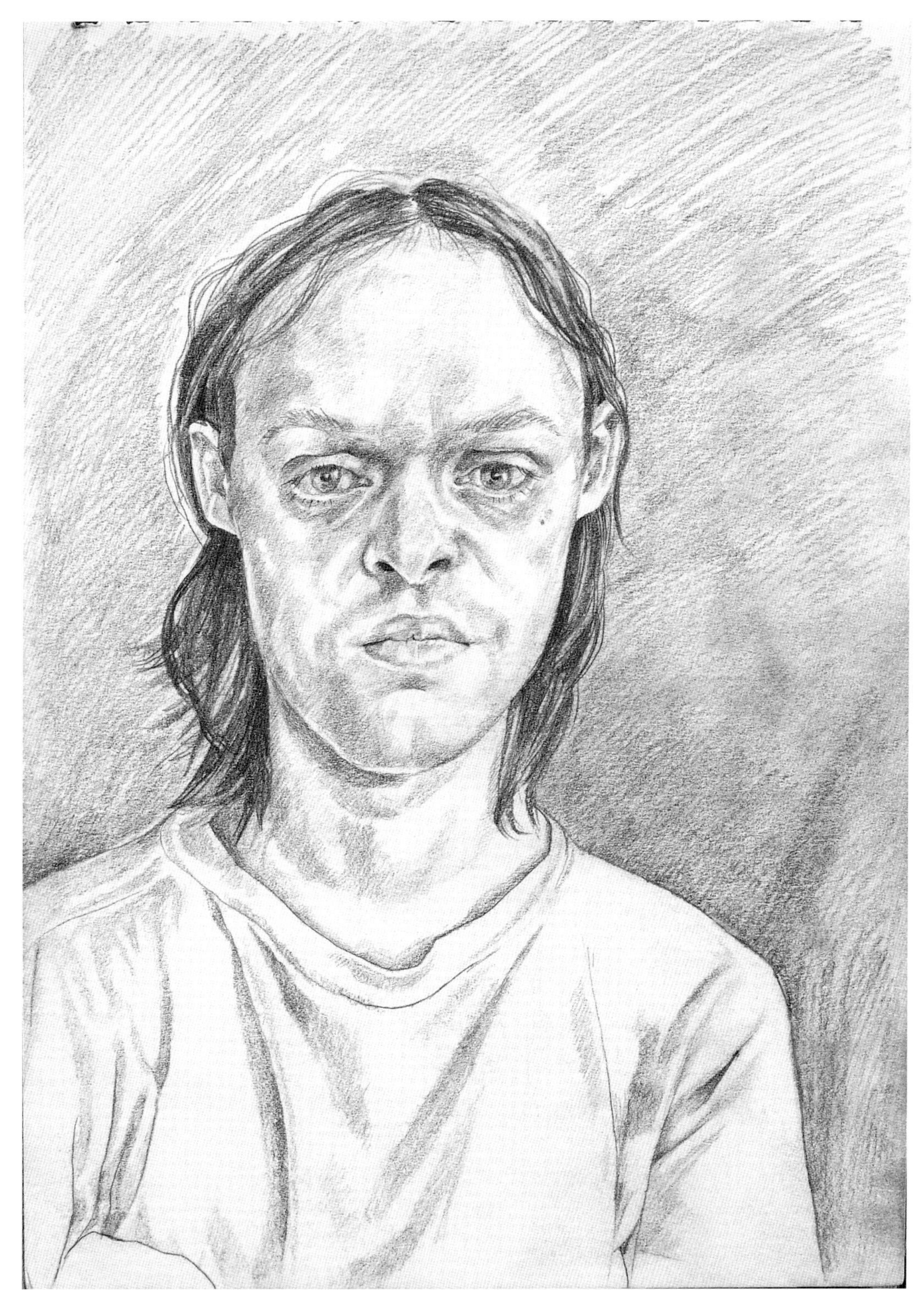

Simon
pencil
210 × 148

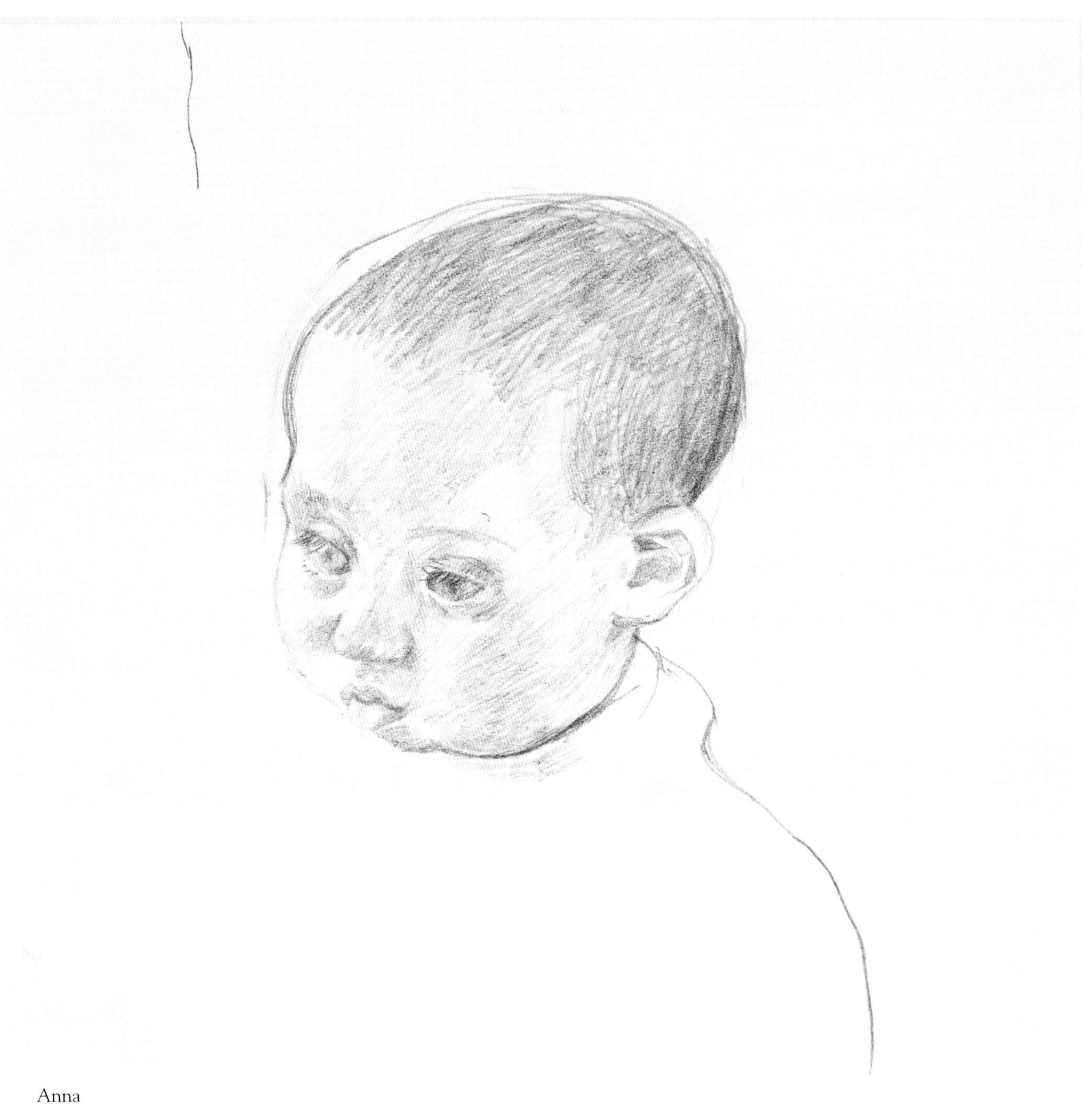

Anna
1991
pencil
140 × 130

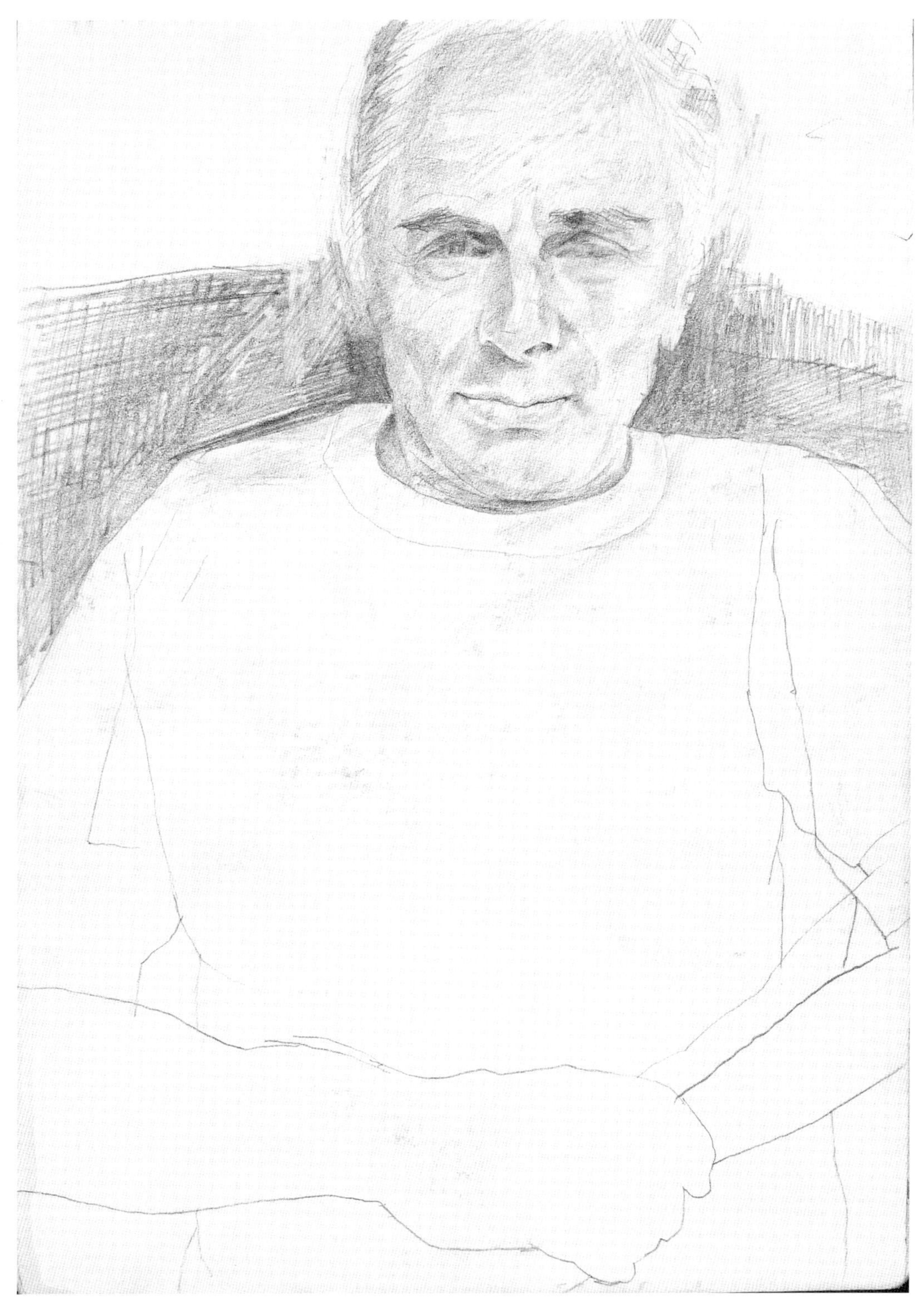

Fred
1991
pencil
210 × 148

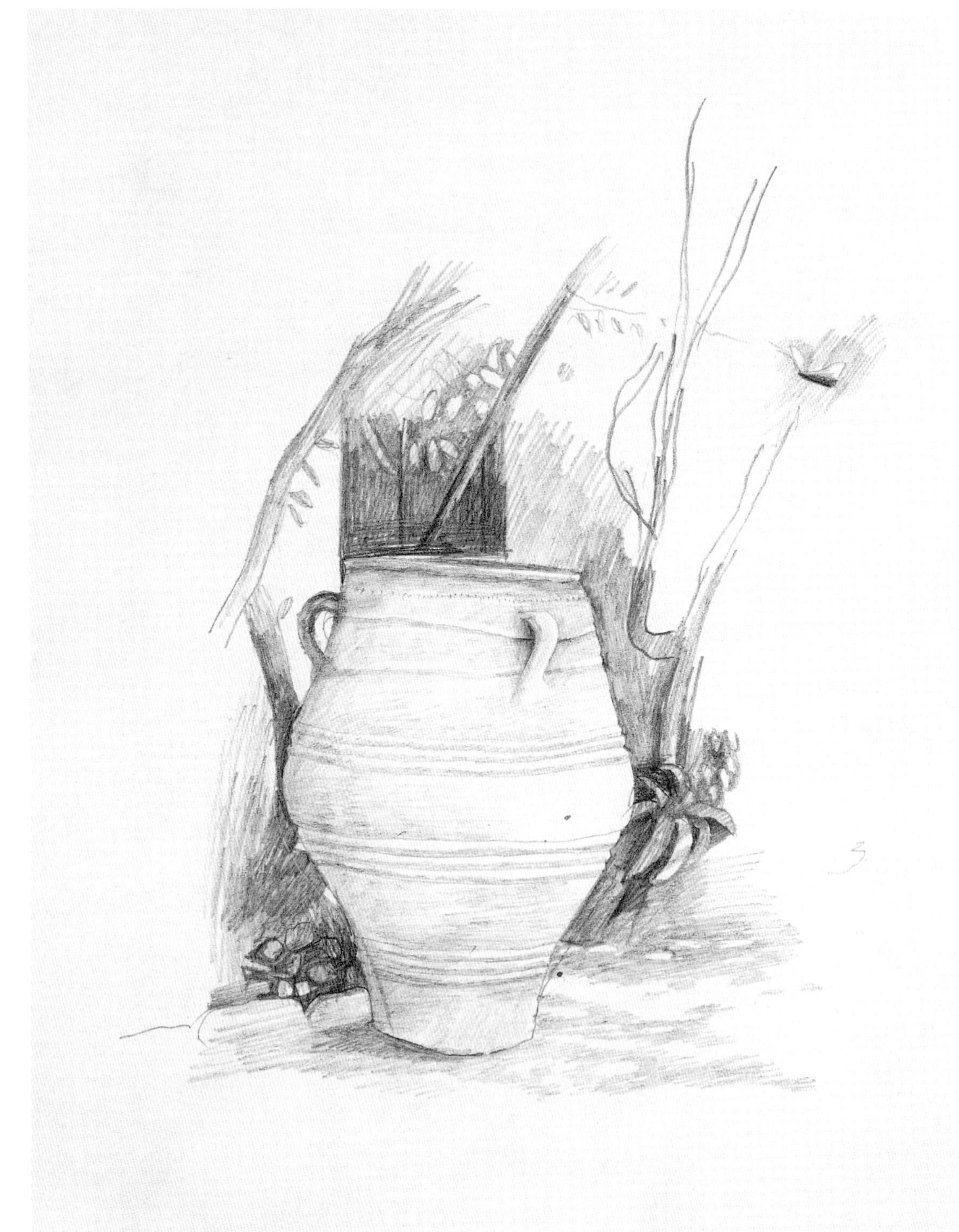

pencil
210 × 148

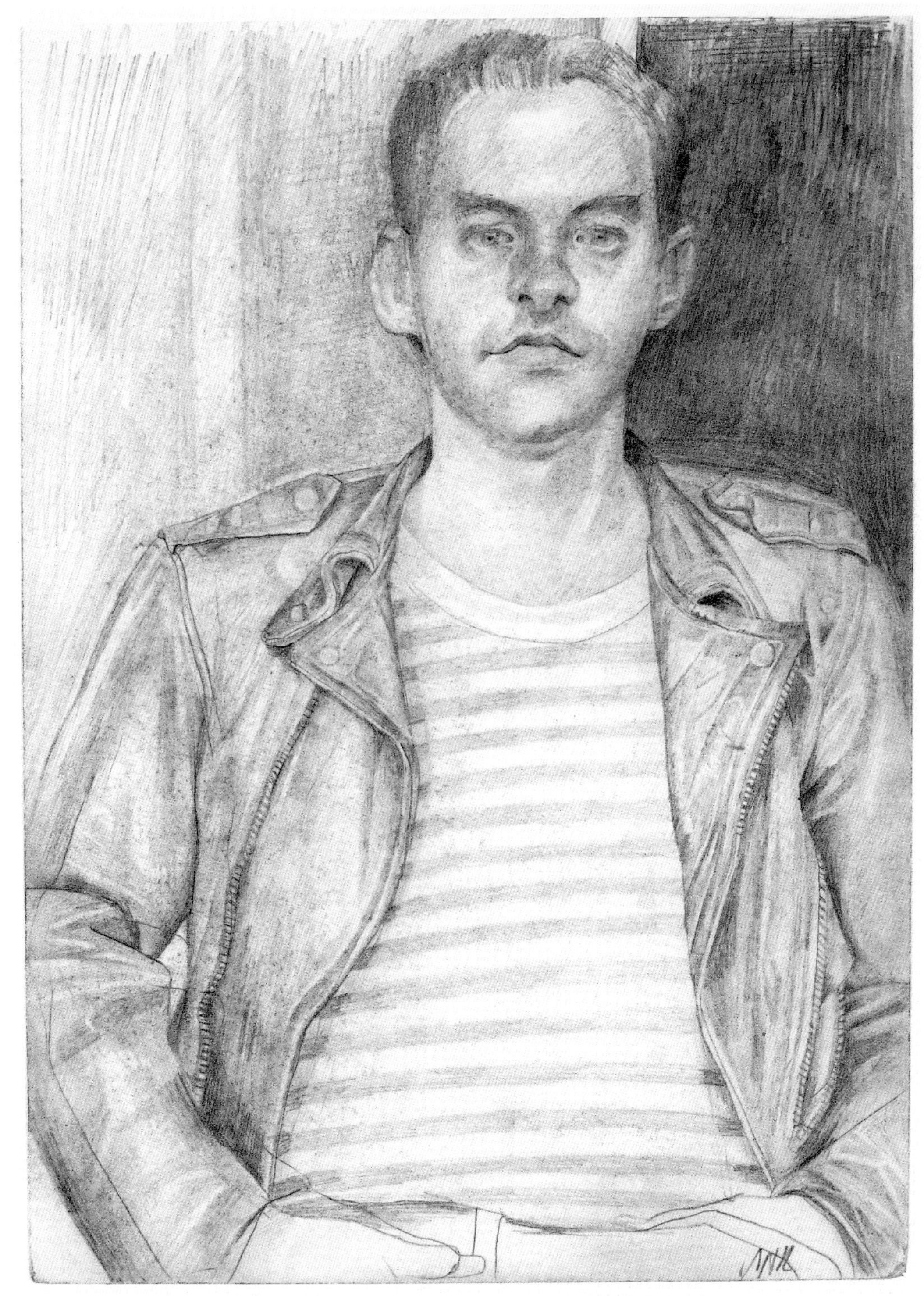

Tony Hande
1991
pencil
200 × 145

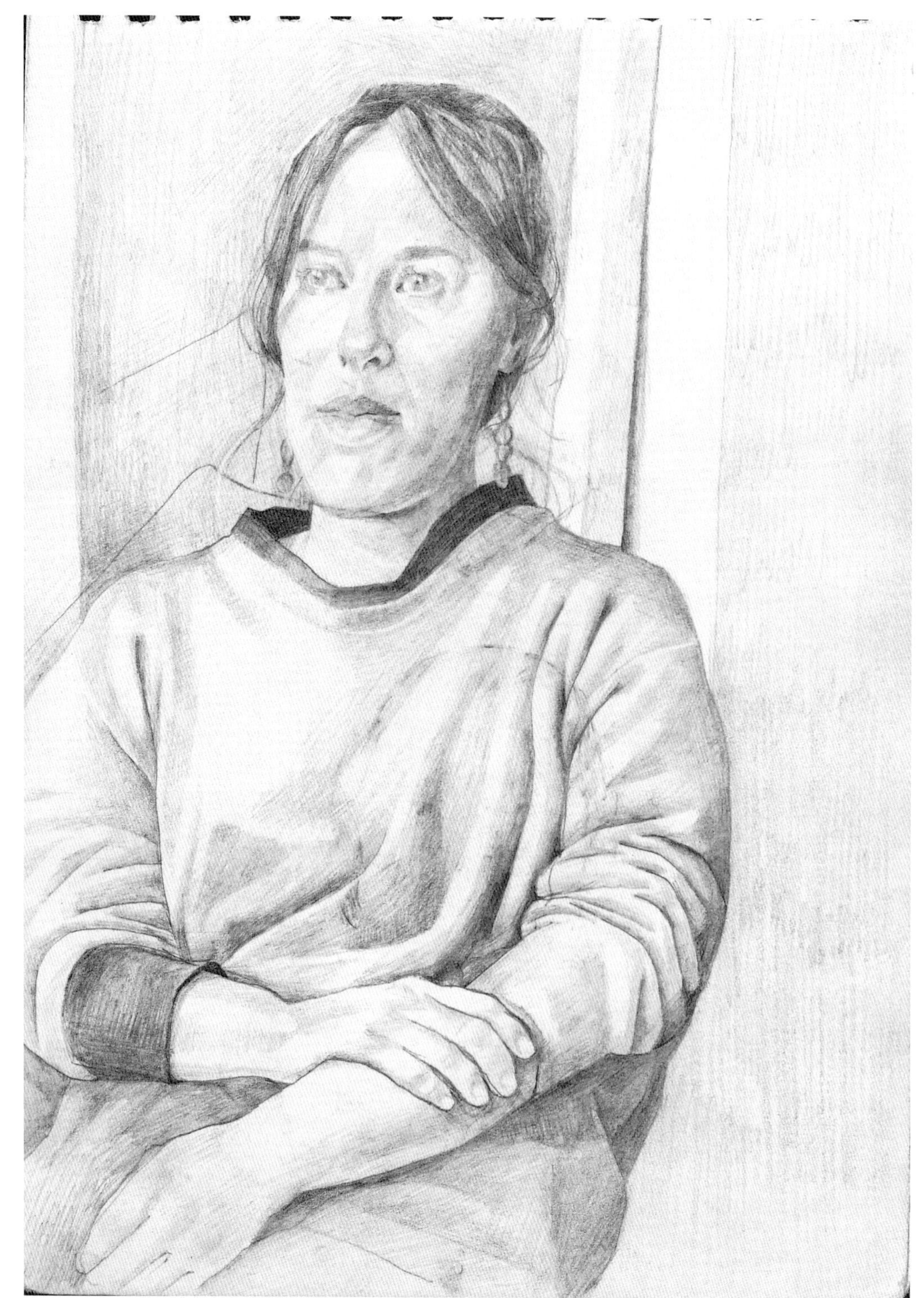

Rebecca
pencil
210 × 148

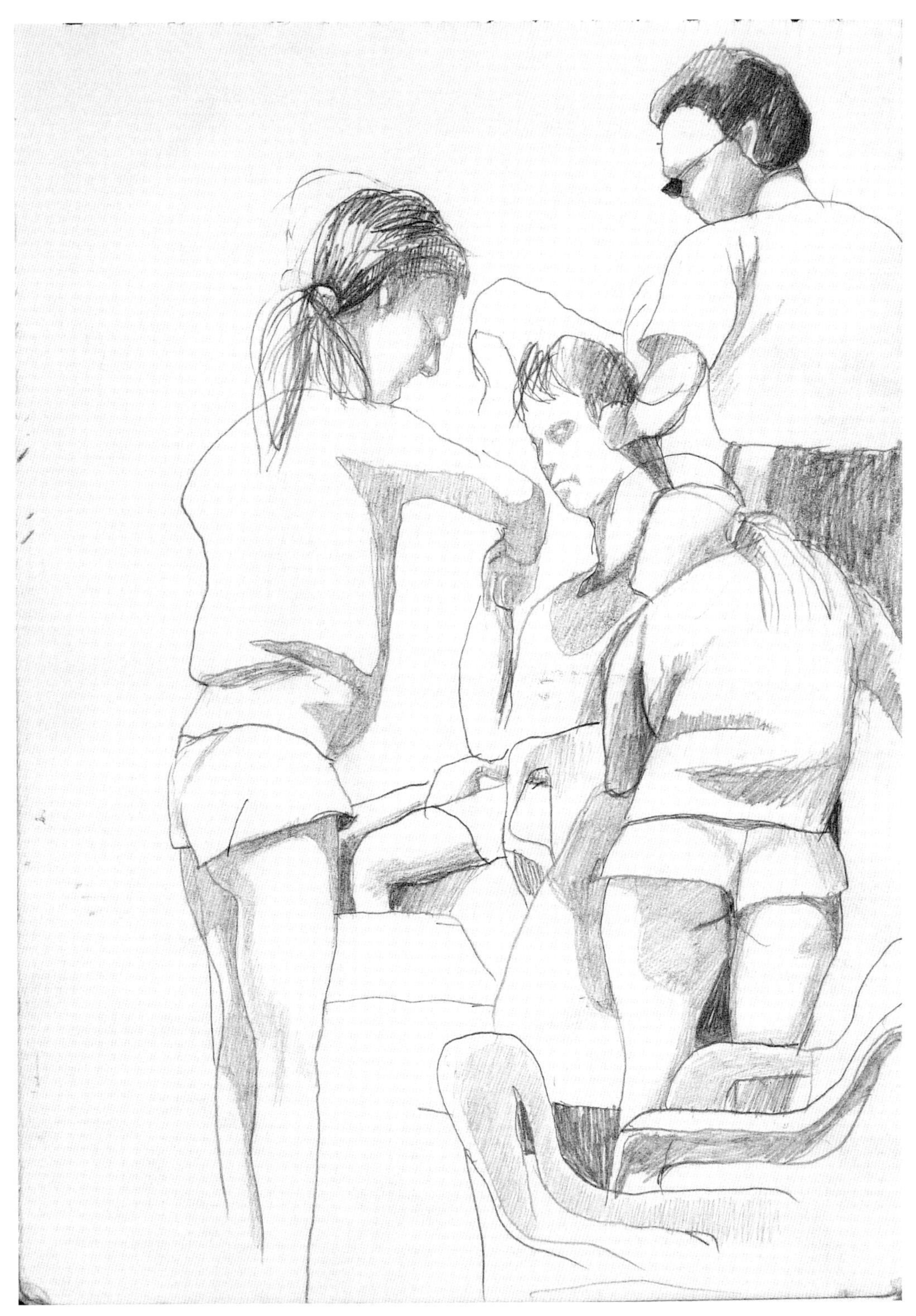

pencil
210 × 148

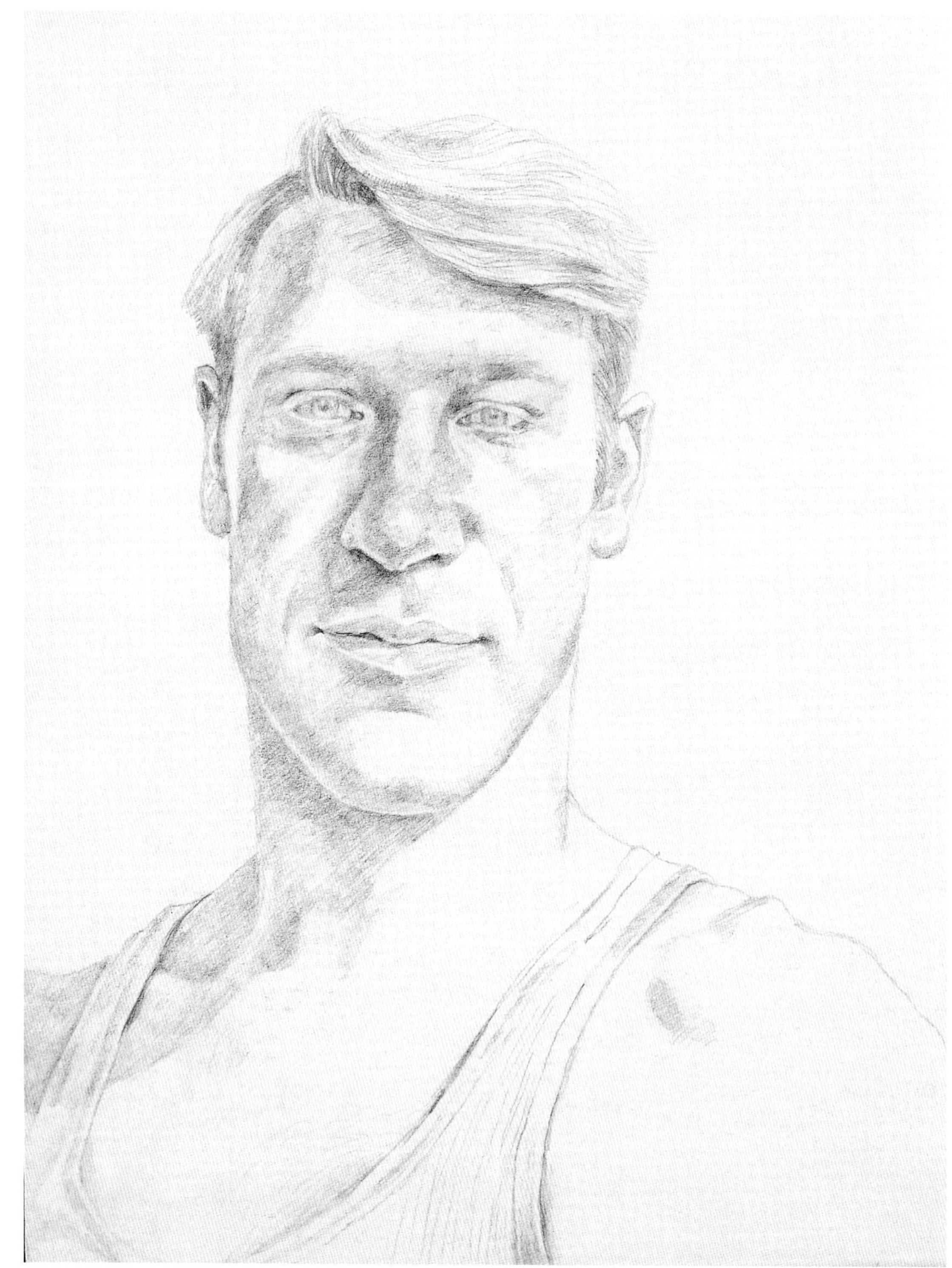

Chris
pencil
210 × 148

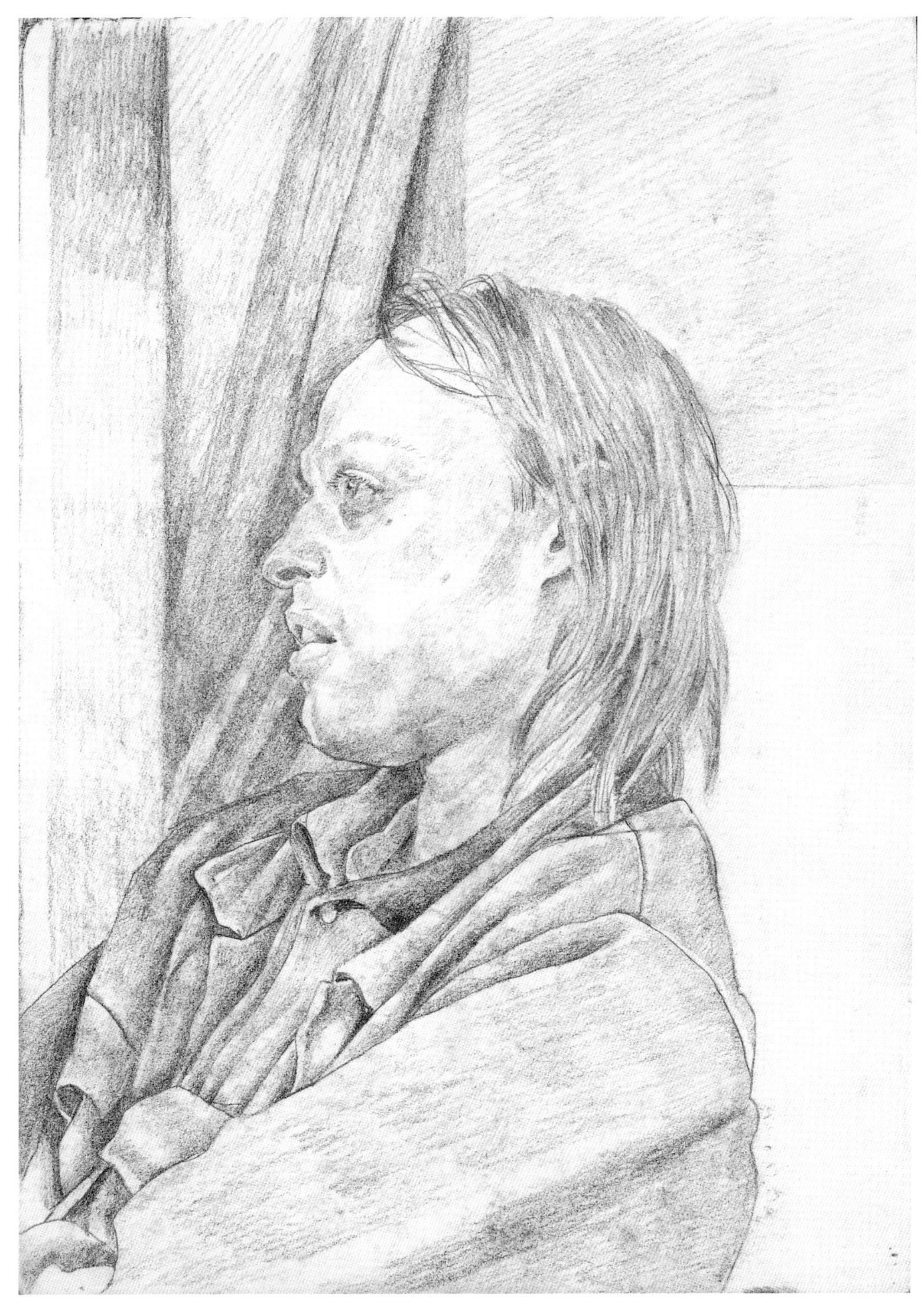

Simon
pencil
210 × 148

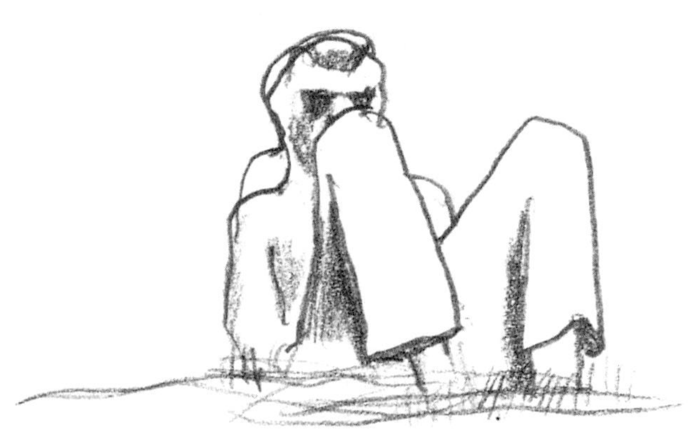

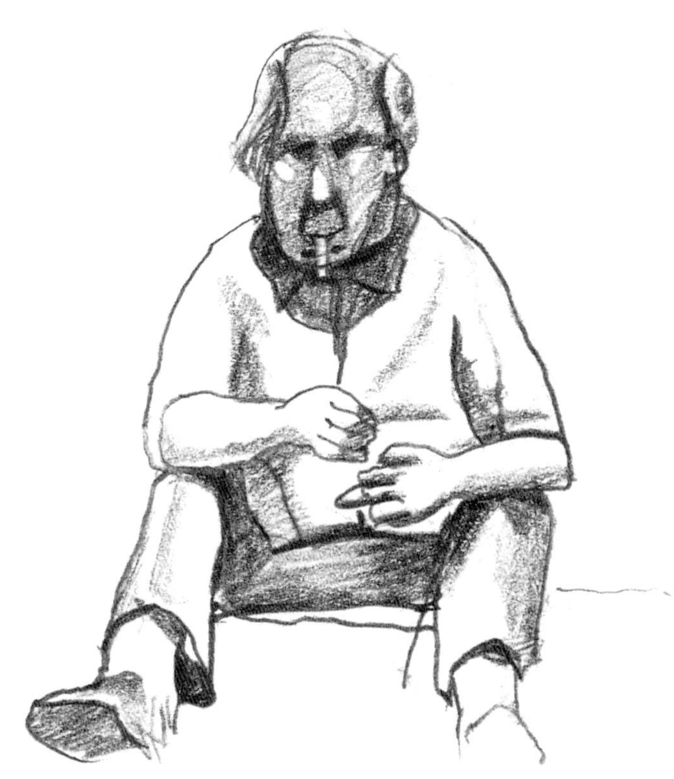

pencil
210 × 148

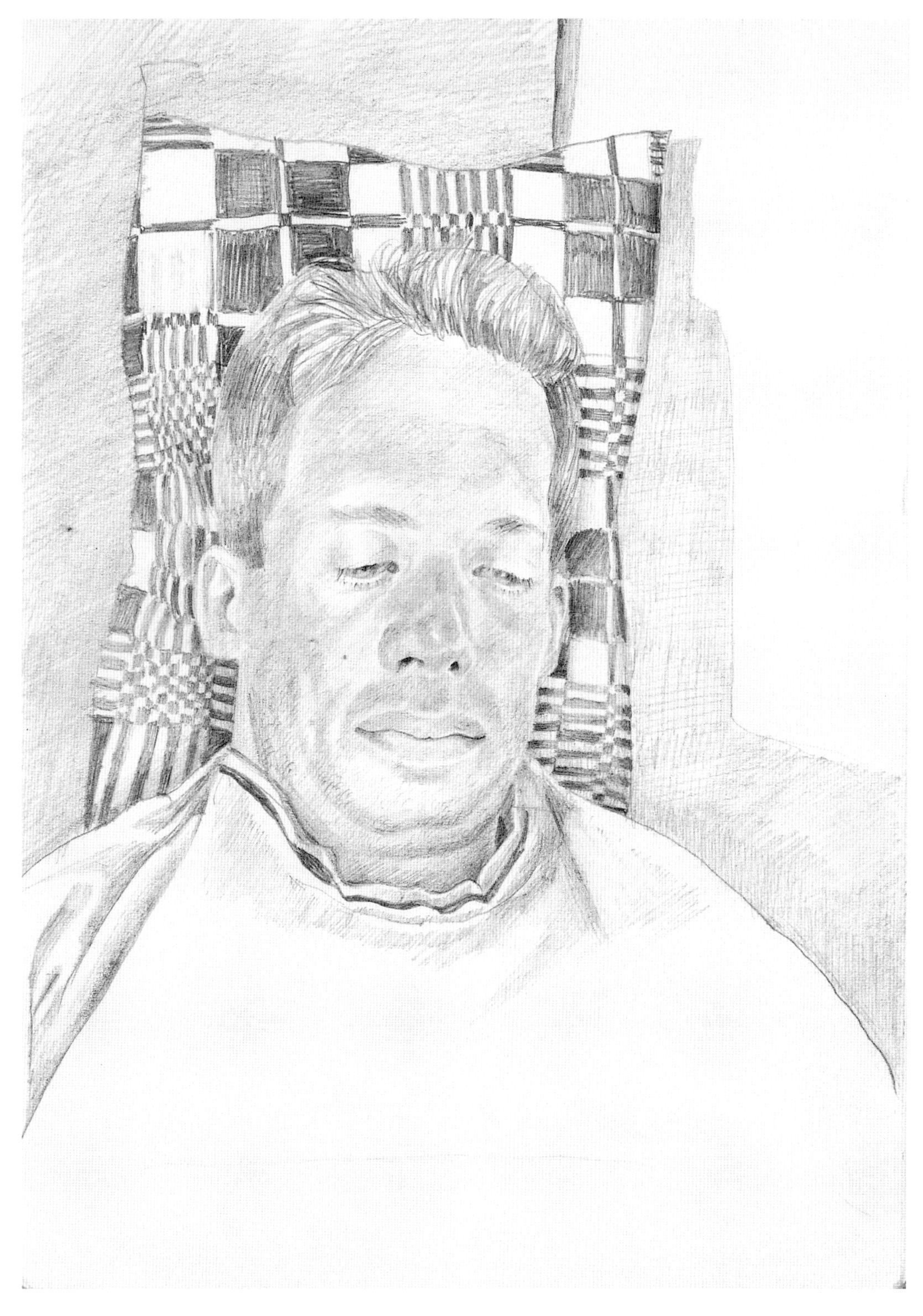

Nick
pencil
210 × 148

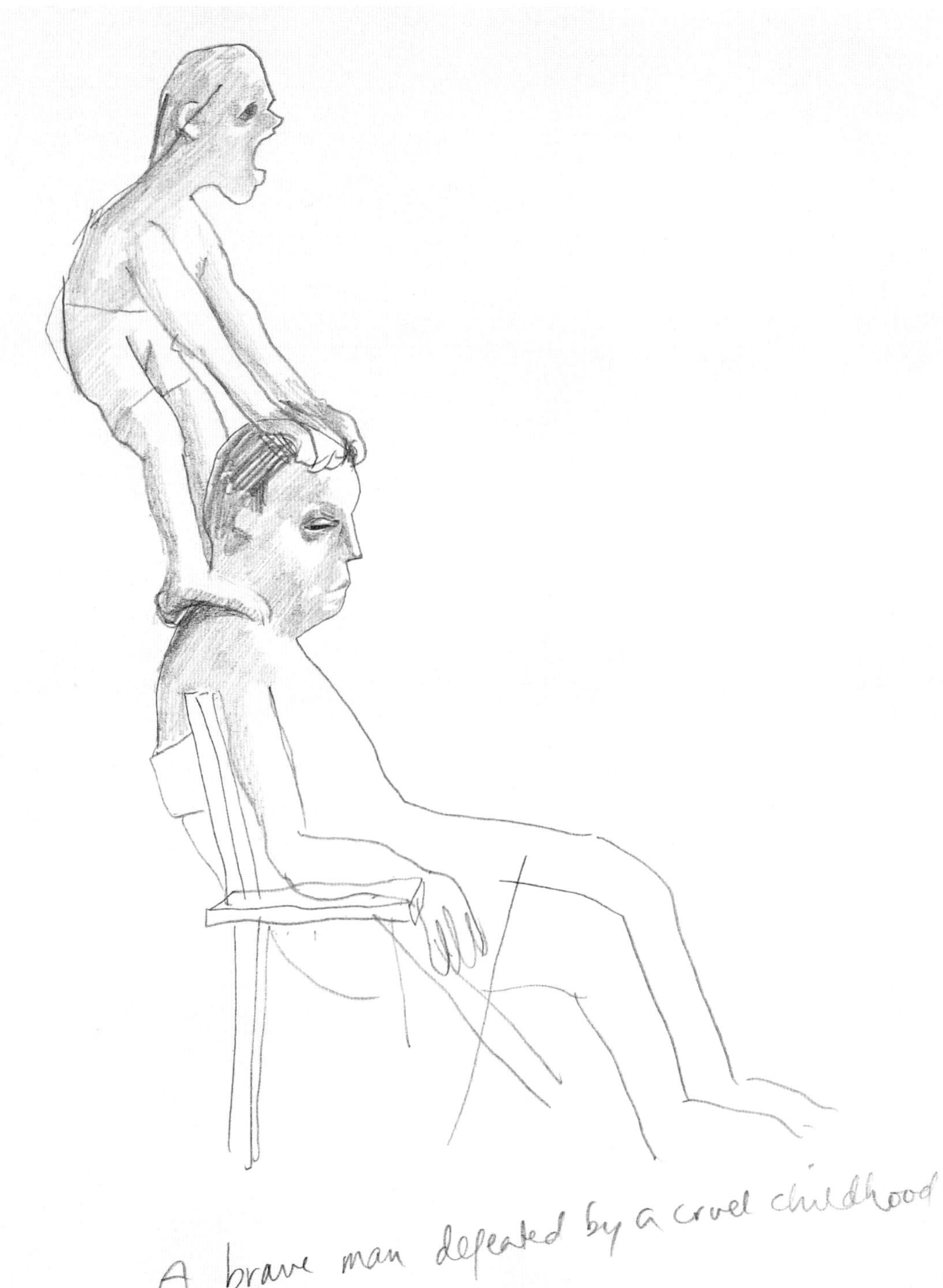

'A brave man defeated by
a cruel childhood'
pencil
210 × 148

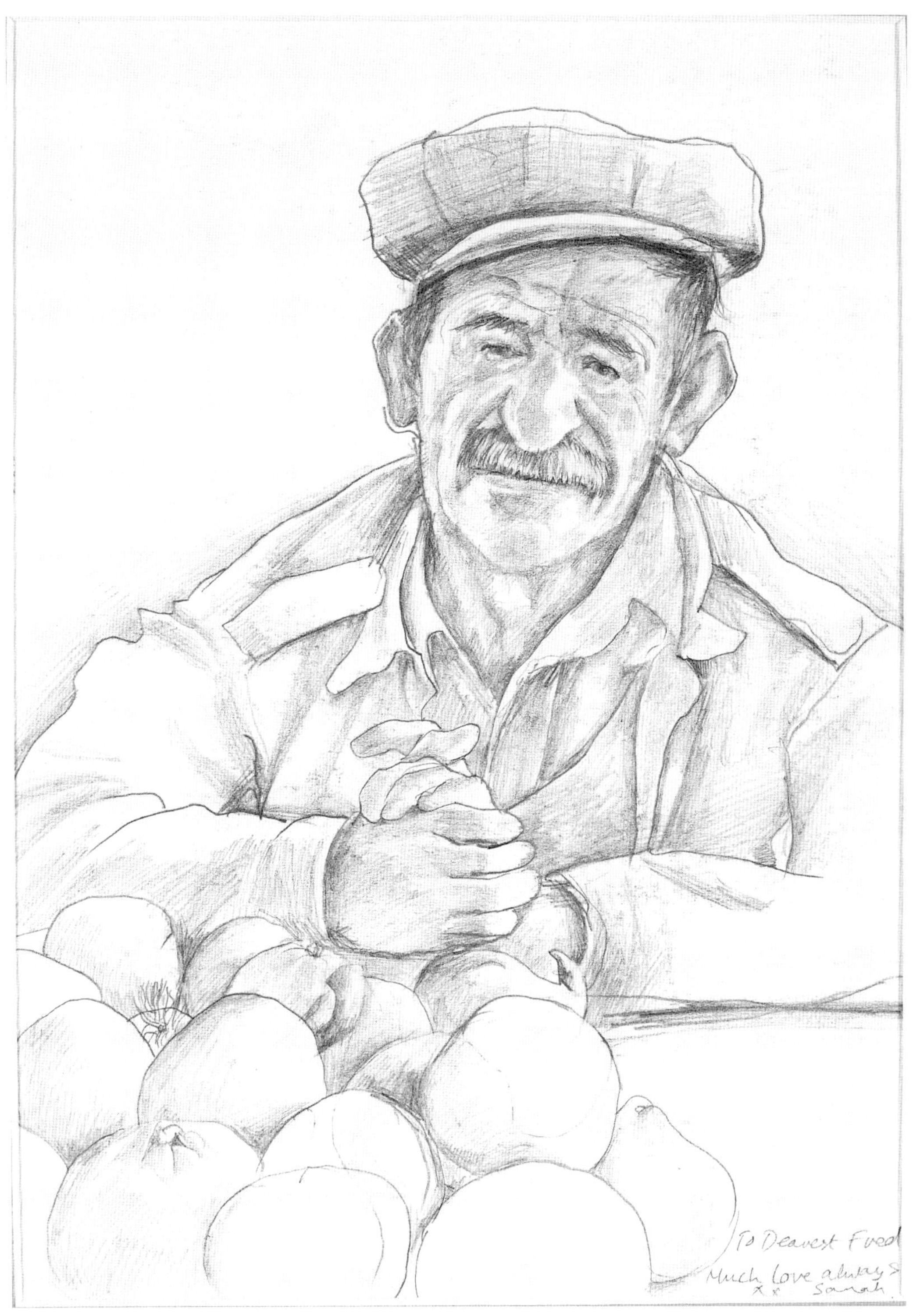

Giorgos Monoyios, Ios
1993
pencil
195 × 140

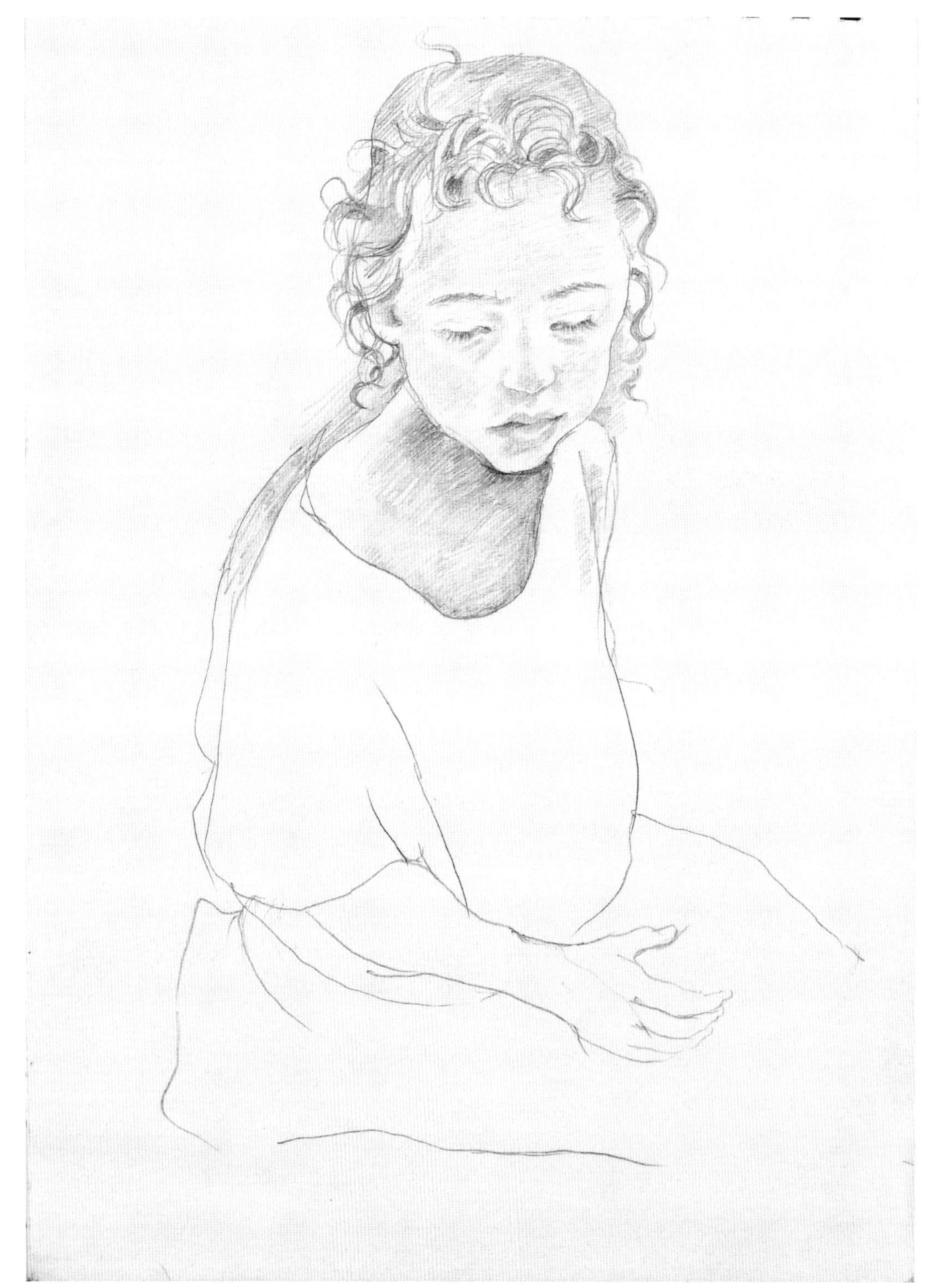

Anna
1994
pencil
210 × 148

64

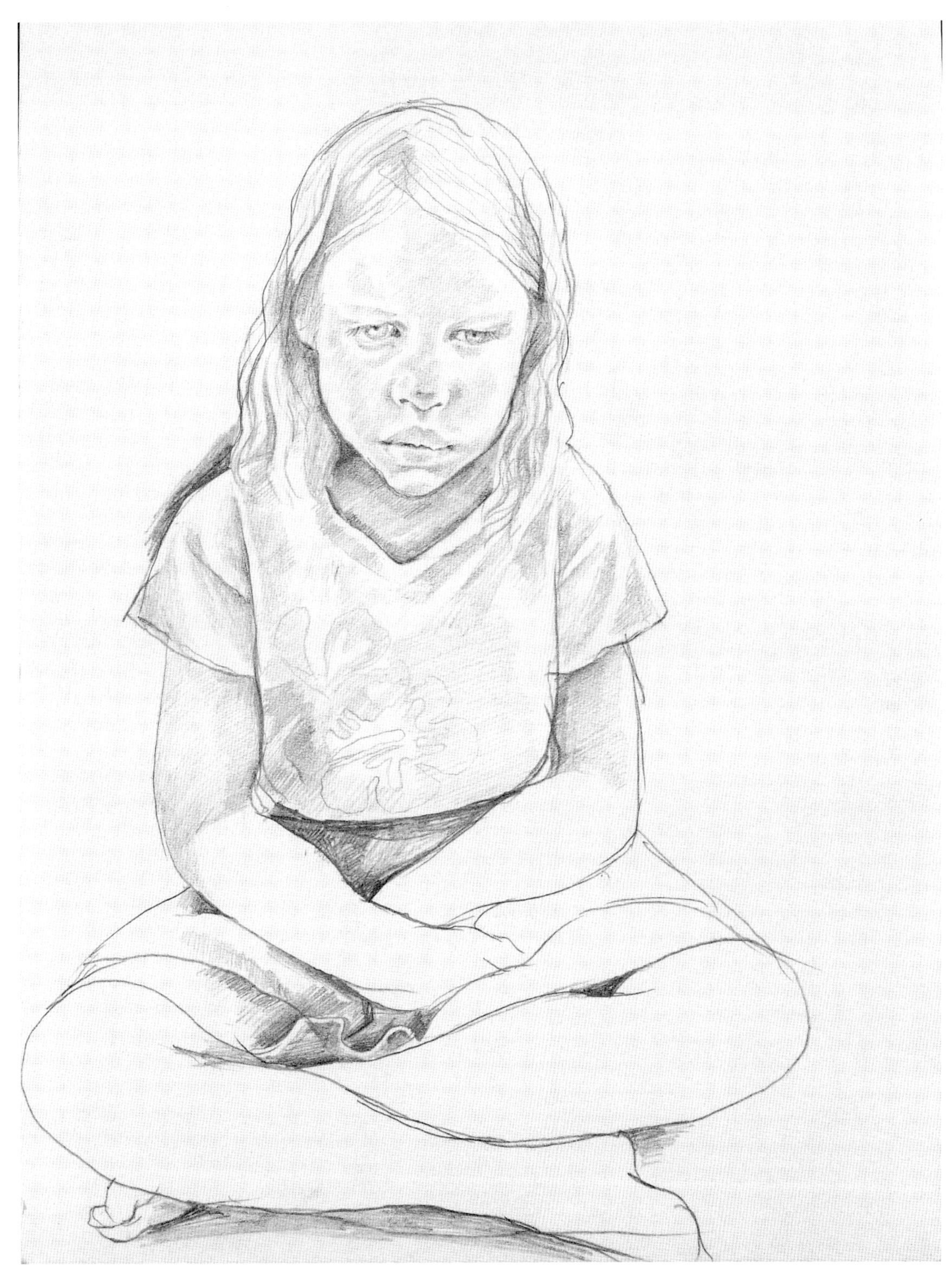

Tara
1994
pencil
210 × 148

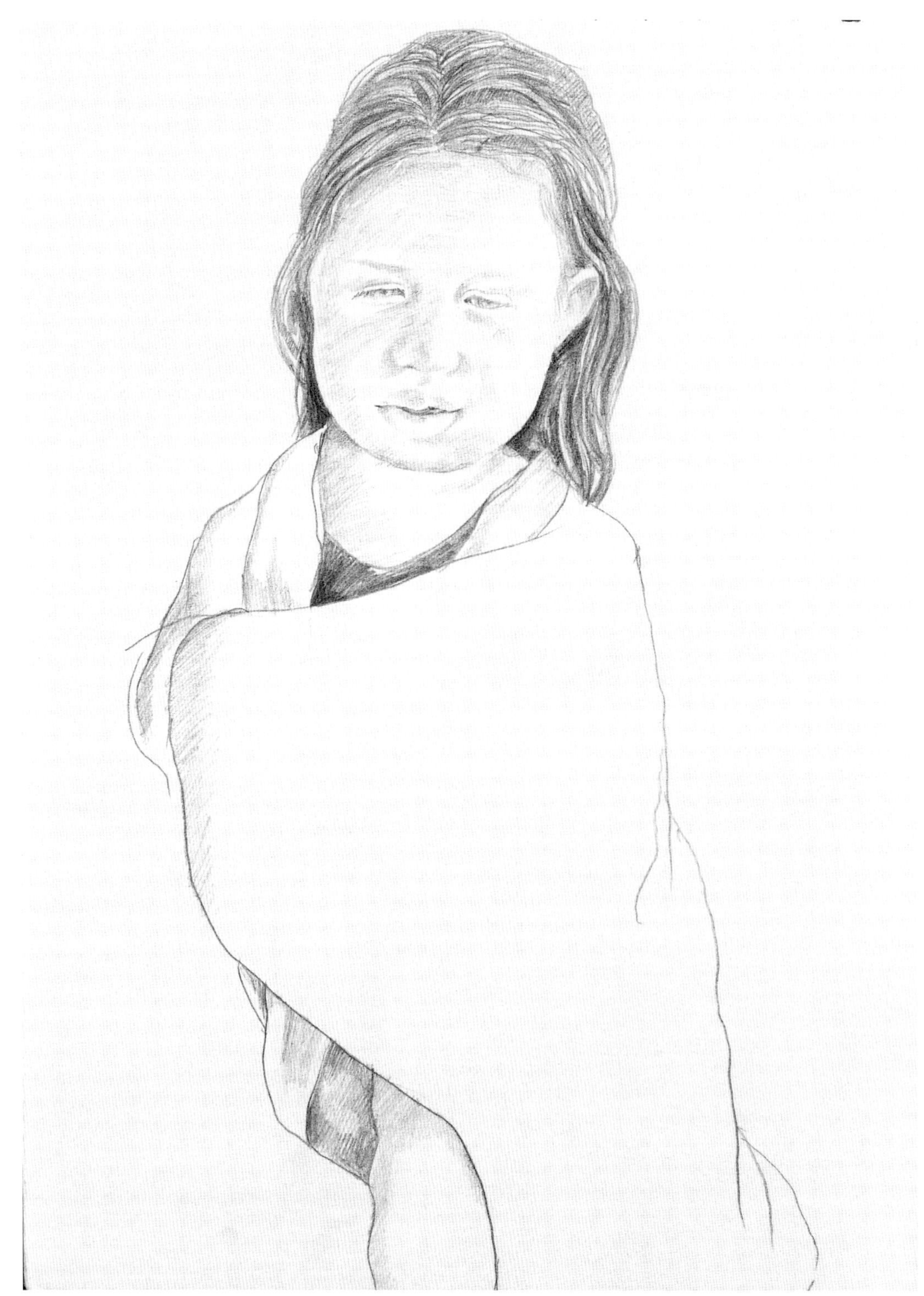

Natasha
1994
pencil
210 × 148

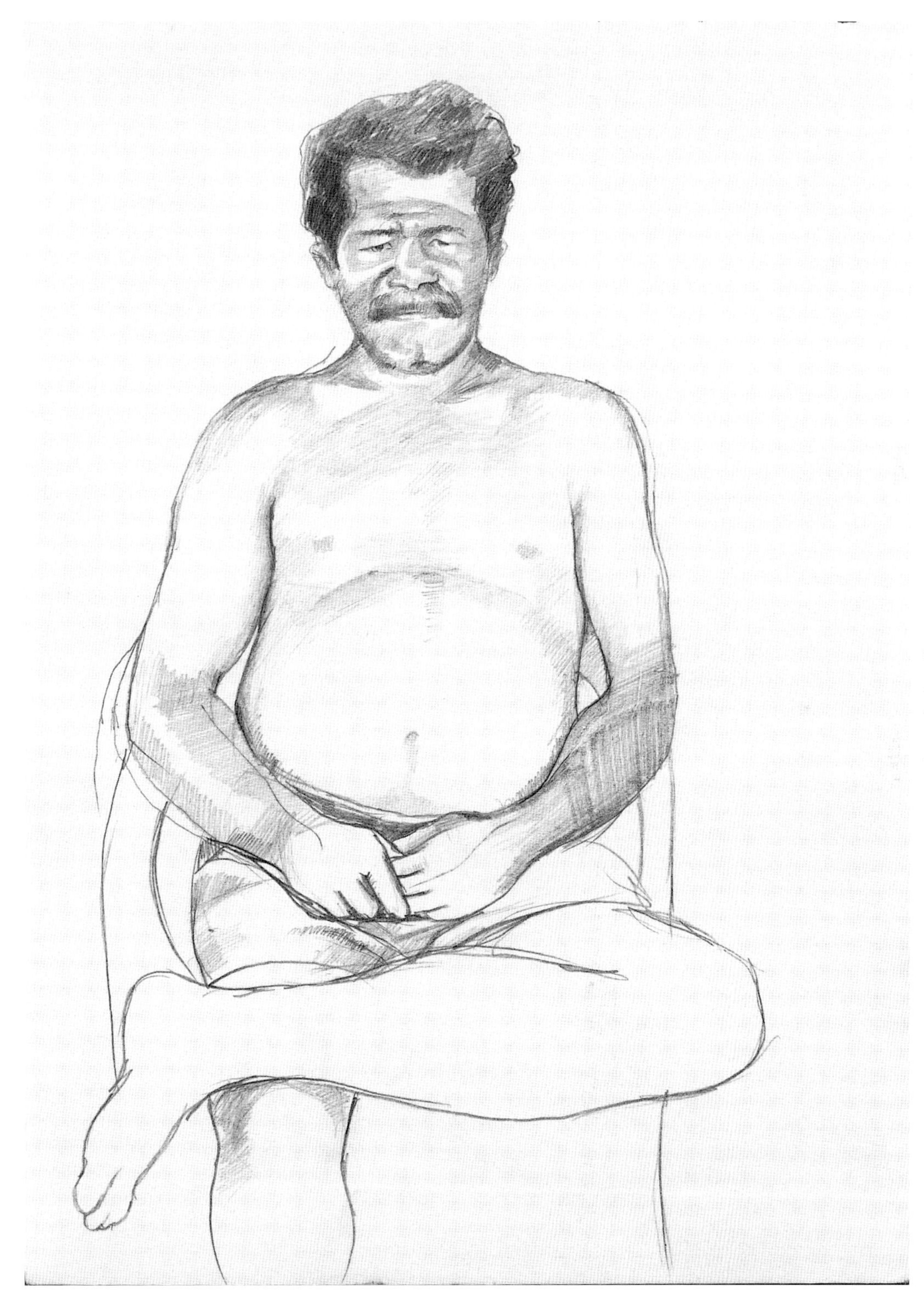

Portrait of a
man in Turkey
1994
pencil
210 × 148

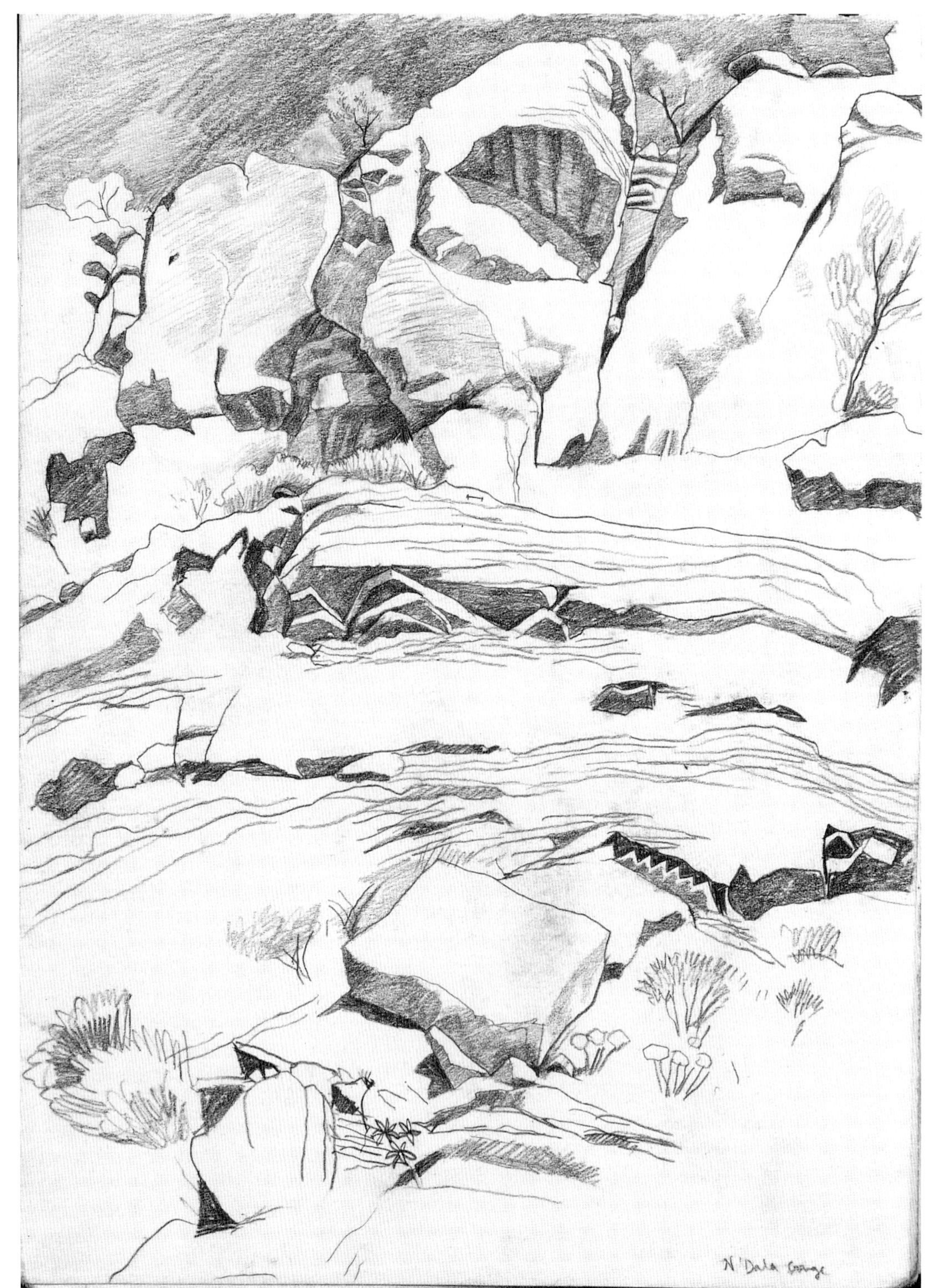

Study: 'N'Dala
Gorge' (Australia)
1994
pencil
210 × 148

68

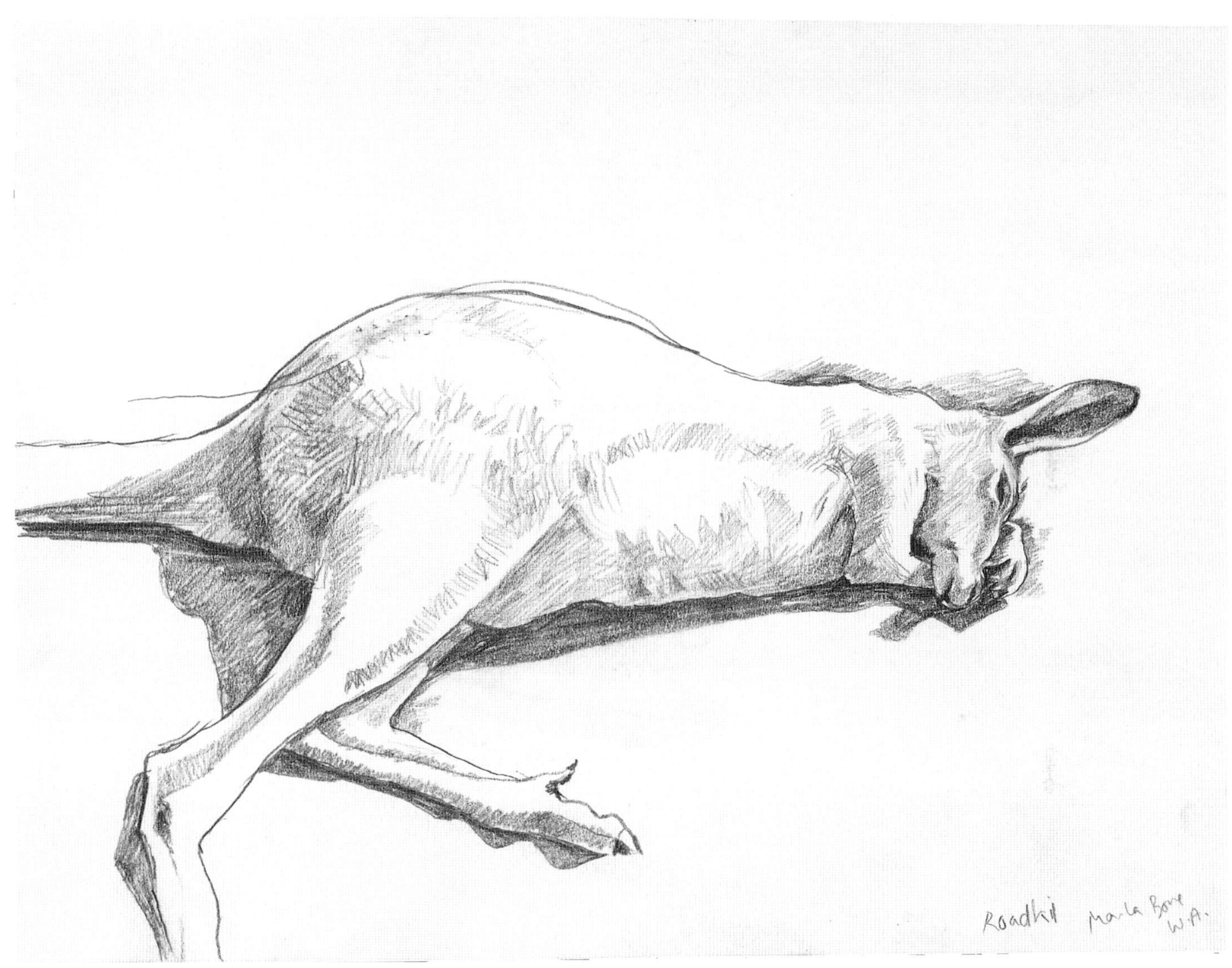

'Roadkill' (Australia)
1994
pencil
148 × 210

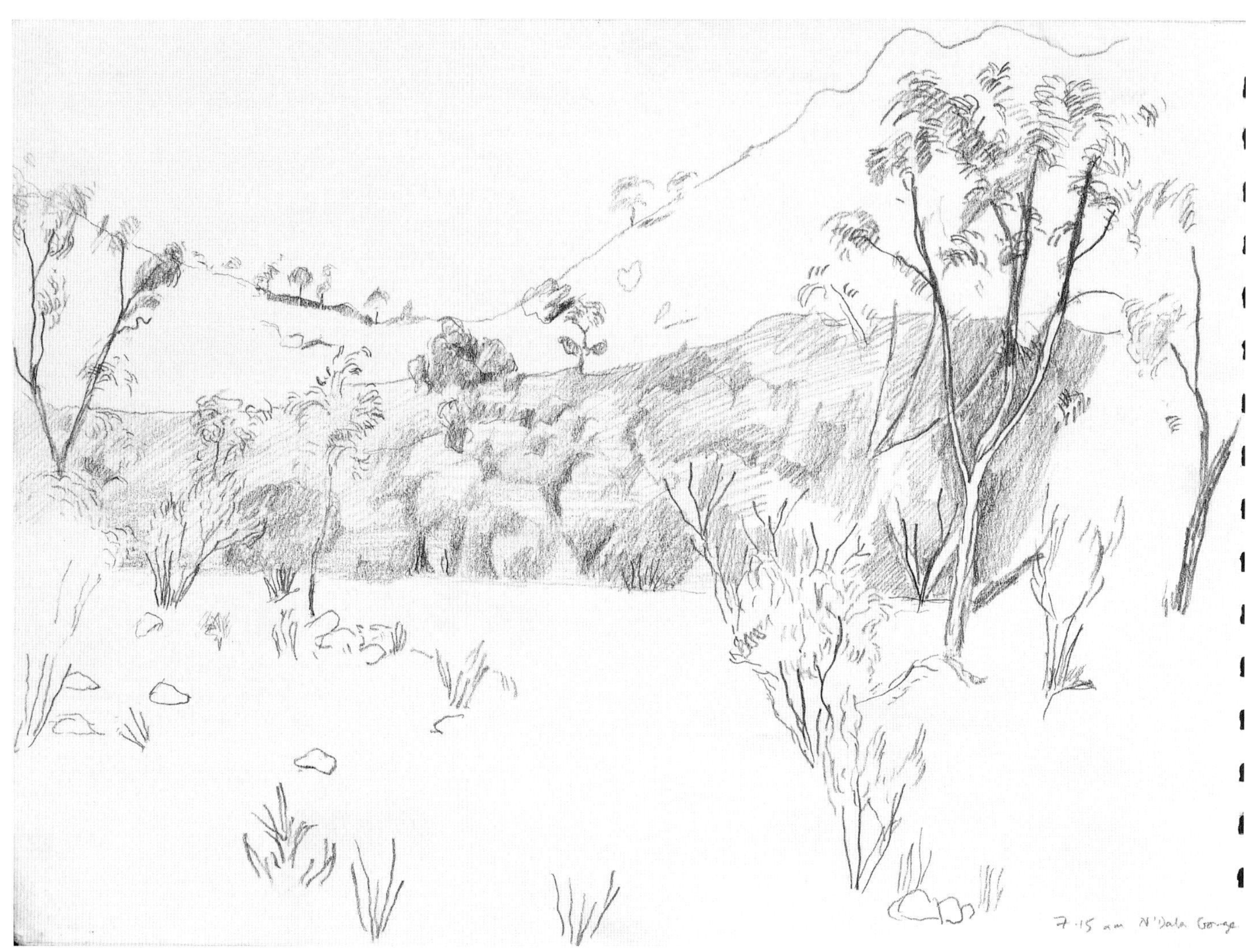

Study: '7.15 a.m., N'Dala Gorge' (Australia)
1994
pencil
148 × 210

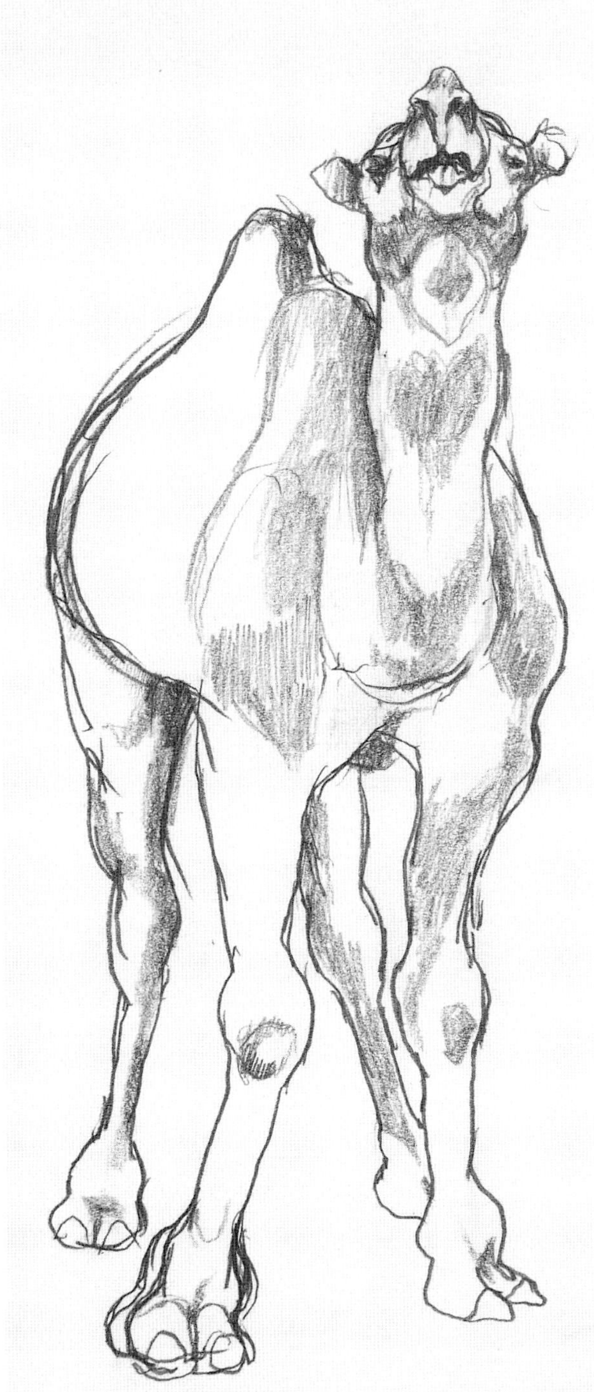

'Ross River
Station'
(Australia)
1994
pencil
210 × 148

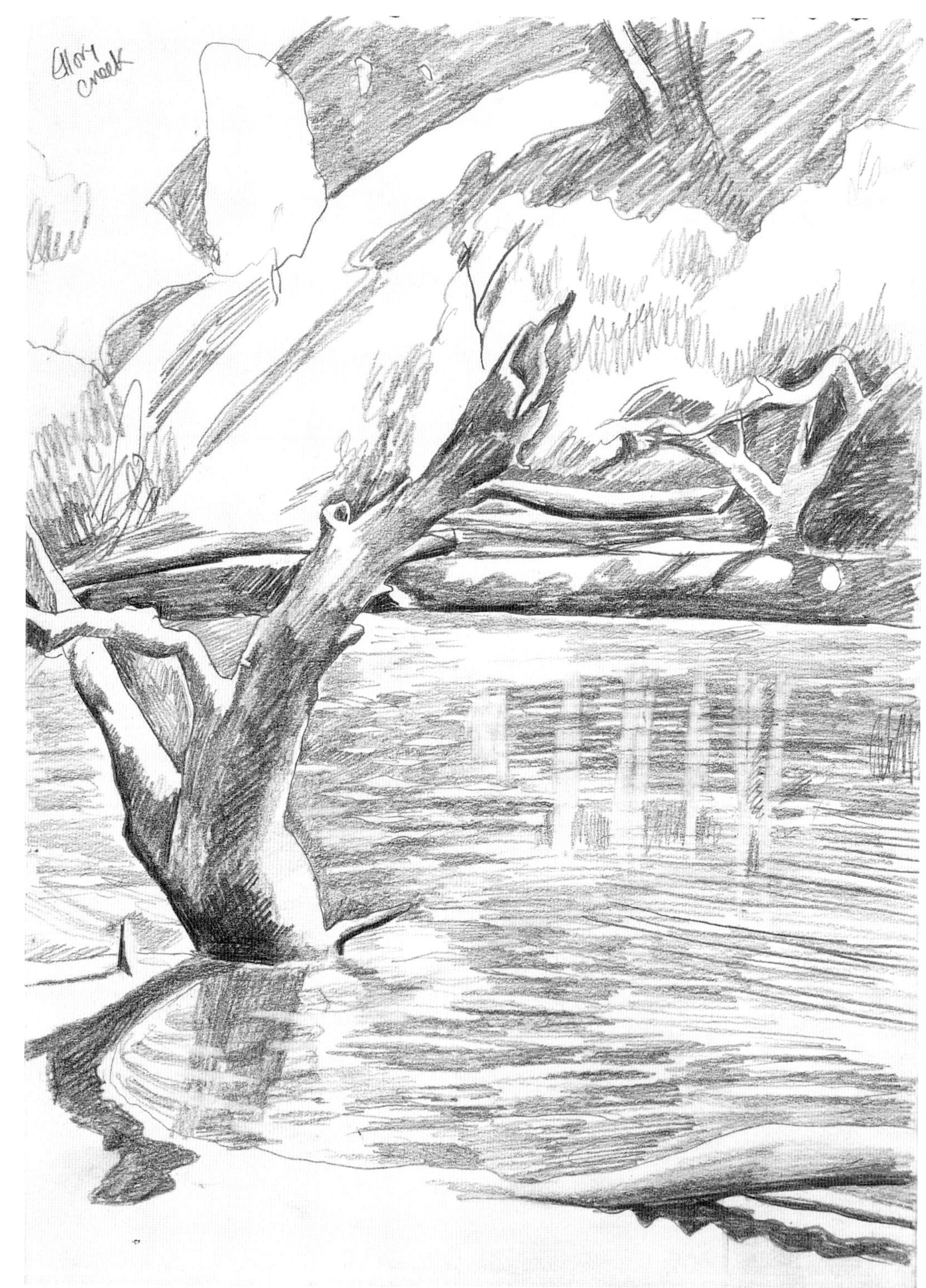

'Glory Creek'
(Australia)
1994
pencil
210 × 148

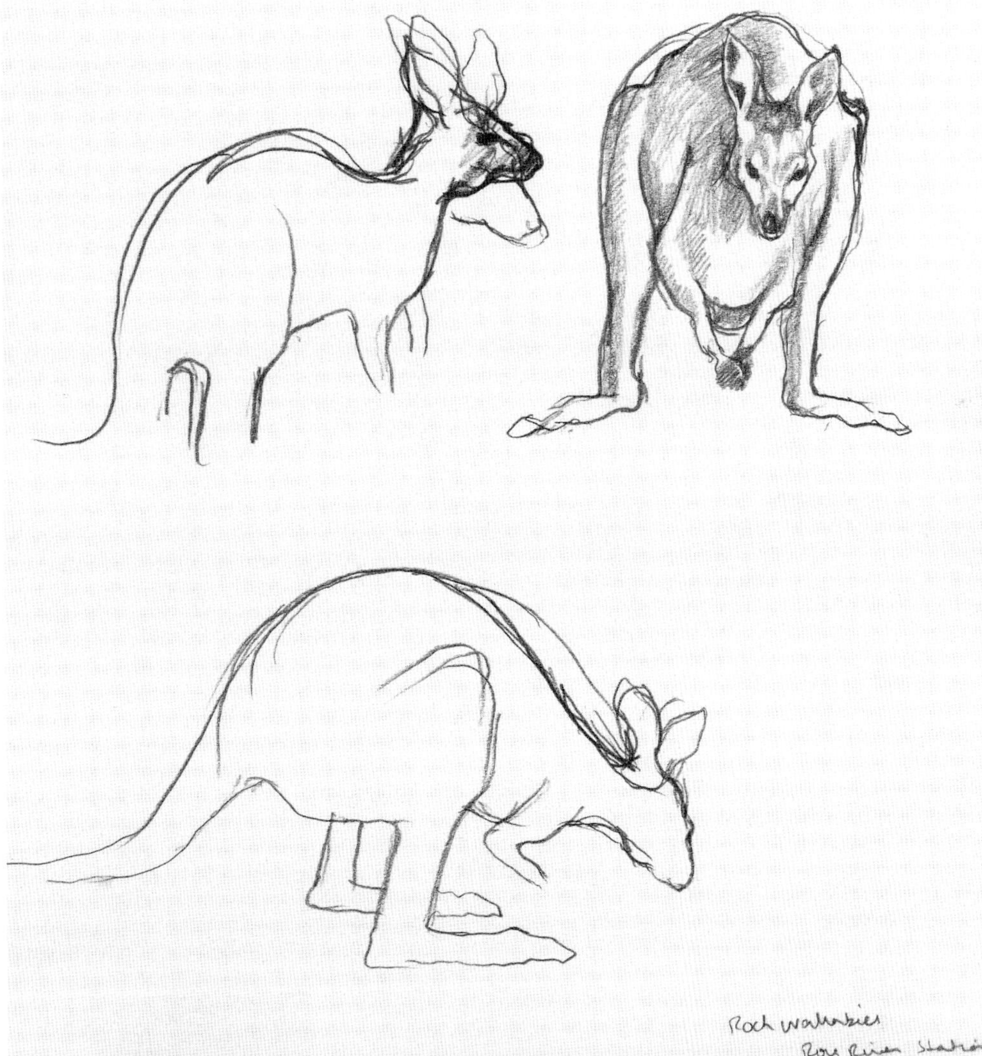

'Rock wallabies,
Ross River Station'
(Australia)
1994
pencil
210 × 148

73

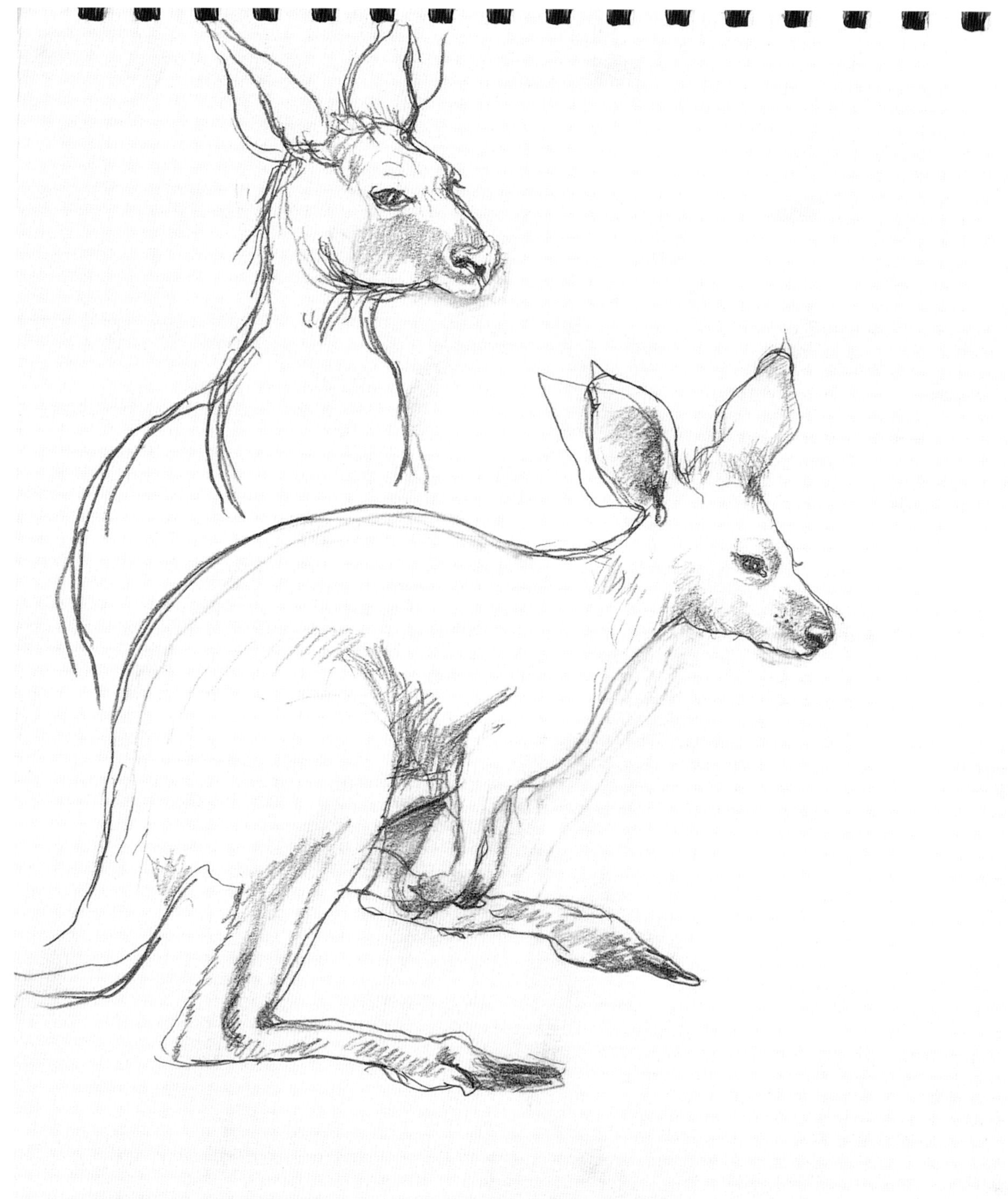

Australia
1994
pencil
210 × 148

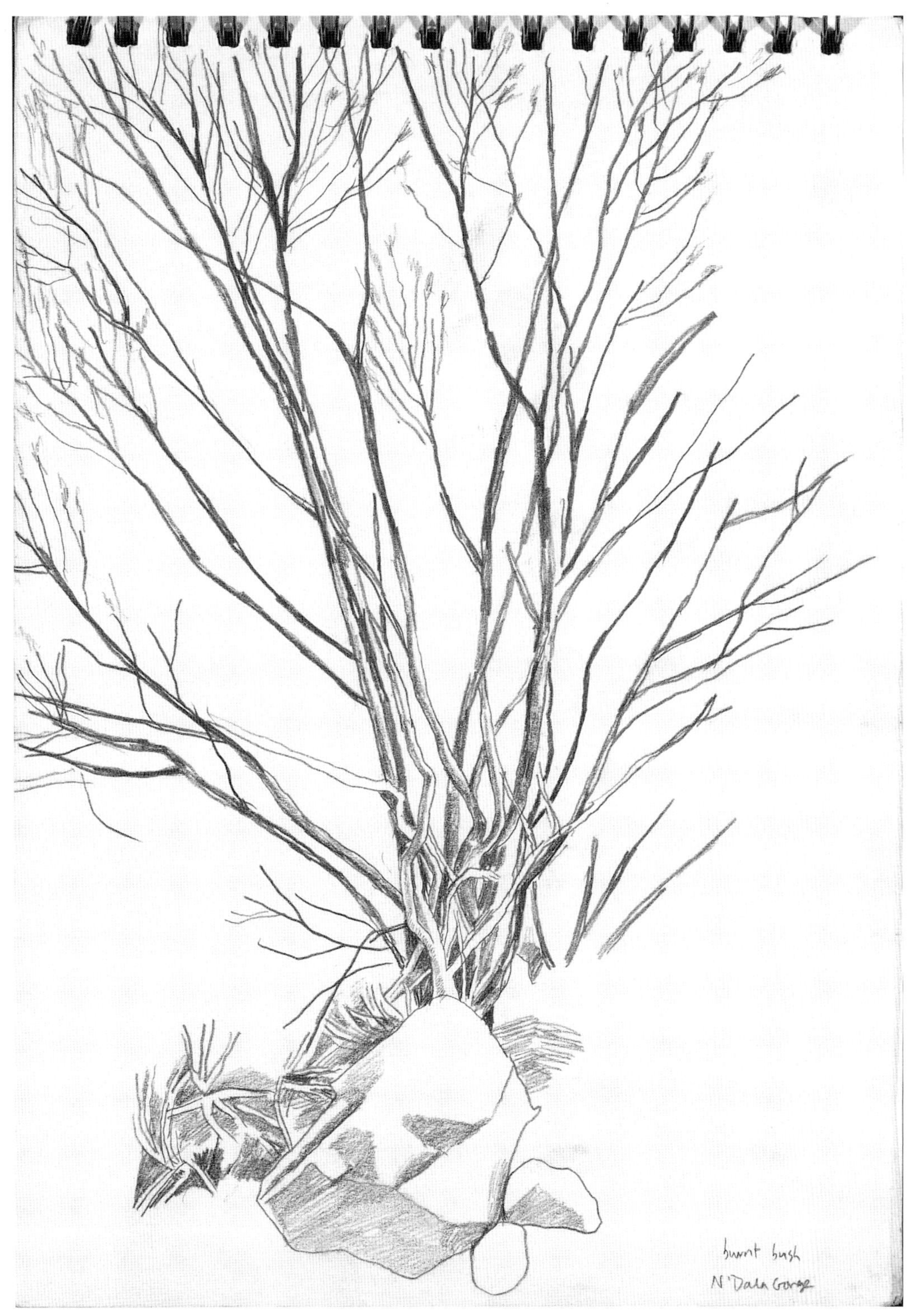

'Burnt bush, N'Dala
Gorge' (Australia)
1994
pencil
210 × 148

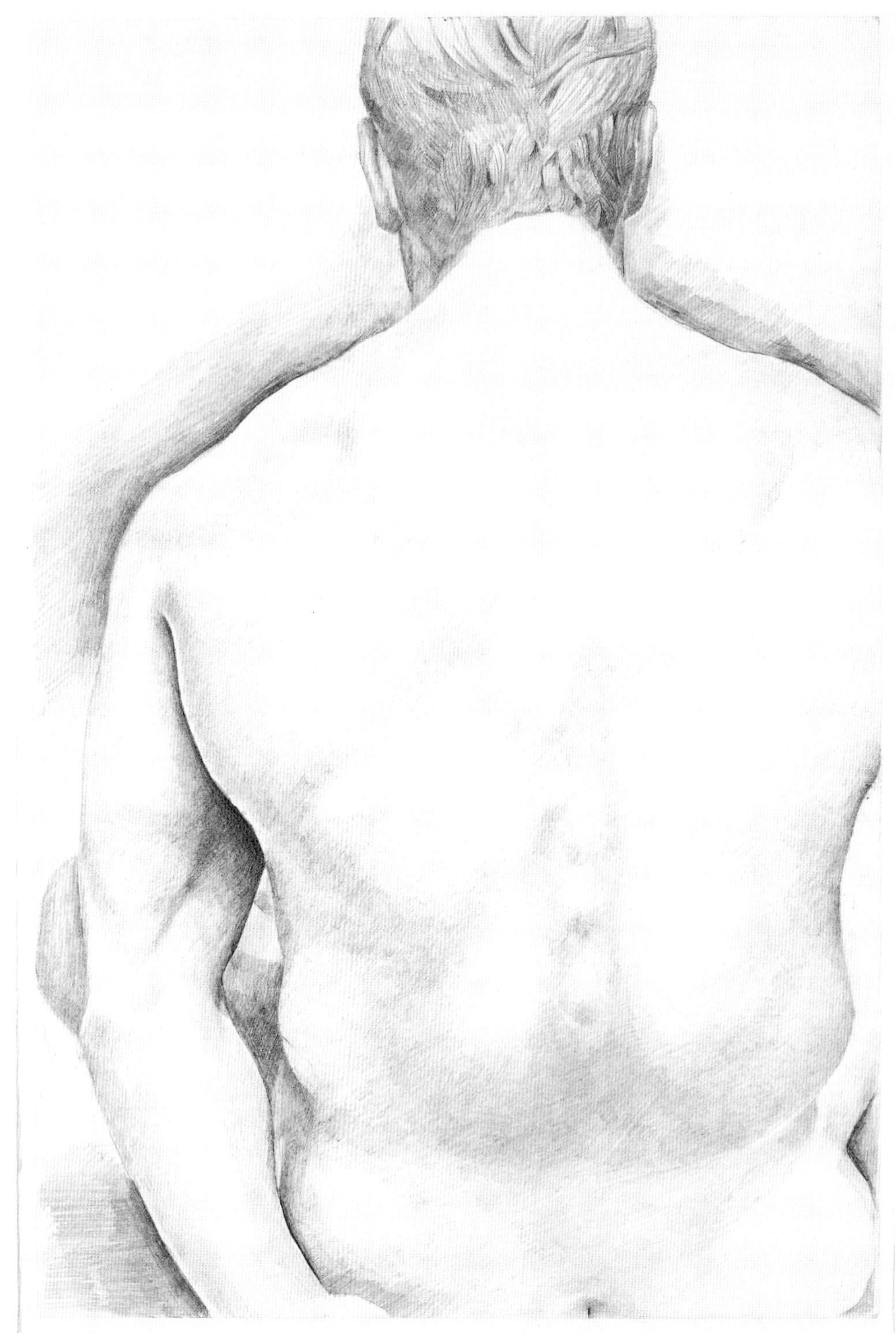

Chris
1994
pencil
250 × 170

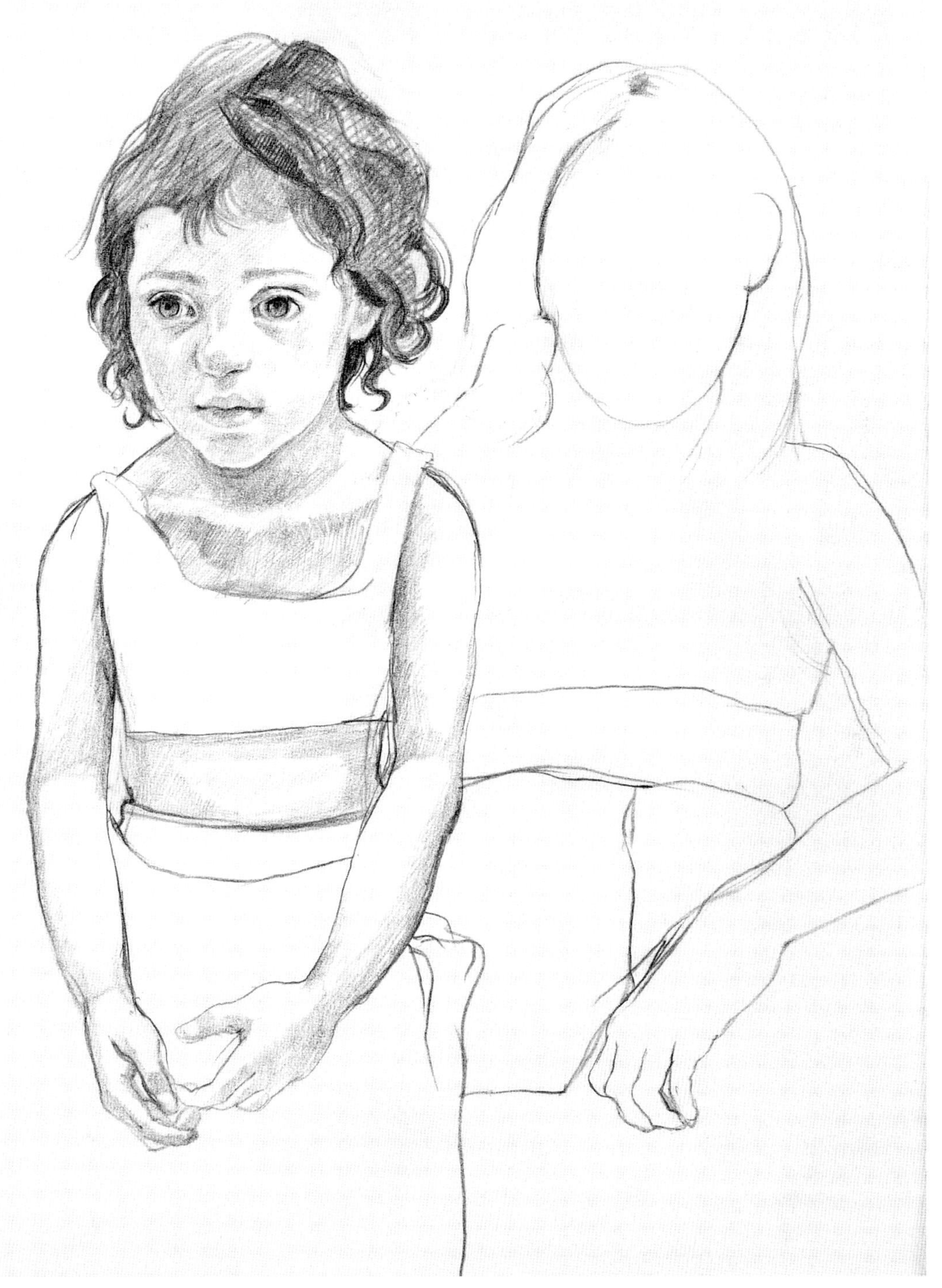

Anna
1994 (?)
pencil
235 × 175

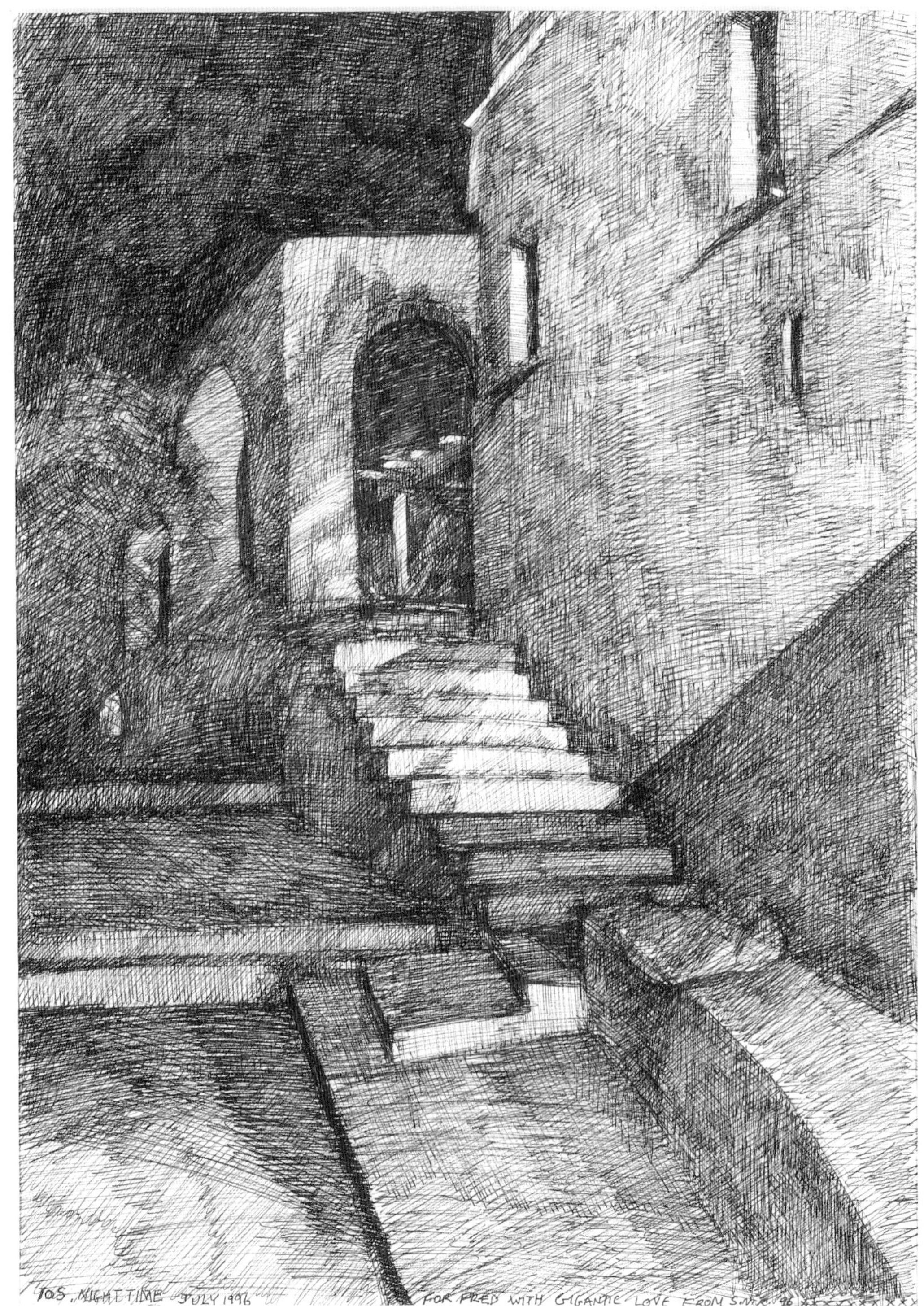

'Ios, night time'
July 1996
pen and ink
285 × 208

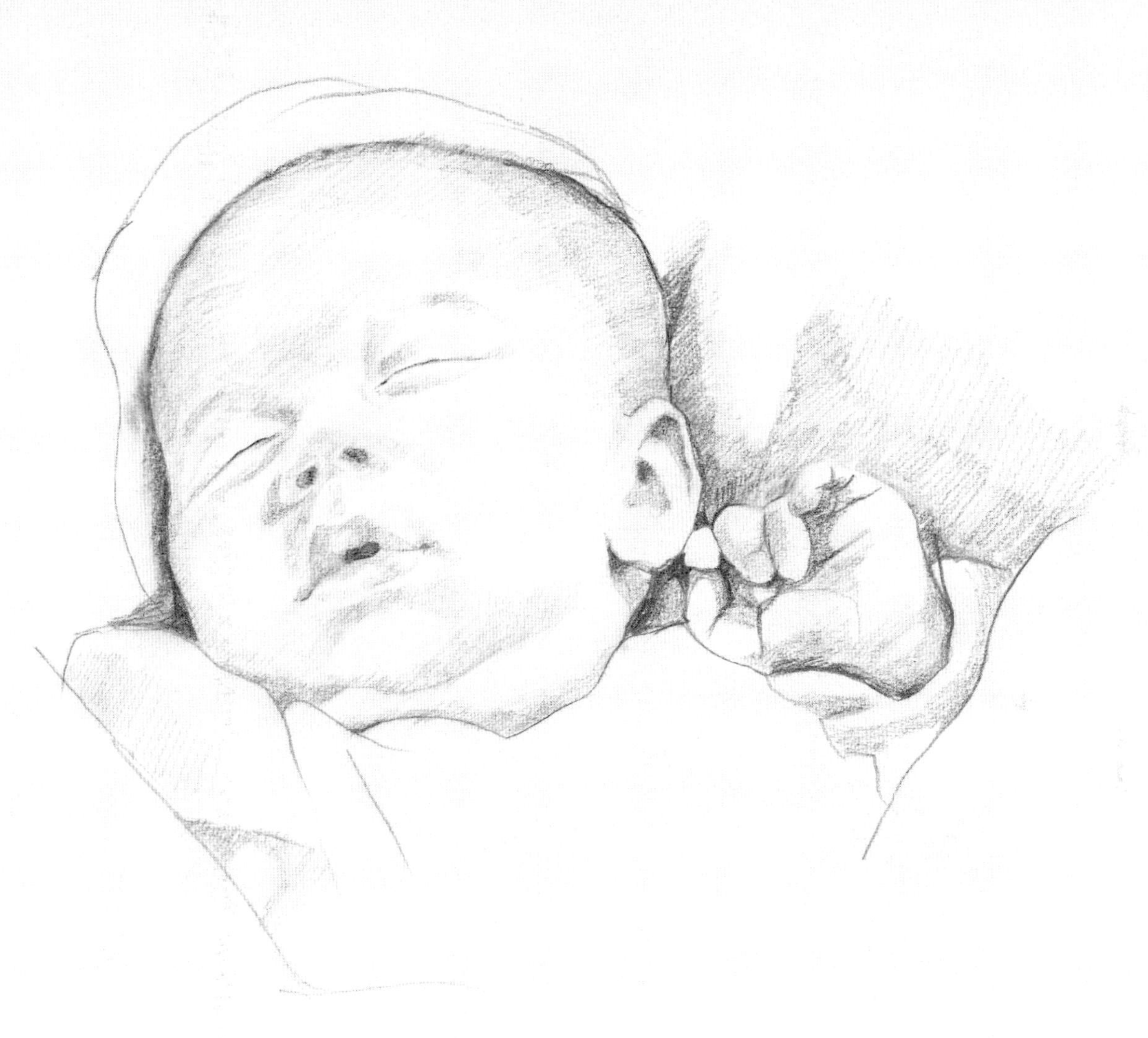

Becky
1996
pencil
290 × 210

79

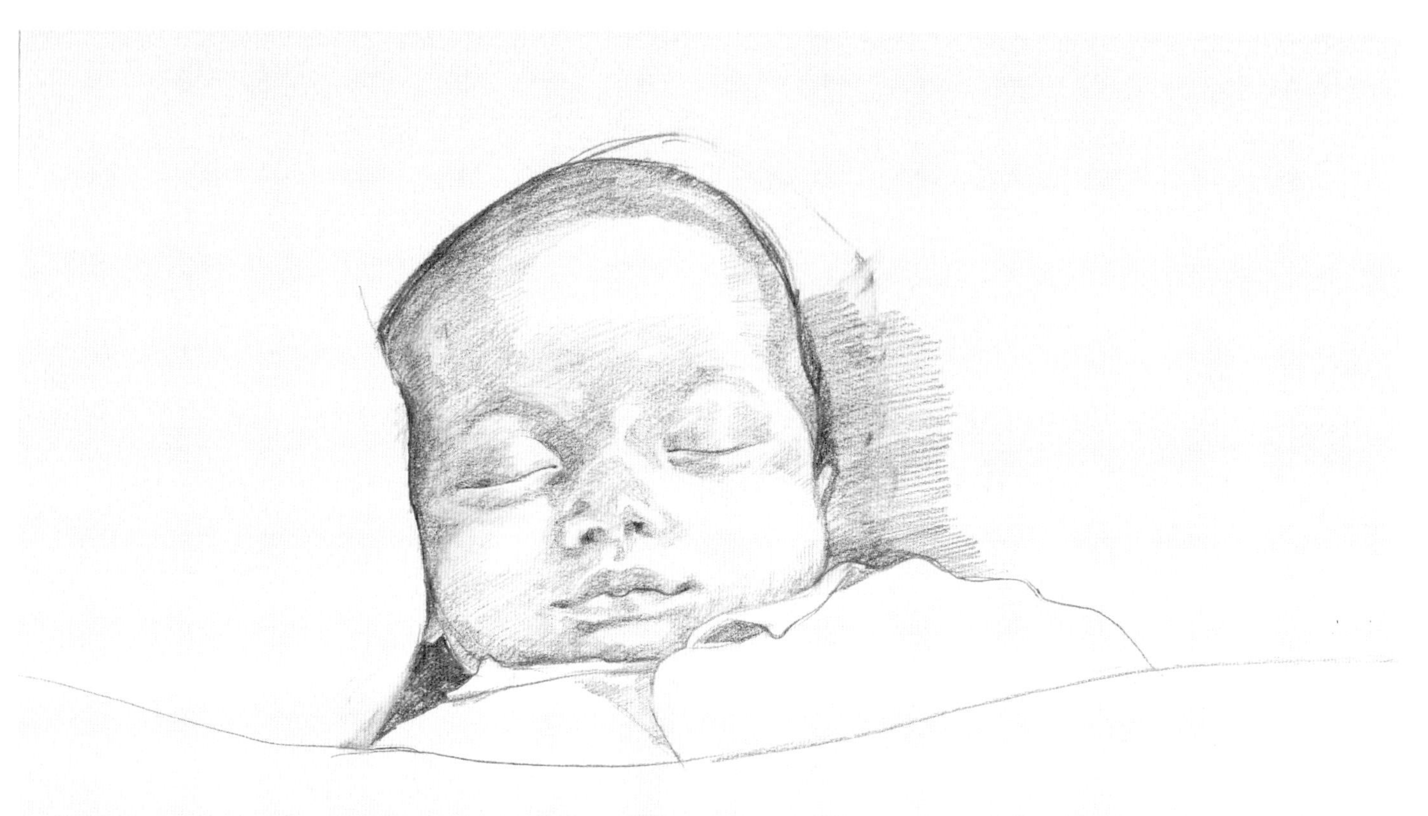

Becky
1996
pencil
210 × 290

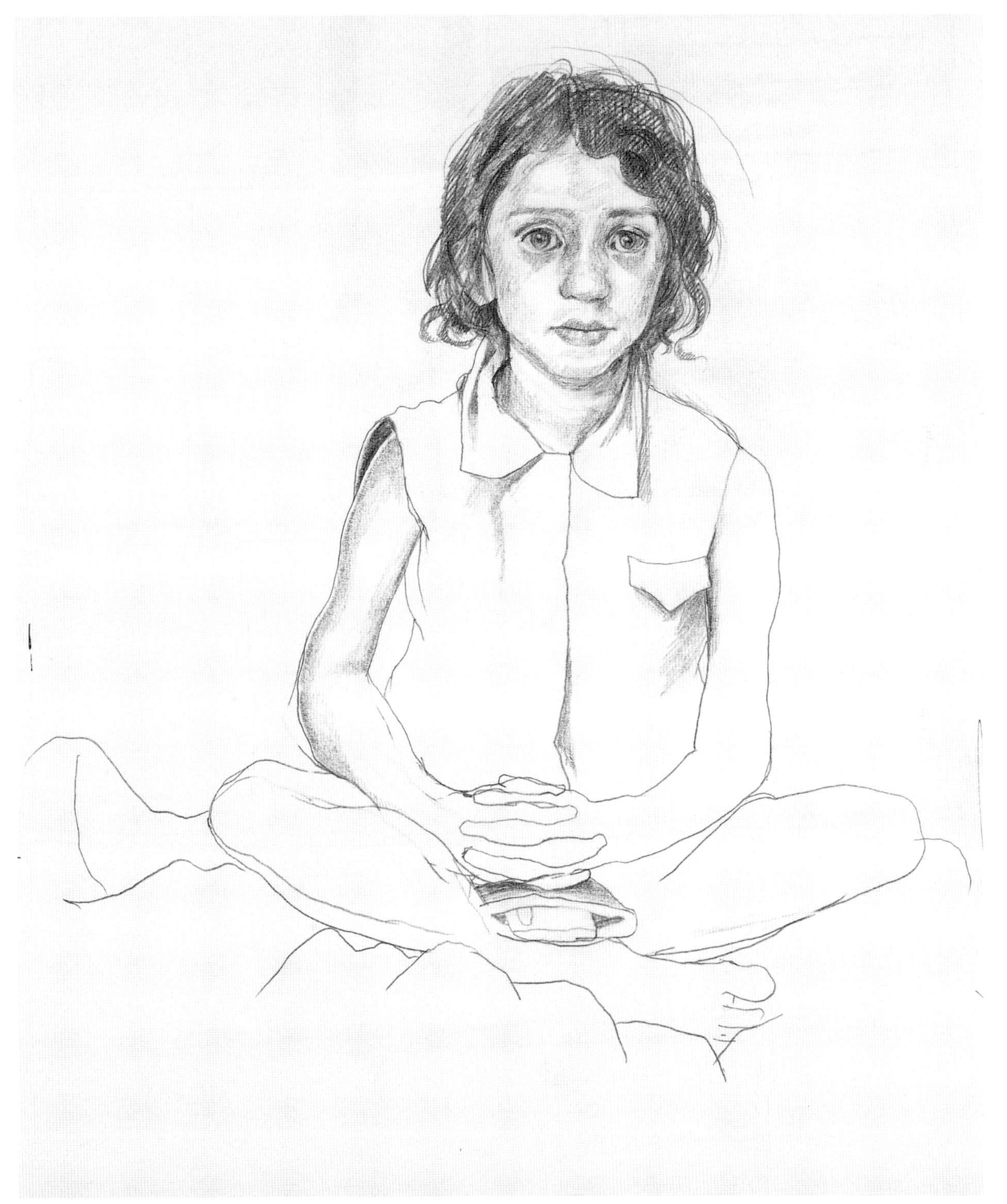

Anna
1996
pencil
290 × 210

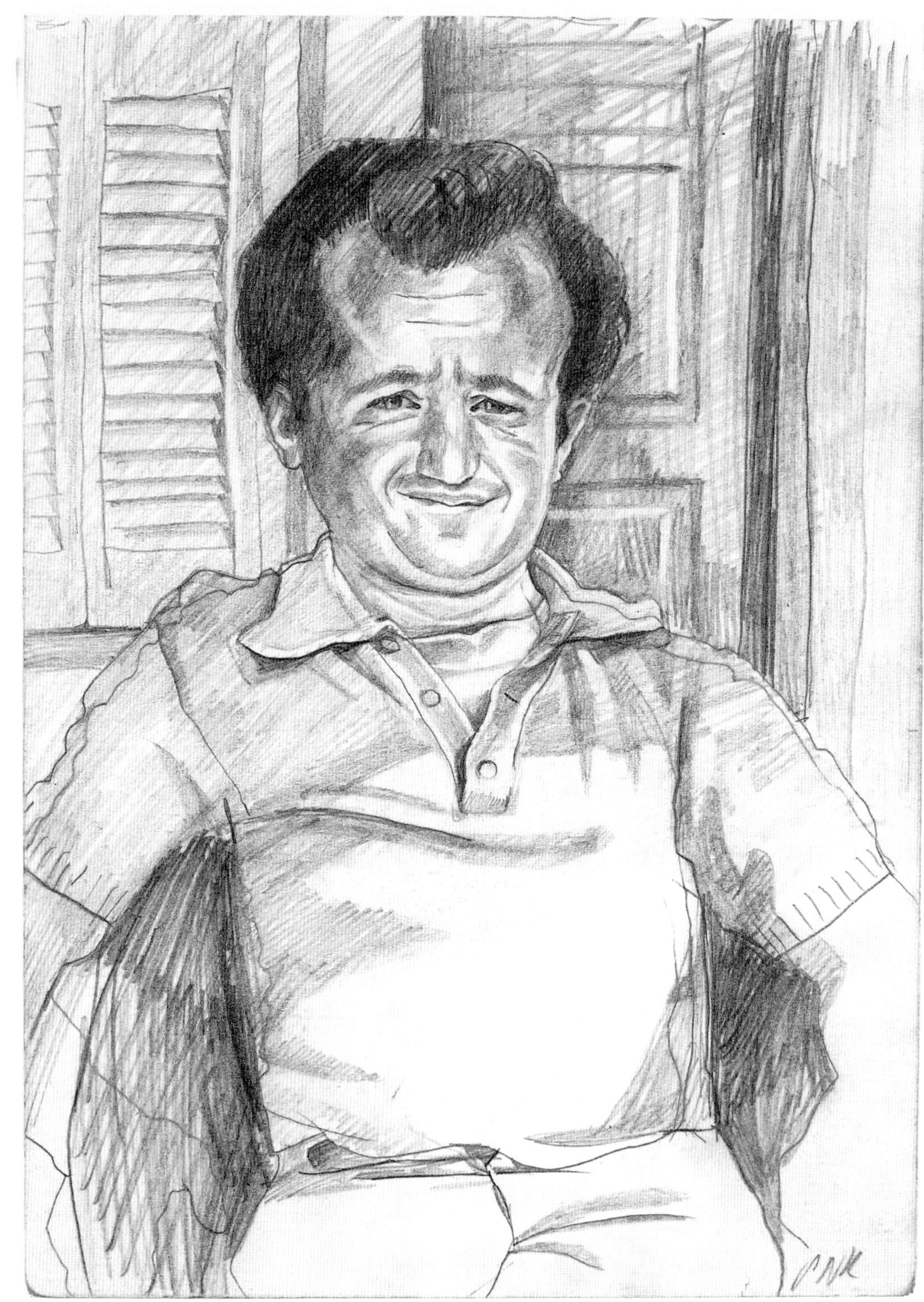

Giorgos, Ios
pencil
200 × 145

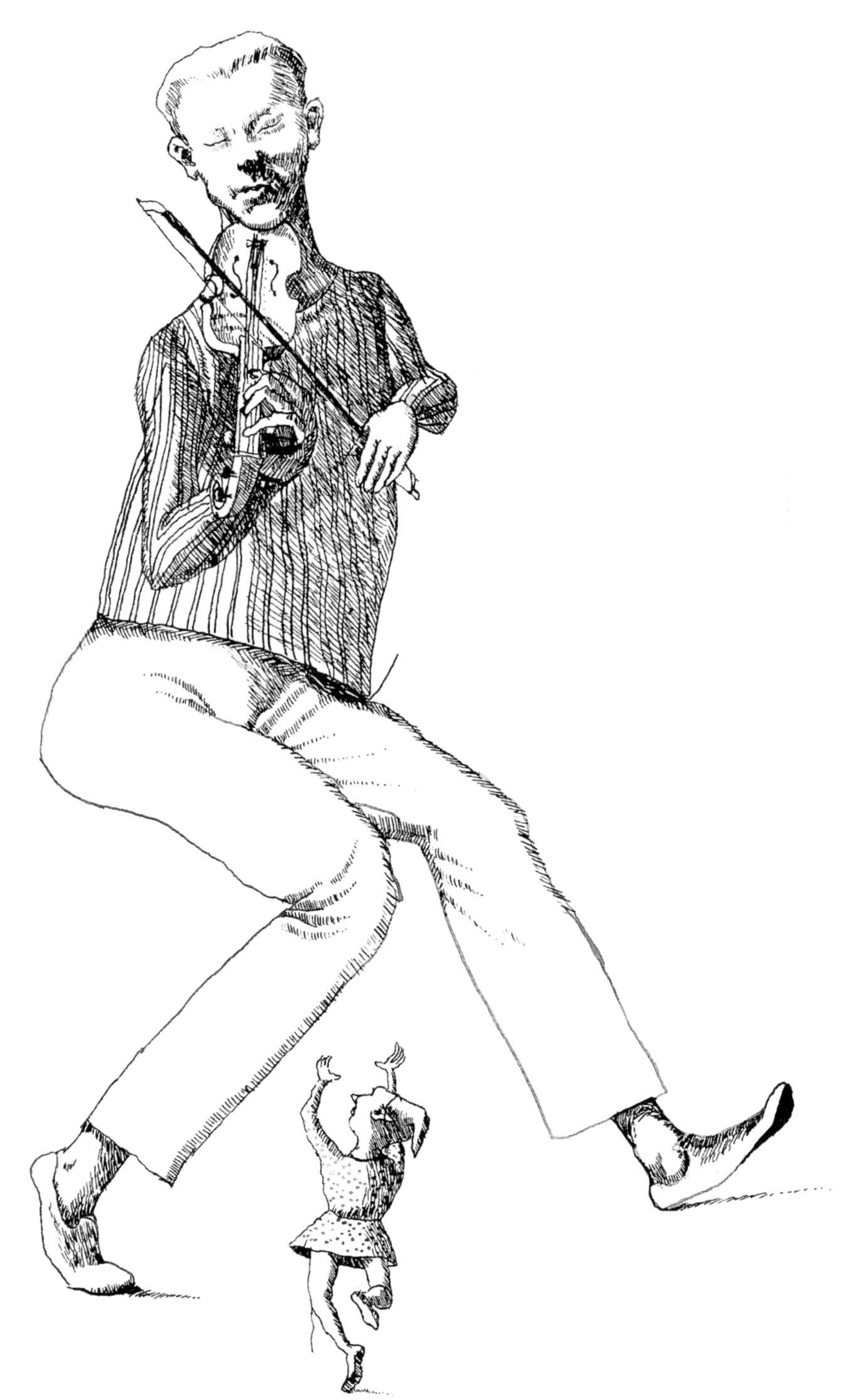

1995
pen and ink
255 × 175

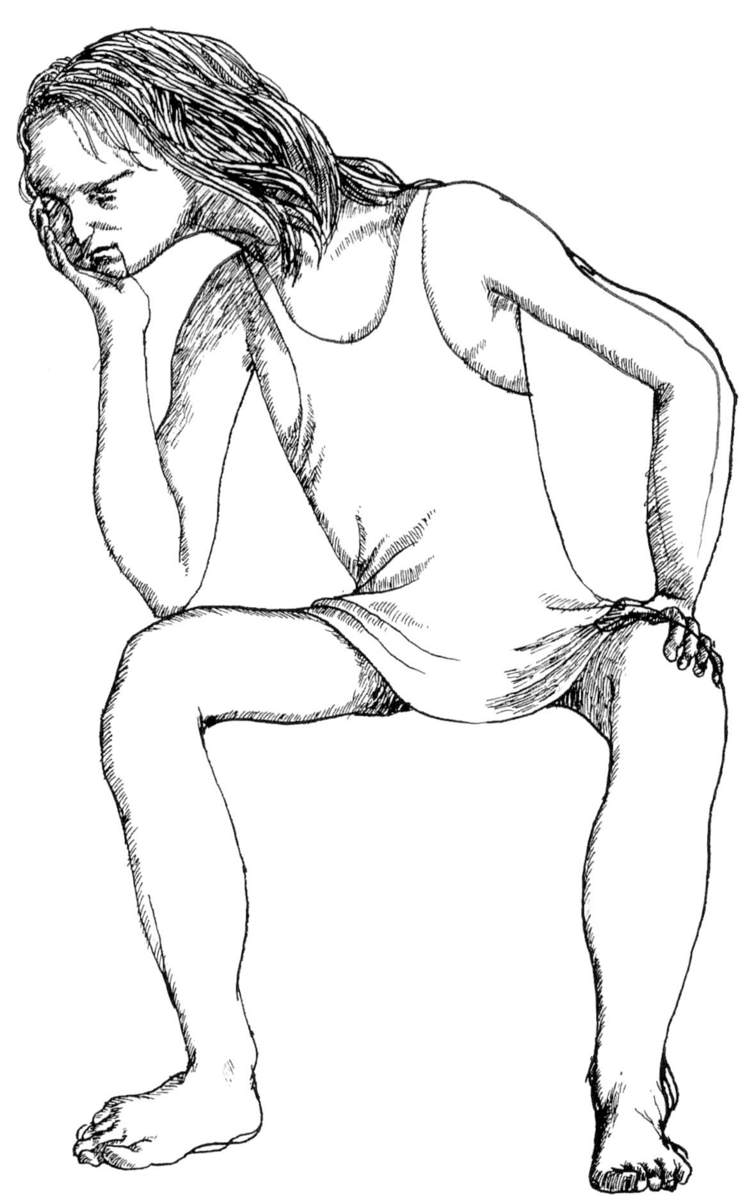

1995
pen and ink
255 × 175

84

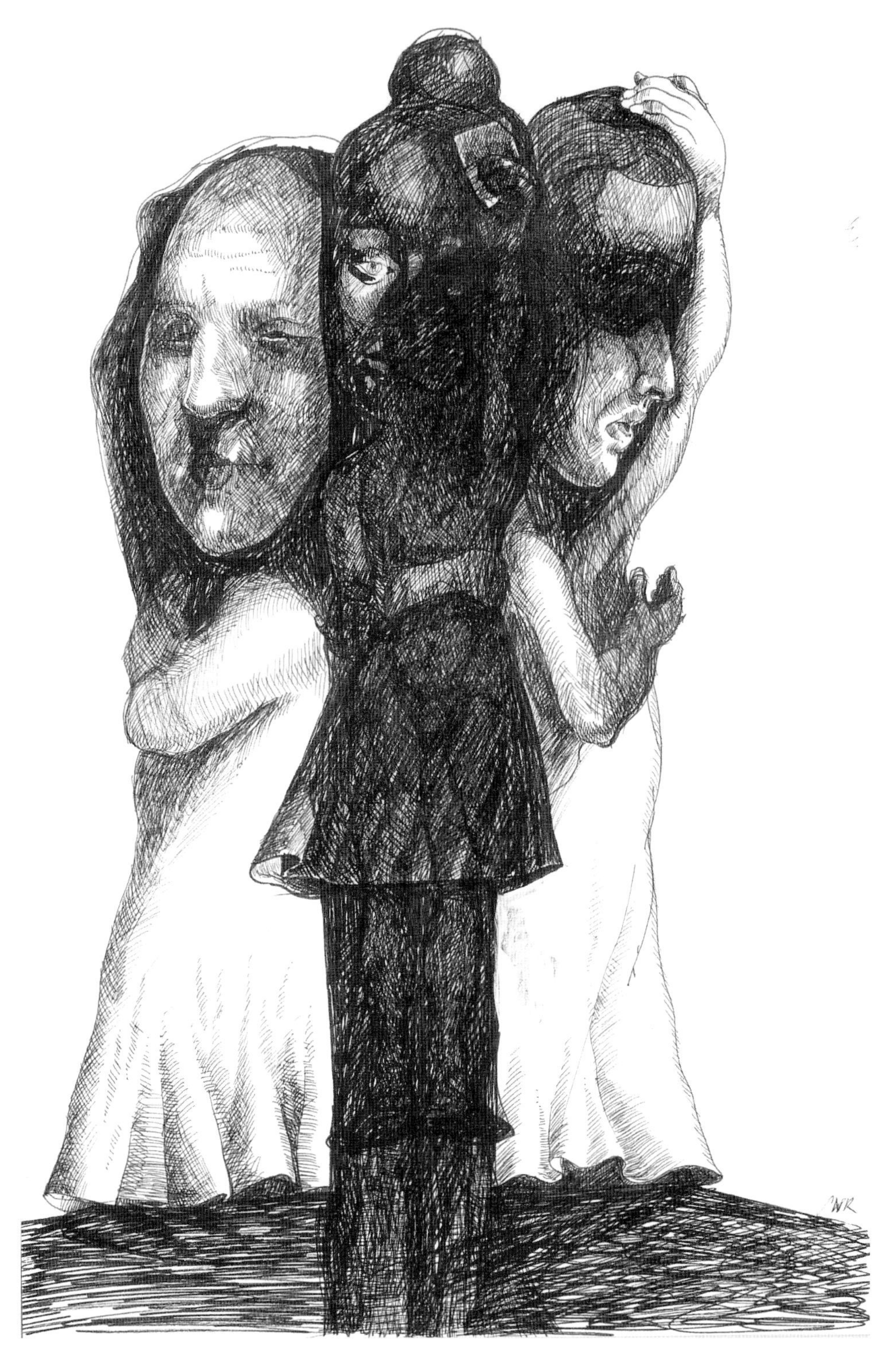

1995 (?)
pen and ink
250 × 170

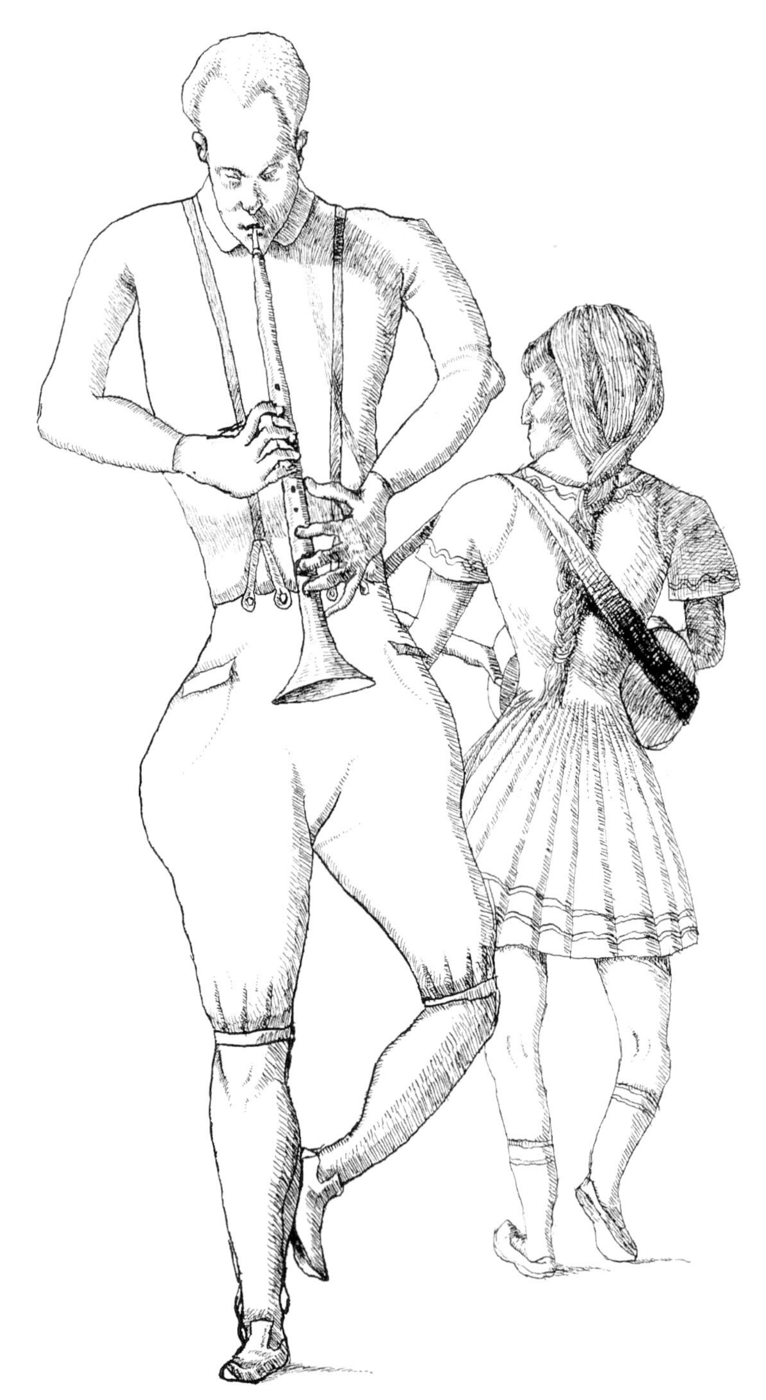

1995
pen and ink
225 × 175

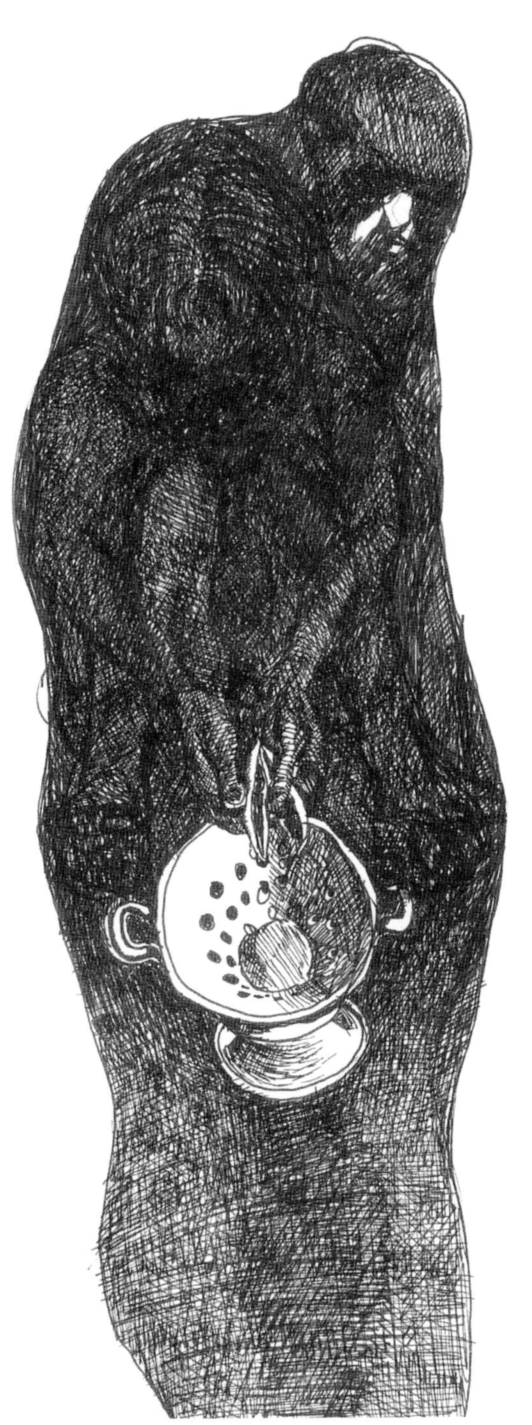

pen and ink
250 × 170

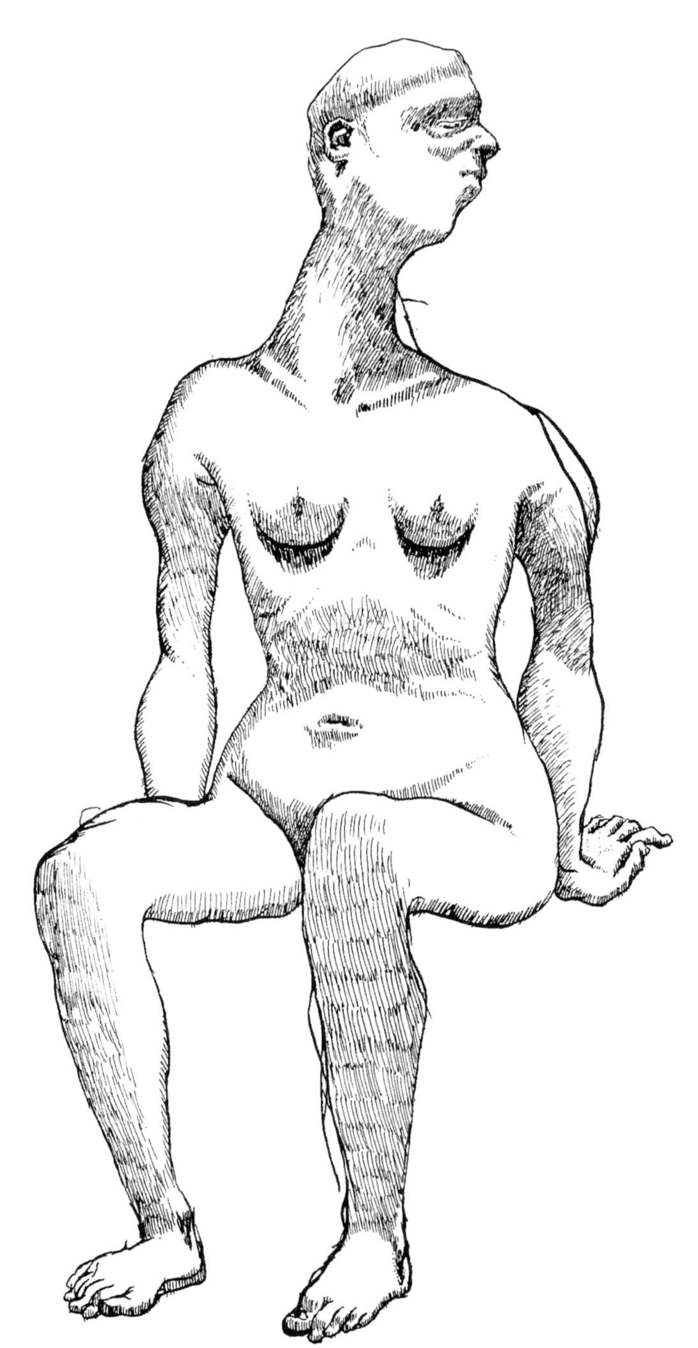

1995
pen and ink
225 × 175

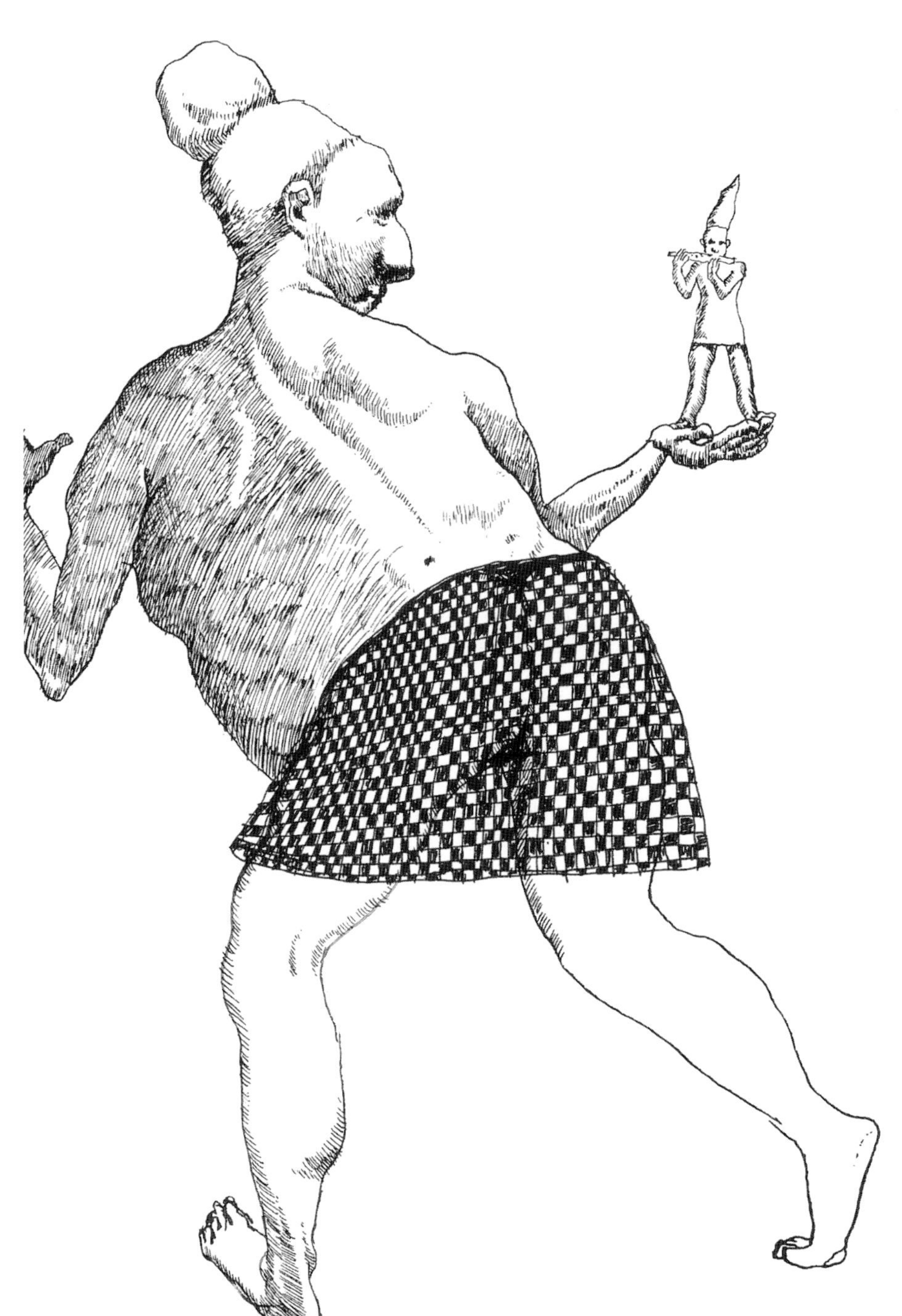

1995
pen and ink
225 × 175

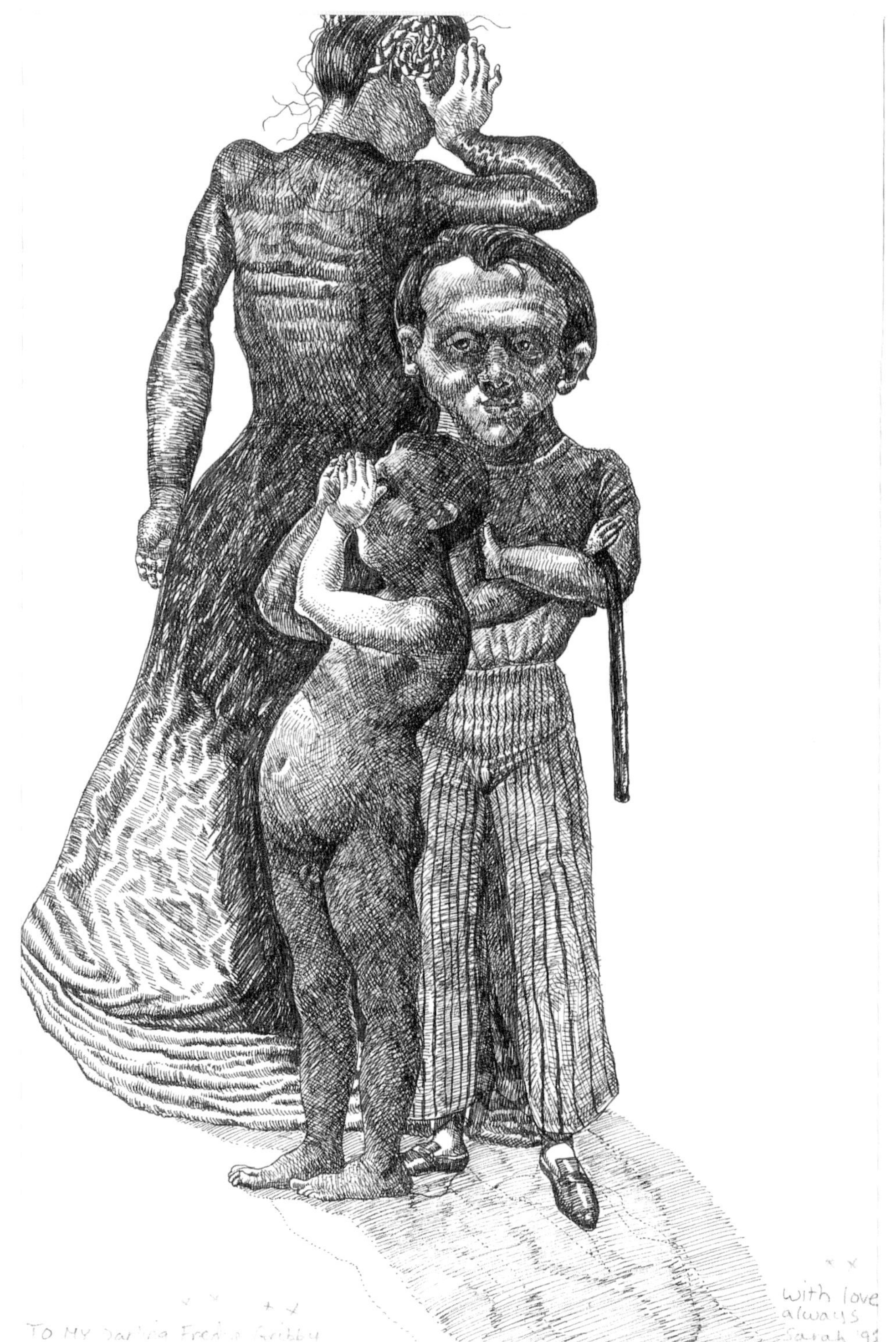

1995
pen and ink
250 × 170

90

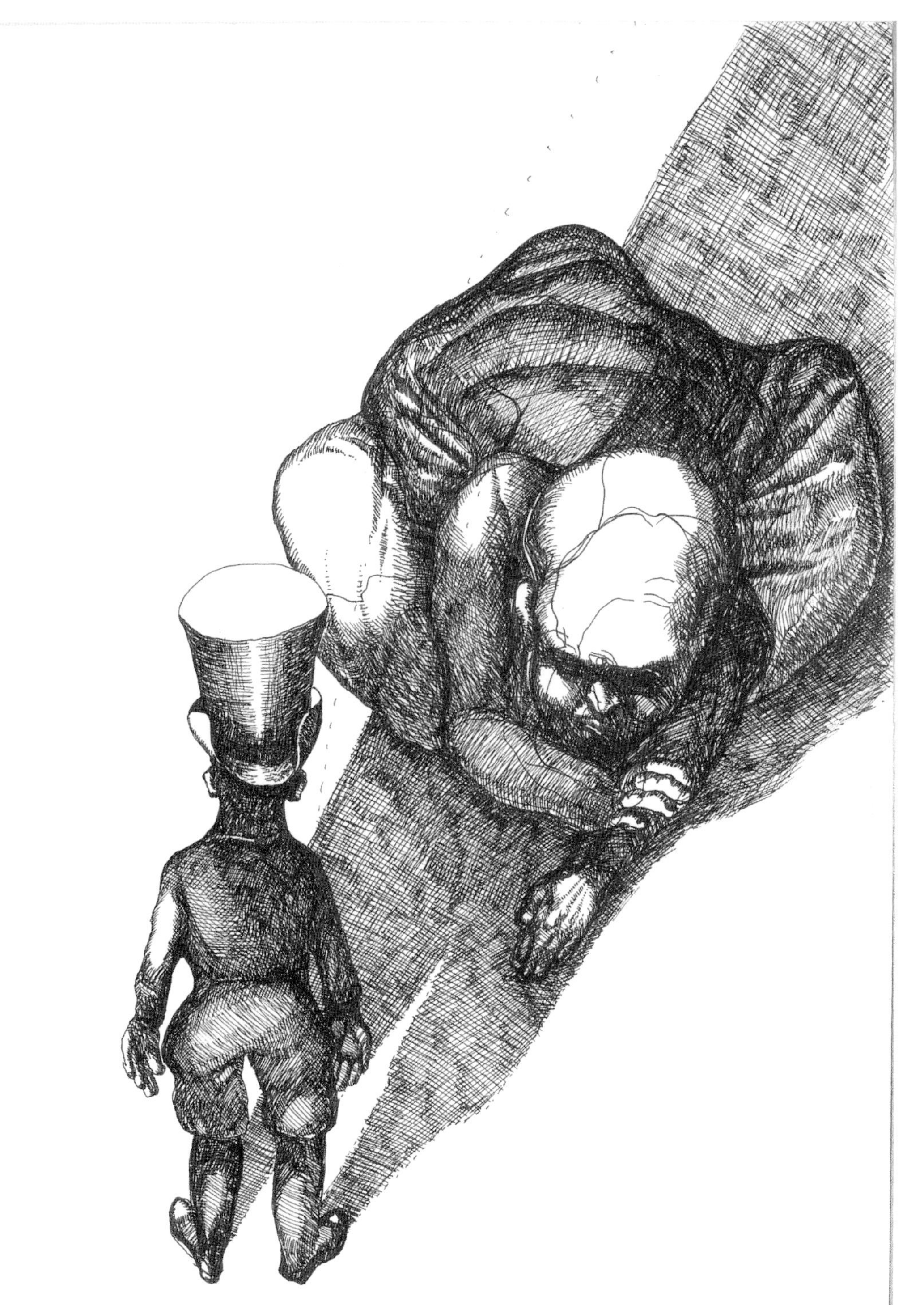

pen and ink
250 × 170

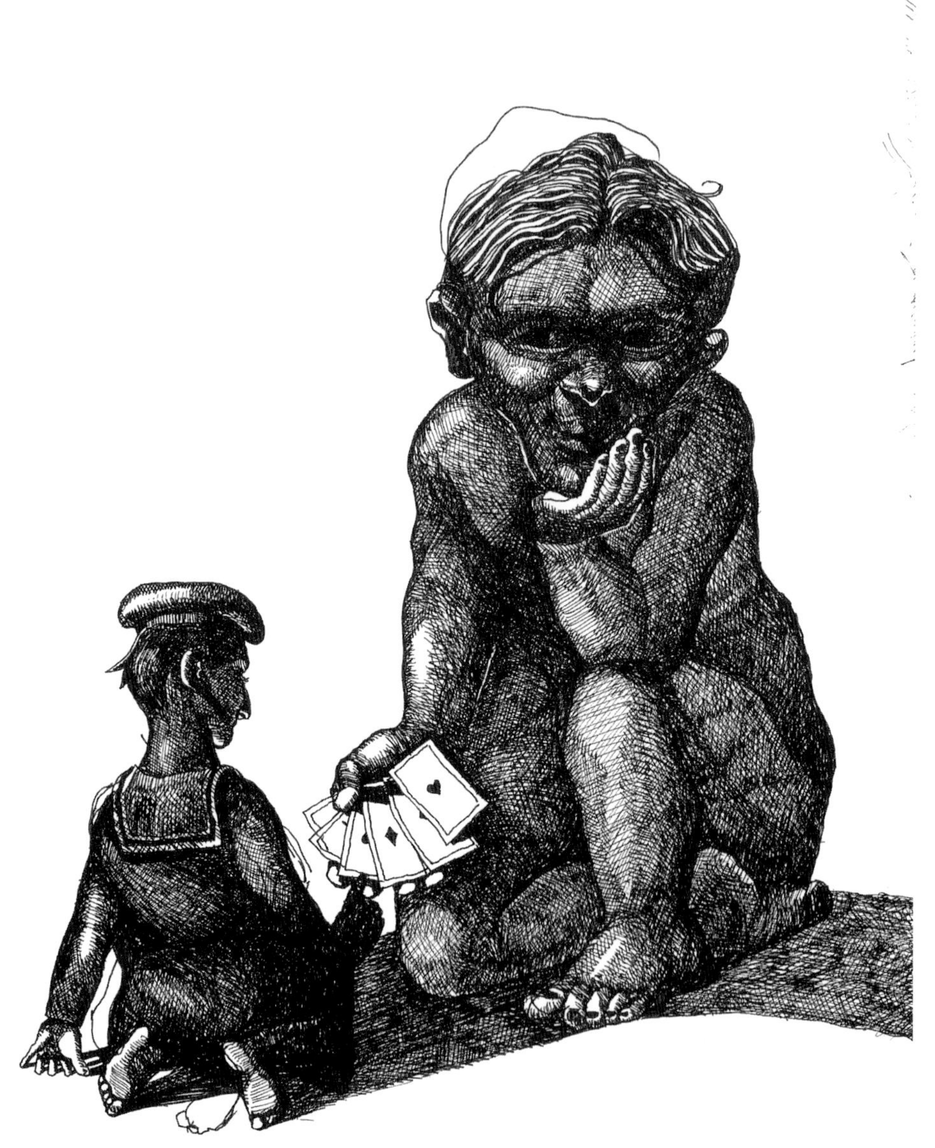

pen and ink
254 × 178

92

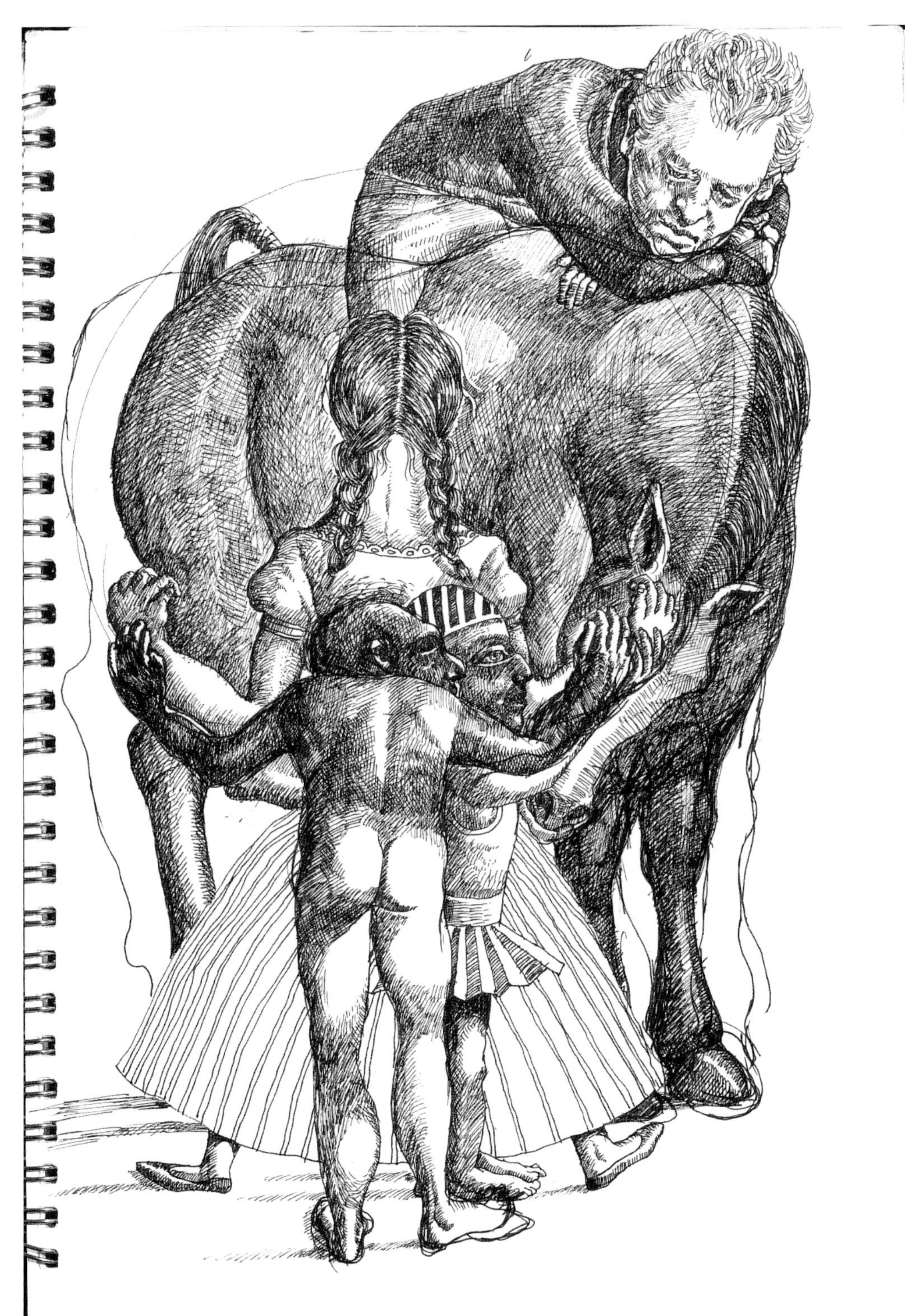

1995 (?)
254 × 178

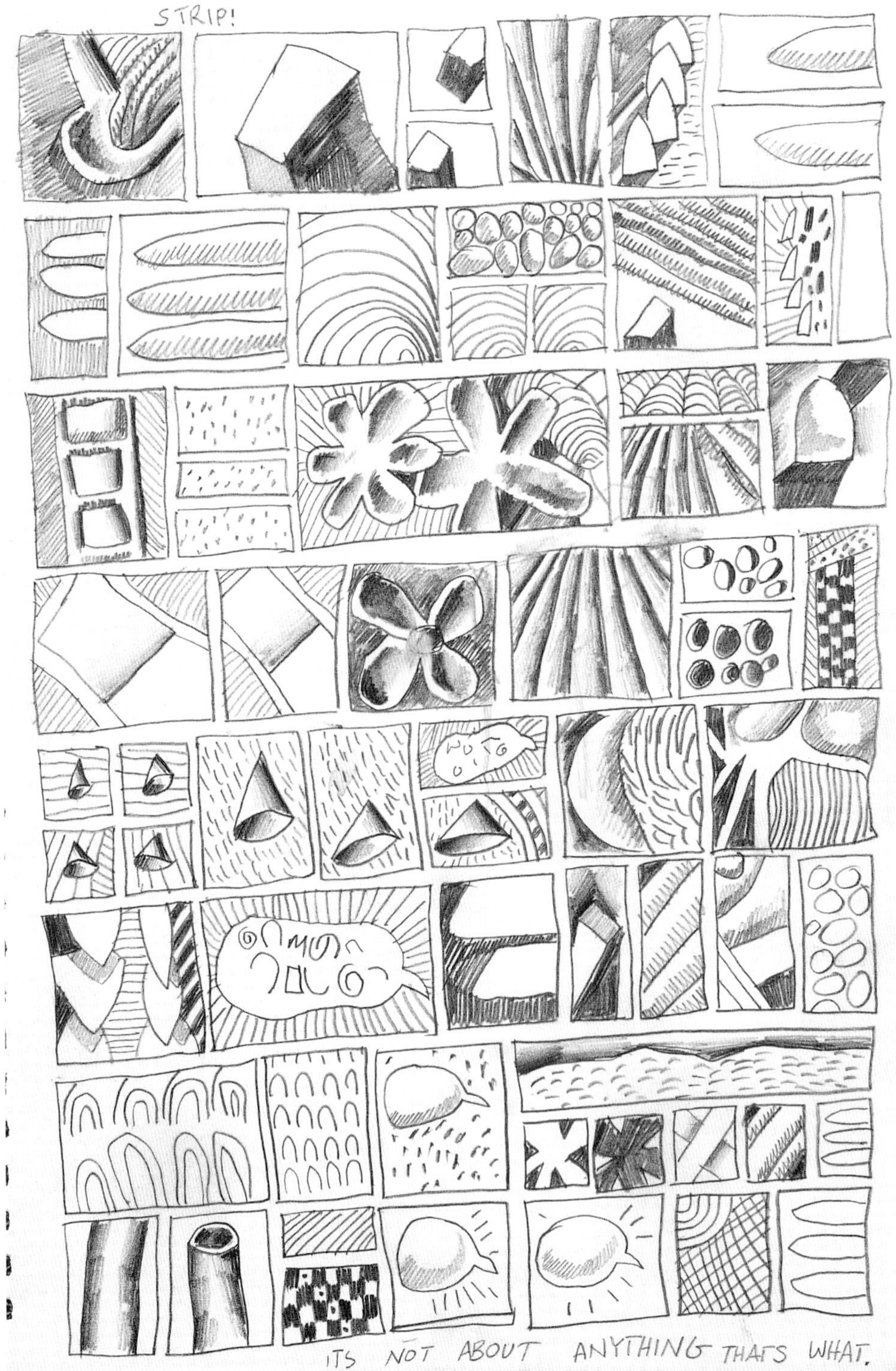

'It's not about
anything that's what'
1995
pencil
254 × 178

94

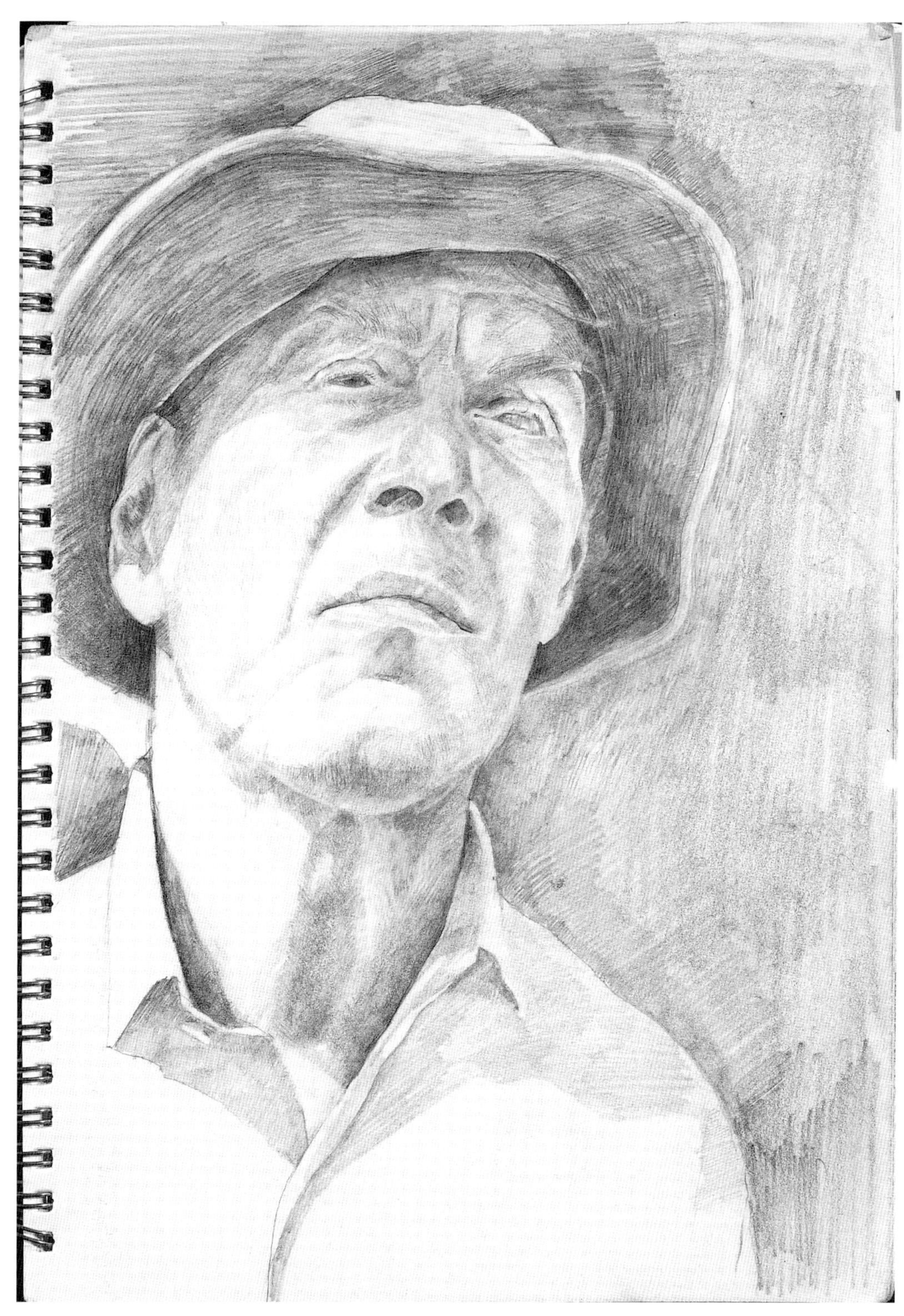

1995
pencil
254 × 178

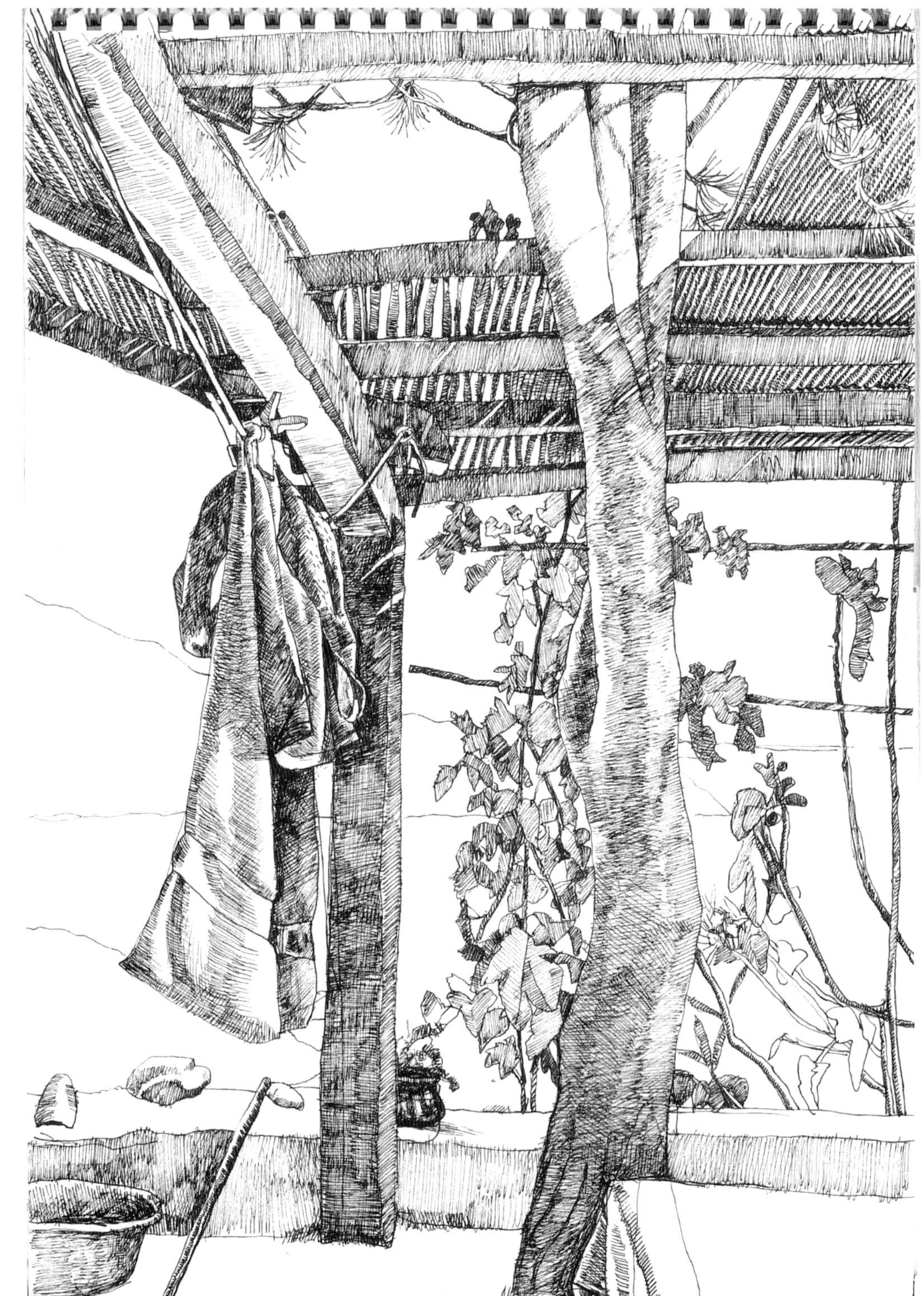

Greece
1996
pen and ink
290 × 210

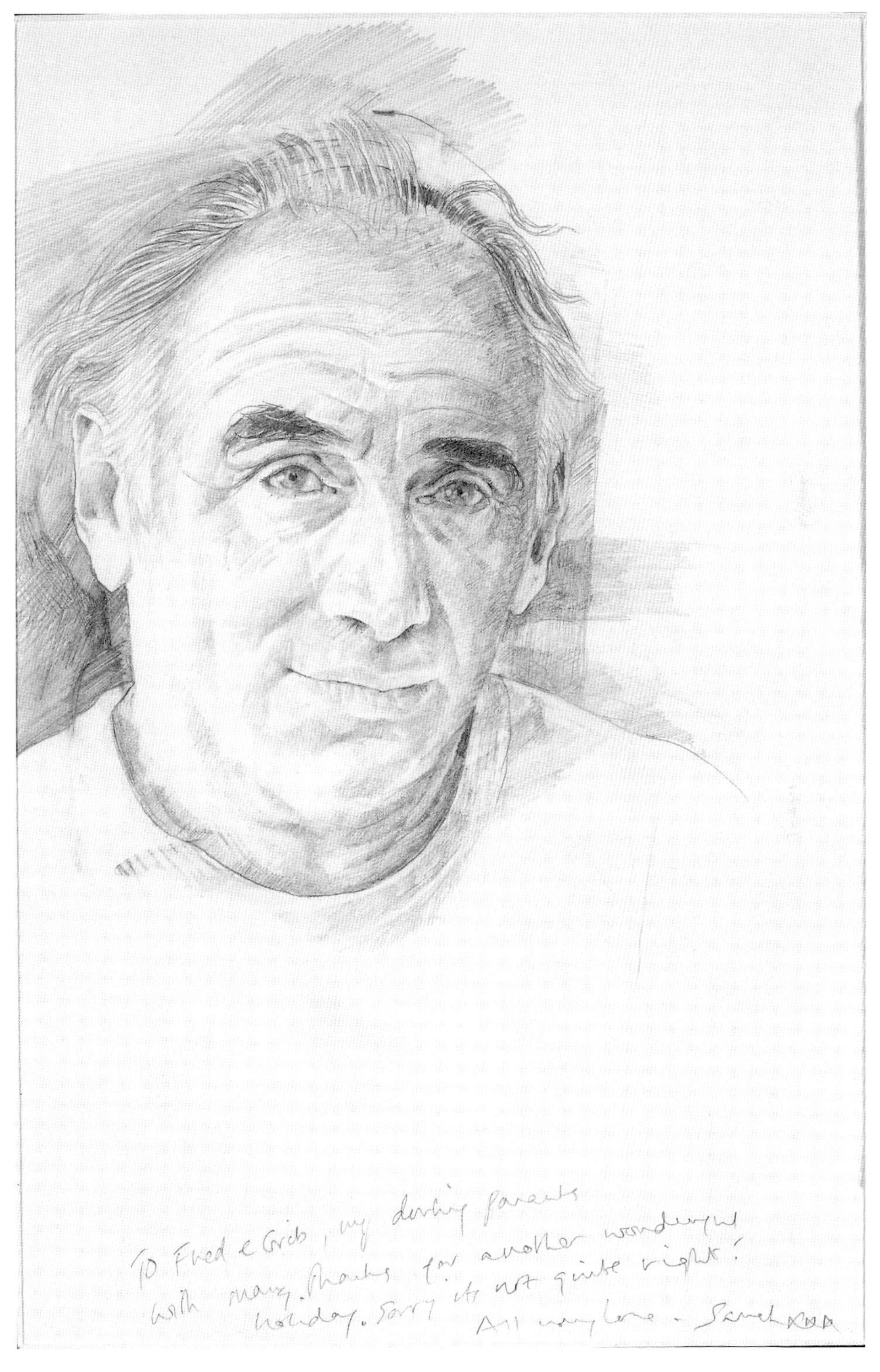

Fred
1997
pencil
250 × 165

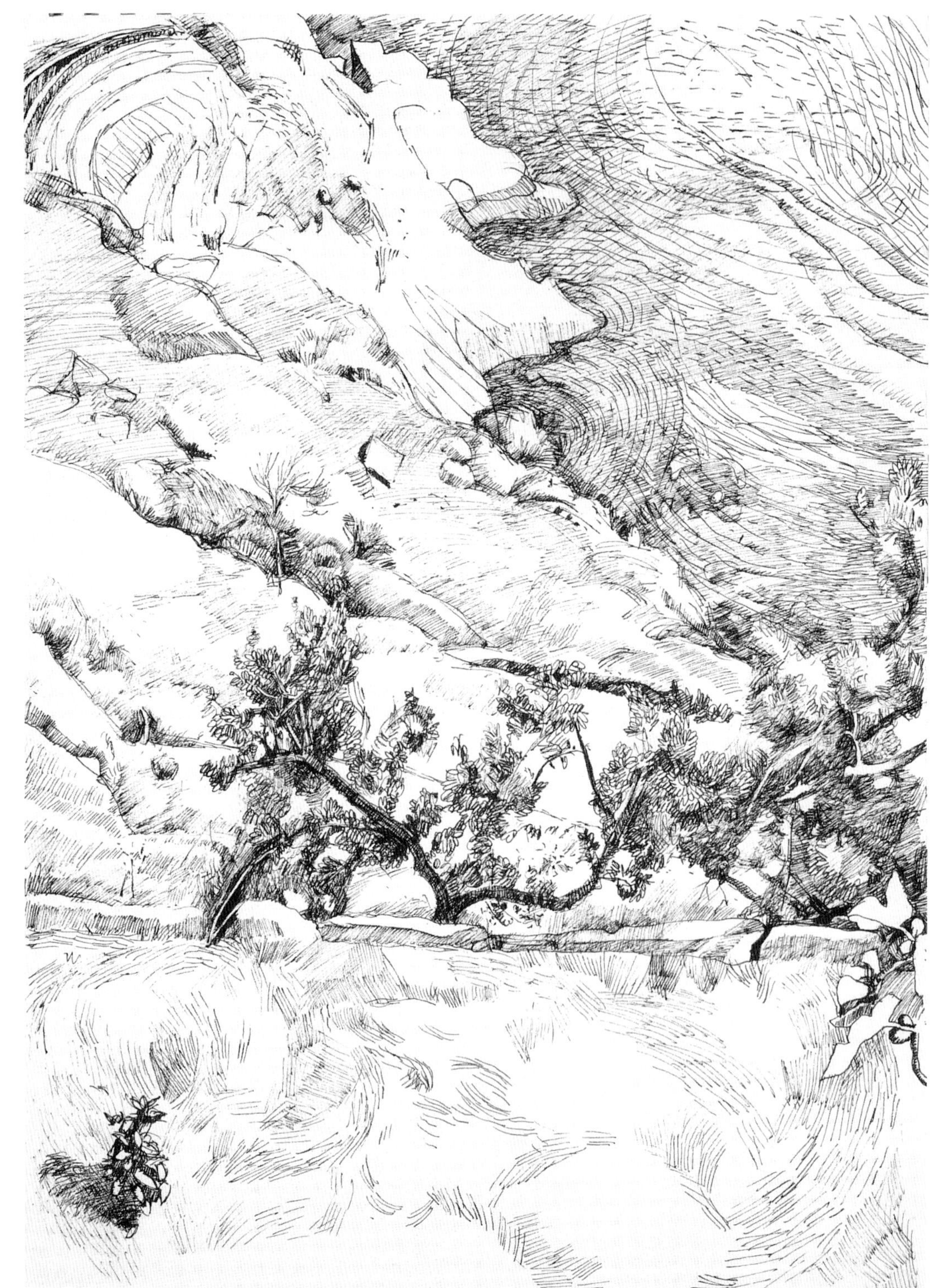

Greece
pen and ink
290 × 210

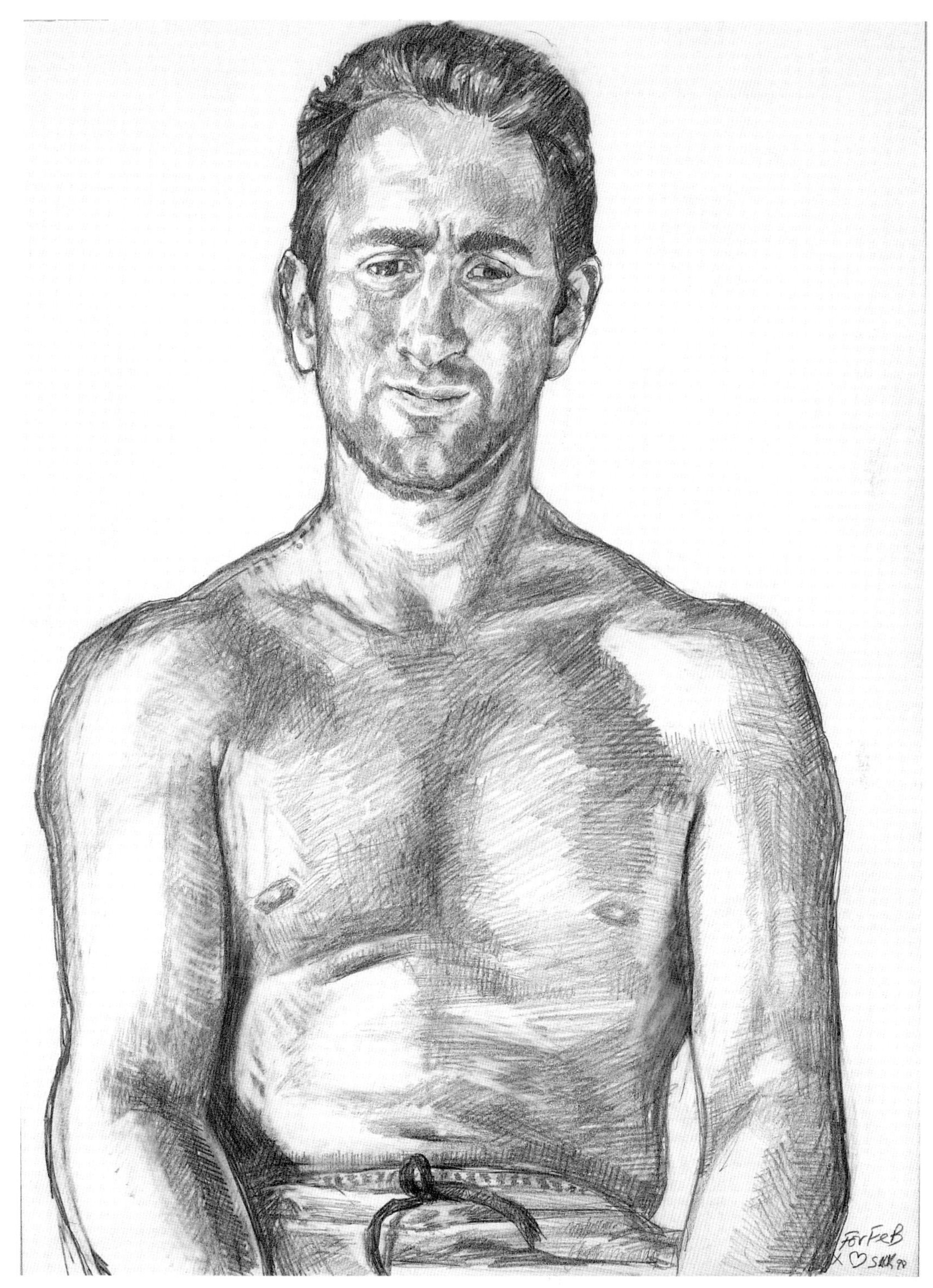

Stee
1998
pencil
278 × 208

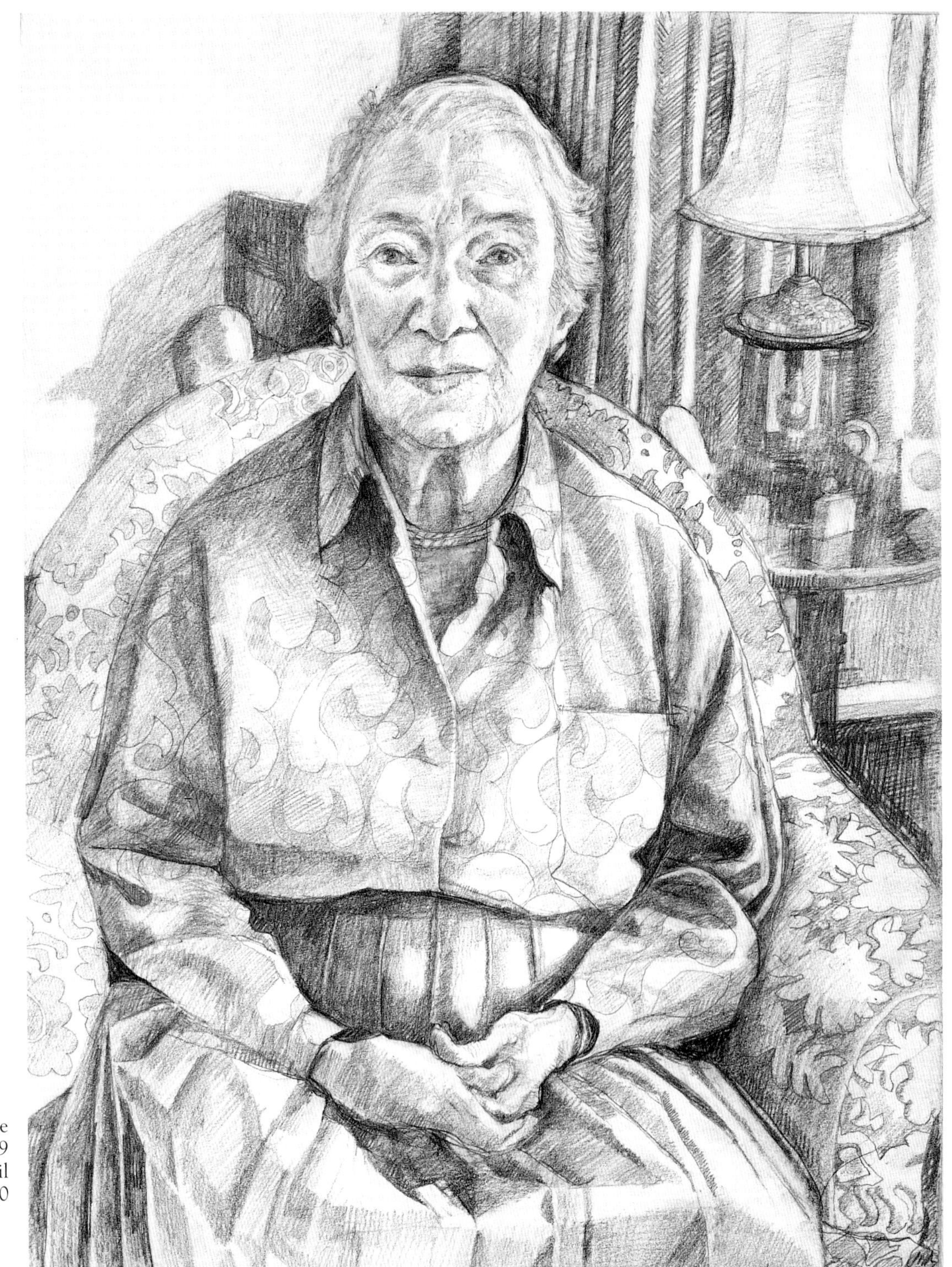

Irene
1999
pencil
320 × 240

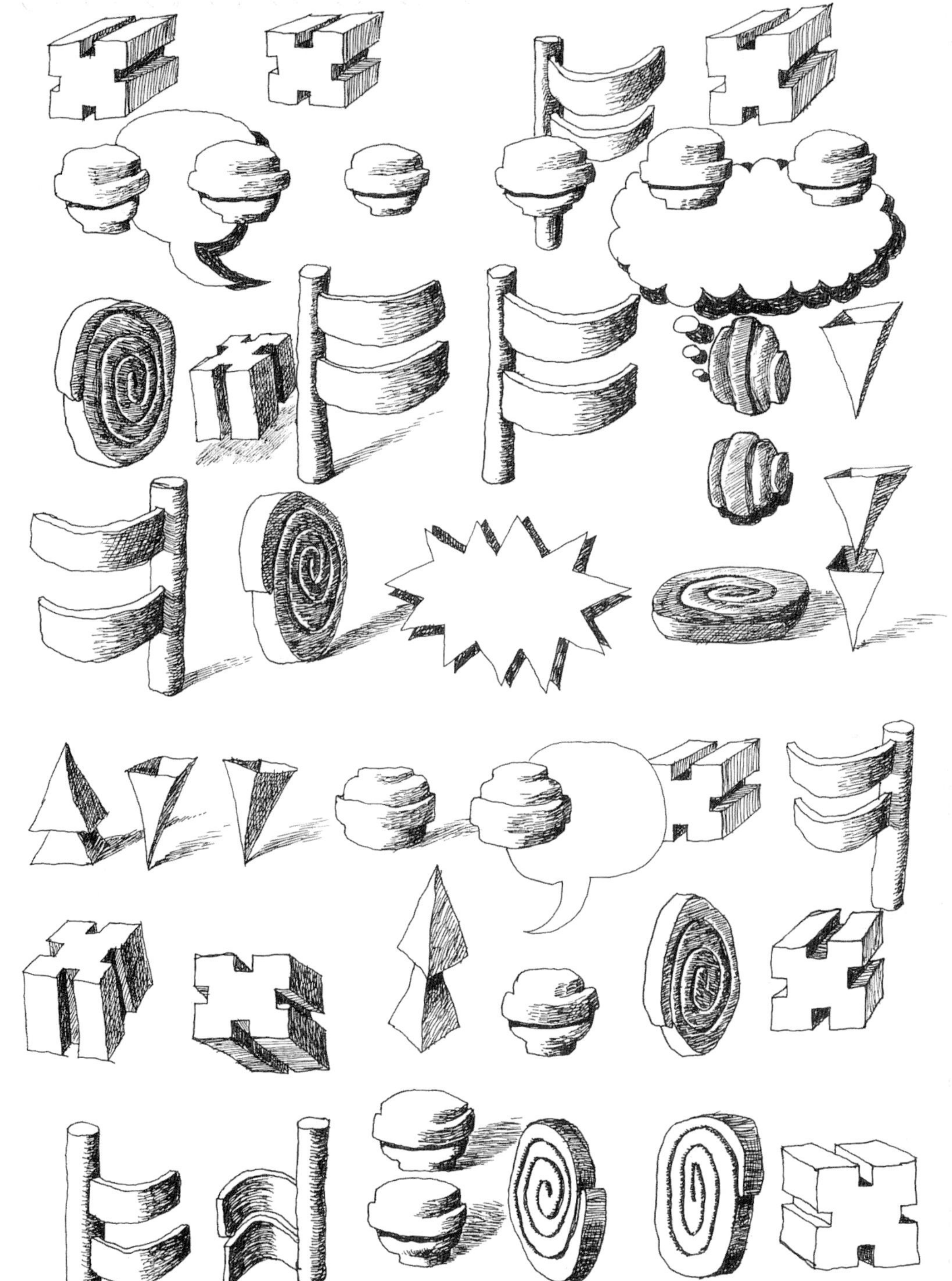

Post-Strip study
2000
pen and ink
290 × 205

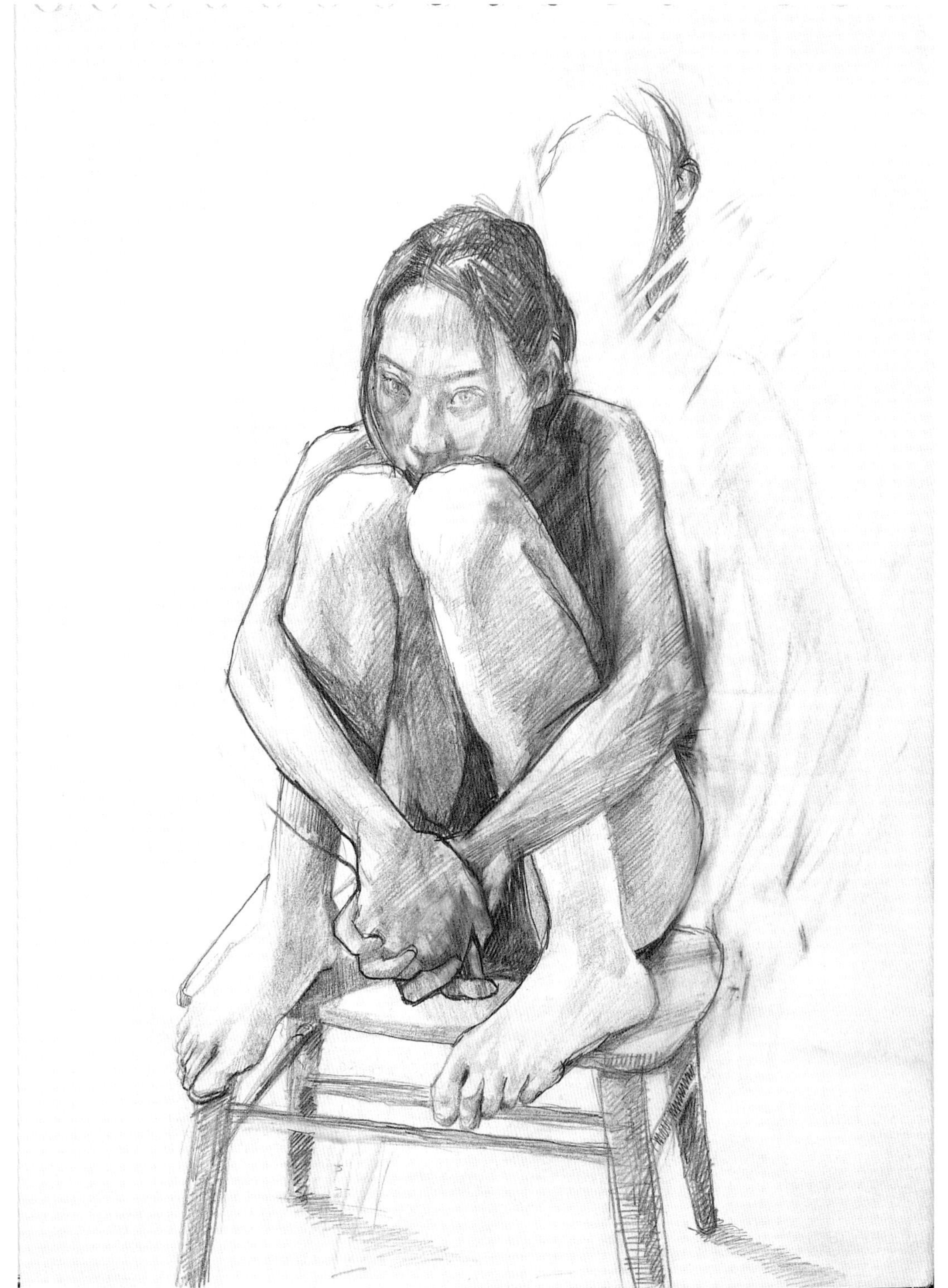

Natasha
2000
pencil
290 × 205

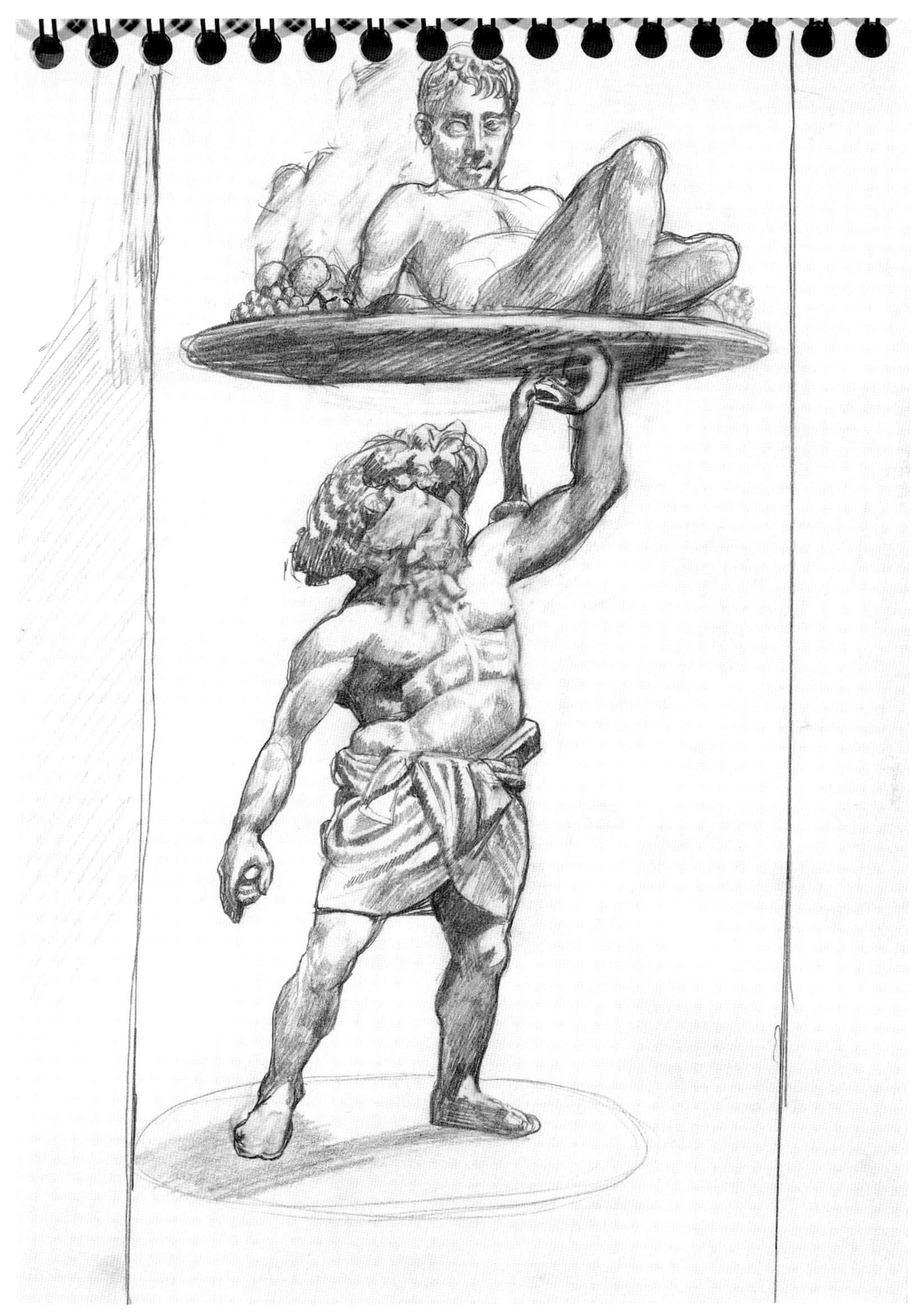

Illustration for
the *Satyrica*
2001
pencil
290 × 205

List of Drawings